THE THEORY
OF GERMAN WORD ORDER
FROM THE RENAISSANCE
TO THE PRESENT

Financial assistance for this book
was provided by the McKnight Foundation

The Theory of German Word Order from the Renaissance to the Present

Aldo Scaglione

UNIVERSITY OF MINNESOTA PRESS □ MINNEAPOLIS

Copyright © 1981 by the University of Minnesota.
All rights reserved.
Published by the University of Minnesota Press,
2037 University Avenue Southeast,
Minneapolis, Minnesota 55414

Library of Congress Cataloging in Publication Data
Scaglione. Aldo D.
   The theory of German word order from the Renaissance to the present.

   Bibliography: p.
   Includes index.
   1. German language — Word order — Historiography.
2. Grammar, Comparative and general — Word order — Historiography. 3. Linguistics — Methodology — History.
I. Title.
PF3390.S3   435   80-16619
ISBN 0-8166-0980-2
ISBN 0-8166-0983-7 (pbk.)

The University of Minnesota
is an equal-opportunity
educator and employer.

CONTENTS

Introduction   3

Chapter 1. The Theory of Sentence Structure   7
    1. Linguistic   7
    2. Stylistic   15

Chapter 2. The Theory of Word Order from the Renaissance to Adelung   29
    1. Renaissance to Steinbach   29
    2. Gottsched to Bodmer   50
    3. Adelung   80

Chapter 3. Modern Theory and Its Nineteenth-Century Background   97
    1. Herling, Bauer, and Becker   97
    2. Behaghel and Delbrück   108
        a. The Behaghel Thesis   109
        b. The Delbrück Thesis   117
    3. Modern Theory   126
        a. The Prague School   126
        b. The Structuralists   133
        c. Transformational Grammar   138
        d. Typological syntax   150
    4. The Practical Paradigms   175

Notes   183
Bibliography   217
Subject Index   233
Index of Personal Names   237

THE THEORY
OF GERMAN WORD ORDER
FROM THE RENAISSANCE
TO THE PRESENT

INTRODUCTION

When modern linguists speak about past linguists they sometimes remind me of the poet Baggesen who, as Kierkegaard records it,[1] said of someone that he was doubtless a good man, but that there was an insuperable objection against him, namely, that no word rhymed with his name. The trouble with past linguists is, indeed, that precious little of what they said jibes with what modern linguists regard as worth saying. Yet there must be some other way of looking at it, and some of us are not afraid of trying. This does not imply that I, for one, believe that "rhyming" with modern linguists is irrelevant.

The theoretical side of this study is concerned with a hypothesis which, if proved functional, could be of interest to the general linguist. To the casual observer the idiosyncrasies of German word order appear to be unique — and uniquely perplexing. Indeed, there is a tradition of regarding German as a language in this respect both unusually systematic and ultimately illogical, even "irrational" — the term that keeps popping up in a recent full-length study by a French linguist, J. M. Zemb (1968). We must start out, on the contrary, with the assumption that whatever happened to German is nothing but a special systematic development of conditions that have affected at one time or another all other languages of the Indo-European group. There is no single feature in German word order that is not common to some phase of other language of the group: not the syntactic differentiation between dependent and main clauses, which was also found in Latin; not the inversion of the subject after the verb when a complement starts out the clause, which was also characteristic of Old French; not the sending of the participle or infinitive to the end of the clause in verbal groups of Auxiliary + Verb or Modal + Verb, which was also found in Old Italian; and not even, if one wishes, the separation of prepositions from verbs with postponement of them, which can be found in limited cases of Modern French.[2] What is characteristic of German is only (and that is, admittedly, a great deal) the strict, systematic nature of these patterns — although this is true only of New High German after 1600, roughly. This systematic regularity still remains a controversial phenomenon, which has been explained alternately through (learned) Latin influence (Behaghel), or crystallization of the devices needed to discriminate between main and dependent clauses — in a language that developed the morphological devices too late and too uncertainly — or, more speculatively, as a way to stress such a discrimination by psychologically grounded devices (Weinrich).

This impressive, though partly mythical, case of systematic regularity has been the main cause of another widespread myth (all "myths" contain a great deal of truth), which is the opposite of the largely French-instigated charge of illogicality or irrationality I have just mentioned. I mean the equally popular notion of German being the philosophical language par excellence, or at least the ideal language for philosophy. Recently, and in the relevant context of a broad-ranging cultural-political interview, Martin Heidegger did not hesitate to allege that "admittedly the French, when they begin to think, speak German, for their own language would not come through."[3] Heidegger was speaking within a specific frame of reference, but the notion has been shared often and by many that Western man thinks German when reasoning or philosophizing.

If this is true (and there is plenty of room for doubt), it is at any rate a relatively recent phenomenon. For at the beginning of the eighteenth century, it was nearly impossible for a German to reason in his own language. To think, he needed to turn to French or Latin, as Leibniz, though a good patriot, did. The years following 1700 were indeed a decisive period for the development not only of the German language, but of the Germans' consciousness about their language. Within a hundred years German became, from an outcast, a ruler in the realm of intellectual commerce. It had been a long uphill fight, for in the very middle of that century Diderot could proudly proclaim to all who could hear that "il faut parler français dans la société et dans les écoles de philosophie; et grec, latin, anglais dans les chaires et sur les théâtres. . . . Le français est fait pour instruire, éclairer et convaincre; le grec, le latin, l'italien, l'anglais, pour persuader, émouvoir et tromper."[4] German, one will not fail to note, did not even appear to deserve a passing mention. And as late as 1784 the Prussian Academy gave the prize to Antoine de Rivarol for his essay that explained the good reasons why French was and deserved to be the "universal" language of intellectual intercourse. Both Diderot and Rivarol, like many others, based their whole argument in favor of French as the language of correctness, clarity, and precision, on its being characterized by "direct word order," to wit, by its basic avoidance of "inversion" (whereas a constitutional addiction to inversion was precisely the intolerable sin of German, as others pointed out). Great changes would seem to have occurred in the relatively short span between Rivarol and the emerging of the situation that Heidegger had in mind.

Much of the rather technical story I am about to unfold is inextricably connected with the effort on the part of educated German speakers and writers to acquire consciousness of their potentialities and of their character, as well as to come to grips with the means they needed to bring themselves up to the highest recognized standards of cultural intercourse. Their language, their grammar, and their style became some of the means to acquire their place as a cultured nation.

My specific purpose is to investigate the analysis of word order and sentence structure as it developed in Germany and in direct reference to the German language. These two topics are both theoretically and historically related as two aspects of what was classically called the theory of composition (in the sense of Latin *compositio*, Greek *synthesis*), and as such they have been the subject of my 1972 study *The Classical Theory of Composition, from Its Origins to the Present: A Historical Survey*.[5] In that book I did not cover German because the space needed for an adequate treatment of such a complex area would have caused the volume to swell to unmanageable proportions. I was, however, hoping to have the opportunity in the near future of filling that gap with a companion volume. The encouraging reception of *CTC* spurred me to pursue this endeavor, especially since more than one kindly reviewer pointed out the advantages of having this gap filled.[6] The present essay is meant to provide such a supplement. The method of investigation remains largely the same, but the nature of German primary literature makes it imperative to give the lion's share to the matter of word order over that of sentence structure.

Like many other areas in the history of what used to be classified as the arts of the Trivium, comprising grammar or linguistics, rhetoric or stylistics, and dialectic or logic, this one is hardly ready for a definitive, comprehensive survey, let alone a fully critical synthesis. Too many particular points still remain so imperfectly known as to defy a satisfactory interpretation, too many primary sources are of difficult access and are rare items even in major German libraries, and the contexts of too many statements remain in doubt because of our limited knowledge as to their national or foreign sources. It will be, therefore, more a matter of realism than modesty to warn the reader about the tentative and conjectural nature of much of what follows. Nevertheless it has seemed worthwhile to map out the field, no matter how inadequate some of the findings may appear to be.

I wish to thank the Deutscher Akademischer Austauschdienst for a grant that allowed me to spend the summer of 1977 in several specialized German libraries, and the Rockefeller Foundation for providing, at the Villa Serbelloni of Bellagio (Italy), an ideal environment for concentrated writing in the summer of 1978. These two opportunities made my work on this essay speedier, more pleasant, and, I hope, better informed. Among the several colleagues who have assisted me I must single out especially Professor Robert P. Ebert of Princeton for his precious advice and constructive criticism.

CHAPTER **1**

THE THEORY OF SENTENCE STRUCTURE

1. Linguistic

Before proceeding to the question of word order, which shall remain our primary concern, we must take at least a cursory look at the broader matter of sentence structure. This preliminary inquiry should help in the attempt to see our main topic in its proper perspective, since, within the sentence, the structure of the part and that of the whole are intimately related. The potential ramifications of the problem demand that we approach it on two separate levels, the linguistic and the stylistic, or the grammatical and the rhetorical. We shall therefore go, though quickly, twice over the historical sources, first considering the essential stages in the development of periodic syntax at the hands of the grammarians.

Our understanding of the basic nature of syntactic structures hinges on the theoretical hypotheses that have been proposed time and again within the last two centuries in different forms. They remain as open questions and are still occasionally debated in modern linguistics. They combine the genetic point of view with the synchronic assessment of sentence articulation and organization.

Ever since Schlegel and, particularly, Thiersch 1826 and then Delbrück 1900,[1] many historical linguists have held that hypotaxis evolved from parataxis. Allegedly, primitive languages operated by juxtaposed independent clauses, and subordinate clauses evolved gradually from the expansion of complements, phrases, or parts of speech as elements of an independent clause. This view would be reflected in the current habit of referring to dependent clauses as substantive, adjective, or adverb clauses, a nomenclature that replaces the traditional logically based terms of subjective, objective, final, causal, temporal clause, etc. A particular case is that of relative clauses, which can be regarded as an expansion of adjectives and appositions (*God the creator of the world* → *God, who created the world*). (The transformationalists' tendency to look on relative clauses as underlying deep structures of adjectives and appositions, i.e., *Dieu créateur* < *Dieu, qui créa le monde*, is, in a sense, an opposite alternative to the preceding.)[2] In this view, there would be a logical and natural parallel between the structure of the clause and that of the sentence. But another possible way of envisaging the genetic question is that of positing subordination as principally a process of adding conjunctions expressing logical relationship to clauses once simply juxtaposed and coordinated to other equally main ones.

In the past, as grammarians attempted to speculate on the peculiarities of German syntax and style, they often tended to attribute to the nature of the language what was due to a particular set of historico-cultural circumstances. They spoke of style while they thought they were speaking linguistically. They were impressed that after 1600 official German, administrative and literary, became progressively addicted to complex periodicity. But the grammarians could hardly realize that this was a radical reversal of the previous natural state of the language — and one still witnesses the original trends in the dialects and in the patterns of popular usage. Generally speaking, it might not be unfair to assume that German is naturally less rather than more hypotactic than most neighboring languages.[3]

As basic nomenclature for what follows, I propose the term of Juxtaposition for a syntactic method that omits conjunctions and *mots-outils* both in main and secondary clauses — a characteristic of spoken language and of what used to be referred to as primitive languages — : this can obtain both in parataxis and hypotaxis, and in those cases we can speak alternatively of Asyndetic Parataxis or Asyndetic Hypotaxis. The fully explicit coordination or subordination can be referred to as (Syndetic) Parataxis and Hypotaxis, respectively.

I should like to give a few "vulgar" Latin examples of juxtaposition or asyndetic structures, which I take from the recent selection of Pavao Tekavčić, *Grammatica storica dell'italiano*, vol. II (Bologna: Il Mulino, 1972), pp. 588–9. One will note the presence of both paratactic and hypotactic cases. I will show some syntactic equivalences in German.

(Plautus) tantum dives est hic, nescit quid faciat auro
 er ist so reich, er weiss nicht, was er mit seinem Geld machen soll (= daß er nicht weiss, . . .)

(inscription referring to gambling) vincis, gaudes; perdis, ploras
 gewinnst du, freust du dich; verlierst du, tust du dir Leid

(Pompei graffiti) Sarra, non belle facis, solum me relinquis (Italian, non fai bene a lasciarmi solo)
 you do me wrong (by) leaving me alone

Coena Trim. 75,9 Iam curabo fatum tuum plores
 I'll see to it (, that) you'll regret your fate

 " 74,17 Habinna, nolo statuam eius in monumento meo ponas

 " 77,6 credite mihi: assem habeas, assem valeas; habes, habeberis

Latin classical epistolary style displayed the highest proportion of asyndetic parataxis (approximately 57% of the clauses in Cicero, 54% Pliny, 40% Seneca), followed by asyndetic hypotaxis (26% Cicero, 22% Pliny, 18% Seneca) and then syndetic hypotaxis (20% Cicero, 30% Pliny, 20% Seneca). These three possibilities have been analyzed as the basic ones by Adolf Primmer,[4] who labels them respectively as Group, Complex Sentence, Period (*Gruppe, Satzgefüge, Periode*), a classification that corresponds in principle to the classical terms of *oratio soluta, perpetua*, and *vincta*.[5]

The following are clear examples of Group patterns (or, as I choose to call them, asyndetic paratactic structures). They come from Seneca's letters — a writer who was variously praised or censured, on the ground of such stylistic practices, as a master of *harena sine calce* (Caligula), *minutissimae sententiae* (Quintilian), *commaticum genus dicendi* (John of Salisbury, *Metalogicon*, 1.22).[6]

Haec sit propositi nostri summa: / quod sentimus loquamur, / quod loquimur sentiamus; / concordet sermo cum vita (*Ep.* 75, 31-4)

10 ☐ THEORY OF SENTENCE STRUCTURE

Sed ita, ut vis, esse credamus: / mores ille, non verba composuit, / et animis scripsit ista, non auribus. (*Ep.* 100, 21-3)

Within the evolution of German syntax, the articulation of hypotaxis was enhanced by Latin influx: Middle High German was both relatively free and unstructured, therefore limited, in this area. Instead of using formal conjunctions, as in New High German, one could handle hypotactic relationships simply through the subjunctive mood (hence we can regard the tradition of defining the subjunctive as the mood of subordination, which we will find to be the norm down through the eighteenth century, as a reflection of this archaic state of affairs), an *und*, or no sign at all of subordination.[7] Some examples follow:

Ouch trûwe ich wol, si sî mir holt (Wolfram, *Parzival* 607, 5), 'Auch vertraue ich fest darauf, daß sie mir hold ist';

Ich erkande in wol, unde saehe ich in (Hartmann von Aue, *Gregorius* 3896), 'Ich würde ihn sicher erkennen, wenn ich ihn sähe';

Ir sult wol lâzen schouwen, und habt ir rîche wât (*Nibelungenlied* 931.3), 'Ihr sollt nun sehen lassen, ob ihr prächtige Kleidung habt';

Von iu beiden ist daz mîn ger, ir saget mir liute unde lant (Thomasin, *Welscher Gast* 1581), 'Euch beiden gegenüber ist es mein Wunsch, daß ihr mir von Leuten und Land erzählt.'

The *Konditionalsatz mit Spitzenstellung des Verbs* (e.g., *Hilfst du mir, helf ich dir*) is a remnant of this simple OG hypotaxis. Learned Latin is responsible to some extent for the rich system of *Nebensatzkonjunktionen*, even to the point of introducing many conjunctions that the average user never or hardly ever employed (*zumal, indem, falls, sofern, sowie, soweit, soviel, insofern . . . als, als daß, auch wenn*). (Polenz, p. 99.)

Following the impact of humanistic Latin and the other learned vernaculars, New High German underwent in the seventeenth century a drastic increase in syndetic hypotactic patterns, with a parallel reduction in asyndetic parataxis. Although this originally Baroque character of Modern German never has been eliminated, the process of modernization that started in the eighteenth century was essentially a reaction against the excesses of the seventeenth century as well as a methodical attempt to adopt the best French and English examples of "plain" style by reducing periodicity or *Einschachtelung* and reviving some of the more functional possibilities of juxtaposition. The first master of modernity, the philosopher Thomasius, was still conspicuously a slave to the heavy-handed, overbearing incapsulating habits of Baroque prose even in his *Monatsgespräche* of 1688–9, the first literary periodical in the German language.[8] We shall have more to say on this question further on.

The terminology and axiology of *Satzlehre* is of particular importance for German, since the pivotal role of word order in this language (semantically and syntactically) can neither be grasped nor defined without a proper understanding of the difference between main and secondary clauses, along with all the peculiarities of their respective organization and transformations. It will therefore come as no surprise that, in answer to that need, it was the Germans who first used methodically the basic terms and concepts of *koordinierte* and *subordinierte Sätze* in the modern sense, as Manfred Sandmann has tentatively proposed, tracing them for the moment as far back as Theodor Heinsius 1819 and S. H. A. Herling in 1821.[9] In 1826 (in the third edition of his 1818^2 *Griechische Grammatik*) Friedrich von Thiersch for the first time used *parataxis* and *syntaxis* (this latter, rather strangely, as the equivalent of *hypotaxis*) as a parallel pair to the preceding. *Coordination* was used in French for the first time in the *Grammaire française* of the Swiss Cyprien Ayer (Lausanne, 1851), but it appeared in France only in 1862 in Pierre-Auguste Lemaire's *Grammaire de la langue française*.[10]

In a learned dissertation by the Swedish linguist K. A. Forsgren,[11] Sandmann's researches have been broadened to cover the whole realm of syntactic terminology. But both Forsgren and Sandmann are so specifically fastened on the terminological end-products of the questions involved that they tend to reduce and distort the earlier phases of speculation leading to modern viewpoints. To complete and correct the picture, we must begin further back. Much of the material can be found surveyed and summarized in the masterly work of Jellinek.[12]

Ancient speculation on sentence structure was found, from Aristotle on, not among grammarians but among rhetorical analysts of style, and it involved the theory of compositional forms, most commonly divided into the loose (*oratio soluta*), the continuous (*oratio perpetua*), and the periodic (*oratio periodica*). When the sentence was treated as a unit (*periodus*), its possible parts were called respectively *colon* (roughly, "clause") and *comma* (somewhat akin to our "phrase"). The formal relationships between these subelements usually were not analyzed in antiquity, but the St. Gall treatise (ca. 1000?) used *comma* for segment of a period that serves (*serviat*) others, and it appears that Siger of Brabant perhaps extended the concept of *regere* to the relationship between two clauses.[13]

Little formal progress was achieved in this area until the middle of the seventeenth century. Port-Royal's grammar (*Grammaire générale et raisonnée*, 1660) brought forward the concept of *proposition incidente* that, introduced by *qui*, *lequel*, and *que*, serves to build up part of the *sujet* or *attribut* of another clause that one could call *proposition principale*. The notion spread and is found, in the German area, in Georg Heinrich Ursin and Aichinger. Let us note here that, aside from the logical origin and context of this discussion, betrayed by the term *proposition*, the distinction of secondary clauses was, for the time being, limited to relative and (for those introduced by *que*) objective clauses. The relative clauses, in particular, were for a long time kept separate from others as if they constituted a special kind of subordination, as illustrated in Nicolas Beauzée (*Grammaire générale*, 1767), who widened the notion of *proposition incidente*, and especially Condillac, *Cours d'études pour l'instruction du Prince de Parme*, first published in 1775,[14] who divided the sentence into *propositions principales*, *incidentes*, and — mark this — *subordonnées*. (The German translation of 1793 had both *Subordination* and *untergeordnet*.) The two latter ones are said to develop (*développent*) the former. The *incidente* qualifies a substantive, the *subordonnée* a verb. Condillac was still following the Port-Royal grammar in keeping the *incidentes* separate. At any rate, Condillac's nomenclature clearly treated sentence structure as an extension of clause structure, and clauses as expansions of complements or phrases. But much earlier, Du Marsais, *Exposition d'une méthode*, 1722, and *Véritables principes*, 1729, had made the analysis of simple and complex sentences central to the study of syntax and grammar.[15]

Meanwhile, German grammarians had developed a timely alertness to matters of analytical terminology. The key terms *Hauptsatz* and *Nebensatz* appear in **Johann Daniel Longolius**, *Einleitung zu gründtlicher Erkäntniß einer ieden, insonderheit aber der Teutschen Sprache* (Budissin: David Richter, 1715), p. 91: "*Periodus conditionalis* oder

THEORY OF SENTENCE STRUCTURE ☐ 13

der bedingende Fürtrag, welcher einen Hauptsatz mit einem gewissen bedingenden Nebensazze proponiret.''[16]

More comprehensive and exemplary, but completely confined within the classical rhetorical terminology, was **Johann August Ernesti** (1707–81), *Initia rhetorica* (Lipsiae, 1750), §§ 367, 369, who gave the following definition of the period, as part of his "Initia doctrinae solidioris":

Universe igitur periodus est, cum sensus perfectus suspenditur per interiecta membra, quae ambitum efficiunt. Id quale sit, clarius intelligitur e formis periodi, et eius structura. Simplex igitur est, in qua est una sententia principalis, sed ita, ut a subiecto ad attributum transitus sit, sive a parte una principalis sententiae ad alteram, per interpositas enunciationes secundarias. Secundariae autem exponunt caussas, conditionem, περιστάσεις temporum et similia [the *circumstantiae*]. Composita periodus est ex antecedente et consequente, vel uno, vel pluribus: unde bimembres, trimembres, et quadrimembres dicunt.[17]

The heritage of classical speculation sounded here loud and clear.

Carl Friedrich Aichinger, *Versuch einer teutschen Sprachlehre* (Frankfurt and Leipzig-Wien: J. P. Kraus, 1754), p. 101, while dealing with *Interpunktionslehre*, used the *Kolon* (:) as a division between main clauses, designated as *Hauptsätze*, and the *Semikolon* (;) as the way to separate the *Nebensatz* or *Nebenglied* from the *Vor-* or *Nachsatz* within a complex (*nicht einfach*) period.

Johann Bernhard Basedow, *Neue Lehrart und Uebung in der Regelmäßigkeit der Teutschen Sprache* (Kopenhagen: J. B. Ackermann, 1759), grasped the nature of subordination as a consequence of certain conjunctions, but without using terms other than *Vorsatz* and *Nachsatz*, *Anhang*, and *Einschiebsel*.[18] In this work, which is noteworthy for its syntax, the concepts of *Subject* and *Prädicat* play an important role. They were adduced by few contemporary grammarians.

More decisive was **Johann Jakob Bodmer**, *Grundsätze der deutschen Sprache, oder von den Bestandtheilen derselben und von dem Redesatze* (Zürich: Orell, Gessner u. Co., 1768), where, in the example *Die Menschen lebeten in Ruhe, da noch keine Säge war*, the latter clause is given as *der verbundene, untergeordnete Redesatz* (with verb and auxiliary, if any, at the end), the other as the *einfacher Satz*; then he showed that turning the clauses around would change the sense.[19] This leans on, but goes beyond, the abbé Gabriel Girard (1677–1748), whose

Les vrais principes de la langue françoise (1747) had been a major source of syntactic analysis and language classification, and who in both cases would simply have spoken of *sense relatif*, without understanding that one clause was subordinated to the other. Furthermore, Girard was properly speaking not of clauses but phrases in his distinctions between *phrases subordinatives* of a *subjectif* and of a *terminatif* kind.[20]

An example of the difficulty German grammarians continued to experience, in classifying conjunctions and distinguishing them from adverbs and even relative pronouns, is to be found in the confused treatment of the matter by **Jakob Hemmer**, *Deutsche Sprachlehre* (Mannheim: Akademische Schriften, 1775), pp. 378, 396–7, 607ff.[21] This is a case of the peculiar German predicament as regards general syntax, since verbal position can be assumed to have been a relative substitute for the weakness of syntactic markers of subordination, such as clearly subordinating conjunctions, as we shall see later on.

It is, finally, with **Johann Werner Meiner**, *Versuch einer an der menschlichen Sprache abgebildeten Vernunftlehre oder philosophische und allgemeine Sprachlehre entworfen von* . . . (Leipzig: J. G. I. Breitkopf, 1781), that the terms *Hauptsatz* and *Nebensatz* acquired functional clarity; they became a firm acquisition of the grammatical vocabulary when Adelung took them over from Meiner. They were, however, rendered somewhat confused (and still remained so with Adelung) by their being flanked by the competing though heterogenous distinction between *Vorsatz* and *Nachsatz*, which came from the rhetorical theory of the "period."[22] Meiner, p. 81, called *Nebensätze* "unmittelbar abhängige Sätze" or "Sätze der ersten Ordnung" and "mittelbar abhängige Sätze" or "Sätze der zweiten Ordnung," according to whether they depended on a *Hauptsatz* or another *Nebensatz*.[23]

This refinement on the analysis of subordination leads us to the first comprehensive theory of the clause-species (*die Satzarten*), which is found in **A. J. de Sacy**'s *Grundsätze der allgemeinen Sprachlehre in einem allgemeinen faßlichen Vortrage . . . übersetzt von J. S. Vater* (Halle and Leipzig, 1804), and even better in **Vater**'s (de Sacy's translator) own *Lehrbuch der Allgemeinen Grammatik besonders für höhere Schul-Classen* (Halle, 1805). Here we find the beginnings of a development that usually has been attributed to **S. H. A. Herling**, *Erster Kursus eines wissenschaftlichen Unterrichts in der deutschen*

Sprache (Frankfurt/Main, 1828).[24] The *Kursus* was soon followed by Herling's *Syntax der deutschen Sprache* (Frankfurt/M., 1830, 3 vols.). In the most carefully researched study of the term *coordination*, M. Sandmann's "Beiordnung . . . ," 165f., 171ff., the concomitant use of the terms *Koordination/Subordination*, or *beiordnende* and *unterordnende Verbindung*, is traced beyond Herling 1828 to Herling 1821, "Ueber die Topik der deutschen Sprache," *Abhandlungen des frankfurtischen Gelehrtenvereins für deutsche Sprache*, Drittes Stück, p. 342, at least for a clear discrimination in usage, whereas their mere presence could be found at least as far back as 1819 in the "Vorwort" (dated precisely 1819) to **Theodor Heinsius**, *Teut oder theoretischpraktisches Lehrbuch der gesammten deutschen Sprachwissenschaft* (Berlin, 1821). **Ludwig Ramshorn**, *Lateinische Grammatik* (Leipzig: F. C. W. Vogel, 1824, 1830^2), also used *coordinirt* and *subordinirt*.

The fact is that around 1800 the notion of syntactic subordination of clauses becomes fairly clear, even when the terminology used does not precisely coincide with later practice. For example, G. M. Roth, *Systematisch deutsche Sprachlehre* (Giessen, 1799), distinguishes between *verknüpft* and *verbunden*, and K. H. L. Politz, *Allgemeine deutsche Sprachkunde . . .* (Leipzig, 1804), is the first that Forsgren has found to use *Koordination* while dealing with *Satzgefüge*, although "he does not make the grammatical distinction."[25] As we have seen above, Condillac 1775, German translation 1793, had used the term *subordination* but not *coordination*. Forsgren's additions and refinements on Sandmann's researches and those of other predecessors are of great value to a precise tracing of the stages in the evolution of these matters. For the period under his review, namely 1780–1830, Forsgren states (p. 21) that he has assembled some 300 titles, as against Jellinek's 141.

2. *Stylistic*

Now that we have gone over the essential stages in the evolution of periodic syntax, we must once again retrace our steps to glance at the developments in the rhetorical or stylistic consciousness of German sentence structure as well as of its literary meaning. The period of most intense speculation on the issues that concern us is between the last decades of the seventeenth century and the third quarter of the eighteenth, and we shall concentrate on that time span. It is an important

16 ☐ THEORY OF SENTENCE STRUCTURE

chapter in the history of German literary self-consciousness, and in this area we are fortunate enough to possess a masterly survey, Eric A. Blackall's *The Emergence of German as a Literary Language, 1700–1775* (1959).[26]

Starting in the sixteenth century and coming to a head in the seventeenth, official and literary usage became heavily influenced by the patterns of periodic Latin style ushered in by Humanism, especially in its widespread Ciceronian varieties. A typical case of this influence can be seen in the use of participial clauses in absolute construction, for example, *Einen Sturm fürchtend, kehrten wir nach dem Lande*; *Diese Arbeit vollendet, ging ich zu Bette.*[27] Hence grew the taste for complex sentences, *mehrgliedrige Periode*, characterized by the "encapsulation" of clause within clause (*Einschachtelung* or *Schachtelsatz*), sometimes on several levels, in a sort of box-within-a-box pattern, and typical of official style, *Hochsprache*. This style could be referred to as *Kanzleisprache* or *Kurialstil* for its highest domain, the court, or more broadly, as *Amtsstil* or *Beamtenstil* when it was applied to the bureaucratese of the administrative quarters — where it became the trademark of the administrative class, or *Dienstadel*, as distinct from the regular nobility, or *Schwertadel*.

Such practices were somewhat parallel to the elevated literary language of both poetry and art prose: This other *Hochsprache*, or *Kunstsprache*, found its most elaborate form in the elitist, periodic, and highly metaphoric (potentially even "precious") language of Silesian Baroque, especially in the "Second Silesian School," which was ushered in by Opitz's separation of the written from the ordinary language to make it distinguished and truly literary — in other words, to bring German culture to the high levels of its more advanced neighbors. In the early eighteenth century, the rationalist, French-oriented critics of the more drastic forms of Baroque style attempted to divorce Opitz and the poets of his generation from the excesses of their successors.

But the reaction dated even from some contemporaries of the Baroque writers, under the banner of **Christian Weise** (1624–1708), who adopted Boileau's rational and classicistic advocacy of a simple, clear, and natural-sounding language, aiming at effectiveness and directness in communication.[28] A basic rationalism and general dislike of *Hochsprache* characterize most of the seventeenth- and eighteenth-century grammarians, who, however, tended to differ from their French counterparts by advocating a learned standard language of literary origin, delimited by social and geographic boundaries, with less emphasis on the practical usage of an educated milieu (this being a typically French idea). The difference corresponded to the different needs of Germany, where the political and linguistic fragmentation made the choice of the right "court" less obvious and any form of dialectal richness suspicious. Thus, instead of a model firmly based on actual usage, what we hear from these grammarians is more reminiscent of Dante's abstract national canon of *vulgare illustre*. This orientation can be found in the greatest grammarian of the seventeenth century, **Justus Georg Schottelius** (1612–76).

Schottelius inspired in part the most brilliant theoretical work on language in the German area, that of **Gottfried Wilhelm Leibniz**, whose *Unvorgreiffliche Gedancken betreffend die Ausübung und Verbesserung der teutschen Sprache* dates from ca. 1697, although it was published by his secretary J. G. Eccard only in 1717, one year after the master's death.[29]

Leibniz proposed three main qualities for style, which could be assimilated to some of the classical virtues of elocution as transmitted and reinterpreted through French classicism, namely, *Reichtum* (*copia*), *Reinigkeit* (*puritas, netteté*), *Glantz* (*elegantia, ornatus*). These notions, in turn, harked back to Leibniz's own Introduction to **Marius Nizolius**'s *Anti-Barbarus* titled "De optima philosophi dictione" (1670).[30] One could find there the conclusive commendation of a *compendiosissima popularitas vel popularissimum compendium* that, in a notably fashionable and baroque chiasmus, expressed a confluence of typically German concern for national and popular identity with the Neo-Stoic ideal of plainness combined with brevity — a Senecan ideal of style that had been brought back to vigorous life by the anti-Ciceronian currents in the late-sixteenth and seventeenth centuries.

But Germans had difficulty in finding their linguistic and stylistic identity in the century dominated by French cultural hegemony. The difficult predicament in the attempt to establish a scientific and cultural vocabulary by naturalizing foreign words or, alternately, substituting German equivalents, is ironically shown by Leibniz's phrase: "Besser ist ein Original von einem Teutschen als eine Copey von einem Franzosen seyn."[31] The nationalistic campaign for purity continued

18 ☐ THEORY OF SENTENCE STRUCTURE

throughout the following century. While the Swiss had their special difficulties due to the archaic substratum of their Alemannic dialects, Gottsched could still speak sarcastically of those princes who "nicht mehr von wichtigen Angelegenheiten ratschlagen, sondern von den *important*esten *Affair*en *deliberir*en müssen."[32]

The growing German concern with matters of vocabulary is reflected in Leibniz's proposal of a *Sprachbrauch* (*lexicon*) for current words, a *Sprach-Schatz* (*cornu copiae*) for technical terms, and a *Sprachquell* (*glossarium*) for archaic and dialectal words. The idea was destined to have long-lasting repercussions in other lands: It will suffice to recall Melchiorre Cesarotti's somewhat similar proposal in the year 1800.[33]

But Leibniz was only theorizing, since most of his works were written in Latin or French. The scholar who started the practical revolution in using German for philosophical teaching (oral and written) was **Christian Thomasius** in 1687, at Leipzig. His contradictory results, however, pale by comparison with **Christian Wolff**'s (1679–1754) success in creating for the first time a truly German style in mathematical and logical terminology. One has only to contrast two contemporary texts: Thomasius' *Einleitung zur Hoff-Philosophie* (Berlin, 1712), a translation of his 1688 *Introductio ad philosophiam aulicam*, and Wolff's Logic (*Vernünfftige Gedancken von den Kräfften des menschlichen Verstandes* . . . . , 1712).[34]

Thus Thomasius, like Leibniz, stressed the concreteness of German terms as being more vivid than French or Latin, yet the German philosophical nomenclature actually was developed in the opposite way, by emptying concrete terms of their pictorial association, the sensual or image quality, and of the metaphorical awareness that had been transmitted by the German mystical tradition, so admired and recommended by Leibniz for linguistic purposes: e.g. *Einfluß auf*, as in Wolff, rather than *in*, as in the mystical tradition, or *Eindruck machen* versus Thomasius' *eindrücken*. With Wolff, the way to needed abstraction became clearly open.[35] Leibniz and Thomasius had been wrong in expecting the German philosophical language to evolve out of its concrete expressions; Hegel was right in praising German for the opposite virtue, that of possessing so many purely abstract, hence potentially philosophical, terms in its everyday popular vocabulary, such as *Sein*, *Nichtsein*, *Eines*, *Vieles*, *Beschaffenheit*, *Größe*, etc.[36]

Thomasius preferred the middle style without rejecting the "scharfsinnige, schutzhaffte und aufgeweckte Schreibart" under the right circumstances and for the sake of "Zierlichket der Rede," and advocated a middle point between the too concise (threatening obscurity) and the too copious (threatening boring monotony). The young lawyer must care more for *res* than *verba* (*Höchstnöthige Cautelen welche ein studiosus juris . . . zu beobachten hat,* Halle/S., 1713, 1729).[37]

The process whereby an awareness of correct and elegant style was produced reminds one closely of Father Bouhours' and the French grammarian-critics' method of painstaking analysis of sentence structure. Without referring such practices to their French models, Blackall offers an excellent example of Bodmer's critique and recasting of a bad sentence of the baroque, encapsulated type.[38] The critique specified word order, subordination, and order of clauses.

The Baroque ideal of a courtly, elitist, ornate language serving above all the purposes of intellect and culture, as sanctioned by Schottel, started to give way at the end of the century to a more "popular" taste for directness and plainness, even among the grammarians, whose efforts thus paralleled those of the reforming philosophers. The Berliner **Johann Bödiker** (1641–95), *Grundsätze der deutschen Sprache* (1690, revised 1723 by Johann Leonhard Frisch, 1666–1743), had peremptorily enjoined: "Sprich, wie du schreibst!" just as the Hamburg poet Barthold Heinrich Brockes (1680–1741) would urge in 1721: "Man muß sprechen, wie man schreibet." It was clearly implied that, if the speaker had to imitate the writer, the writer could not keep a great distance from the speaker. Eventually, it was **Johann Christoph Gottsched** (1700–1766), *Grundlegung einer deutschen Sprachkunst,* 1748 . . . 1776[6], who decisively reversed the Baroque trend by championing usage as paramount (whereas Schottel had made no clear appeal to usage), even while he made himself the oracle of an Aufklärung of French imprint. Toward the end of the century **Johann Christoph Adelung**, the most celebrated of the classical German grammarians, still emphasized usage — which he identified with the habits of the cultivated, like the French court usage of Vaugelas. From Gottsched to Adelung, the cultivated became limited geographically to the upper classes of the Saxon electorate: "Die Mundart der südlichern Chursächsischen Lande, . . . die cultivierteste Provinz in dem ganzen Deutschlande."[39] This standard had been first defined in full detail by Gottsched, who neatly summarized it in the "Vorerinnerung" to the

"Wortfügung" (Syntax) section of his *Deutsche Sprachkunst* (1748): The national literary language shall be based on the deserved priority of Dresden (the best court), Leipzig (the large residential town nearby, formerly the seat of the leading literary academy, the "Deutsche Gesellschaft"), and Meißen (the sweetest sounding dialect); the model then will be the usage of the Dresden court as codified in the rules of the Leipzig academy and as actually uttered by the educated residents of Meißen.

In a famous statement on style, Gottsched condemned the periodic style and the abuse of conjunctions (*Ausführliche Redekunst*, 1728, ch. xiv, § 7). It was a clear echo of the French polemics in favor of the cut style (*style coupé*, à la Voltaire, for example), and the enemy was, of course, the *Kanzleistil*.[40]

The progress of German style toward a modern type of sentence structure is best reflected in the periodicals of the first half of the eighteenth century. Gottsched was justly enthusiastic about the style of Hamburg's *Der Patriot* (Jan. 5, 1724–Dec. 28, 1726), which he polemically contrasted with the uneven and "impure" style of Bodmer's and Breitinger's journal *Discourse der Mahlern* (Zürich, 1721–3). The evident gracefulness of *Der Patriot* was as much the result of logical structure as of musical intonation and rhythm. It had a "natural" movement not deprived of some clear concessions to rhetorical *ornatus*, e.g., hendiadys.[41] A sample will suffice to give a clear idea of how "modern" the periods of that journal could sound: lengthy but noncircular, information being parceled out gradually without final surprises, with first things first, in a smooth and easy-going rhythm — in other words, nearly the opposite of what a German imitator of Ciceronian Latin would have tried to achieve:

Bey dem Römischen Volcke war die Auffsicht über die Sitten und das häussliche Betragen der Einwohner eins von den ansehnlichsten und einträglichsten Aemtern. Ich nehme dieses Amt, als ein rechtschaffener Patriot, bey meiner, der Teutschen, Nation von selbst über mich, und zwar so wenig aus einiger Geld- oder Ehr-Begierde, daß ich vielmehr die Besoldung der vielen hin- und wieder dazu nötigen Schreiber, nebst den täglichen Post-Geldern, aus eigenem Beutel herschieße, und immer hiebey verborgen zu bleiben verlange.[42]

But before turning to grammar, Gottsched had taken his stand on rhetoric, the theory of prose composition, and on poetics, the theory of poetic style. He covered the latter in his *Dichtkunst* of 1730 and the former in his *Grundriß zu einer vernunfftmäßigen Redekunst*, 1729, followed by the revised and enlarged edition *Ausführliche Redekunst*, 1736, again reworked and expanded for the successive editions of 1730, 1750, and 1759.[43]

This successful treatise must be understood against the background of the preceding rhetorics, especially those inspired by the French "Senecan" currents advocating the "Neo-Stoic" virtue of brevity (cut or *coupé* style) without necessarily falling into the obscurity that also was a virtue for the extreme, "Tacitean" wing.[44] The effort to emancipate German culture and its language by assimilating French views and modes was necessarily accompanied by a polemical intent to expose anti-German French prejudice, since French grammarians and stylists tended to regard German style with ill-concealed contempt as irrational and barbarous.[45] Common terms used to classify styles were *natürlich*, meaning the generically loose and unadorned; *sinnreich* for the witty and succinct, broadly corresponding to the Senecan, its clauses being connected intuitively, with sparing use of conjunctional particles; and *beweglich* for the style that tended to express and induce emotion. A middle course in the advocacy of Senecanism without Taciteanism could be detected in the advice offered by **Johann Hübner**, *Kurtze Fragen aus der Oratoria* (Leipzig: Gleditsch, 1701, 1706²), p. 327, in which under the rules for clarity, brevity, and *Zierlichkeit* or elegance (*ornatus*) the orator was urged to seek the audience's approving admiration by pursuing all sorts of brevity without becoming obscure: " (1) Erwecke . . . eine Verwunderung; (2) Befleissige dich in allen Zeilen der Kürtze; (3) Vermeide mit aller Sorgfalt Obscurität."

Benjamin Neukirch took the *Kanzleistilus* to task for its too many epithets, adjectives and participles, unnecessary definitions, synonyms, accumulation of subordinate clauses leading to an illogical conclusion, and unnecessary conjunctions and other connectives: *Anweisung zu Teutschen Briefen* (Leipzig, 1745⁶), pp. 510, 532–45. But one also must avoid excessive curtness, hence both the Ciceronian and the "curt" Senecan modes.[46]

Gottsched's *Ausfuhrliche Redekunst* was divided into a Historical Introduction, a General Part, and a Specific Part, this last one containing translations of speeches and new speeches as examples. In the General Part we are particularly concerned with the chapters on periods ("Von den Perioden und ihren Zierrathen, den Figuren," ch. xiv, pp. 326–357 in 1759 ed., 289–316 in 1739 ed.) and on what was traditionally called *virtutes et vitia elocutionis* ("Von der Schreibart, ihren Fehlern und Tugenden," ch. xv, pp. 358–392 in 1759 ed., 317–346 in 1739 ed.).

But first, the historical introduction begins dealing with Germany at § 22, after a passing mention of Petrarch as one of the first who restored eloquence. Gottsched betrays the prejudice of a son of the Enlightenment and shows his hand as a neoclassicist by denying success to all those who have taken pains to prove that a German eloquence existed in the barbaric centuries, and he refers the reader to the Eighth Part of the second tome of the *Beyträge zur critischen Historie der deutschen Sprache*, No. IV (a journal that he edited until vol. VIII, from 1732 to 1744), namely, the "Dissertation von der Beredsamkeit der alten Deutschen."

He praises Melanchthon's *Rhetoric* especially, and regrets that it has been replaced by the equally good but not superior rhetoric of Vossius. At any rate, it took 100 years to bear fruit, until as late as Opitz, who introduced at last a new taste in both prose and verse ("nicht nur in gebundner, sondern auch in ungebundner Schreibart" — § 25, p. 66 in 1739 ed.). Christian Weise produced more oratorical writings than all the scholars ("Schulmänner") of his time taken together, yet one must assess his impact as a negative one, since he did German eloquence more harm than good by his lack of classical learning and lack of discrimination in the "Mischmasch" of his foreign vocabulary. Gottsched singles out for praise Benjamin Neukirch's book on German letter writing (*Buch von den deutschen Briefen*) as well as his "galante Briefe," but he belongs more to the preceding century than to the current one. All in all, however, if one considers the numerous collections of speeches by leading figures of his time, both in German and other languages (French, presumably), he concludes that the bad outweighs the good ten to one. Since 1720, however, the situation has been changing, and the prospect for the future is a bright one.

Chapter xiv on Periods opens, after the definition of period and its necessary rhythmic divisions, with an attack on the rambling, undivided, unending character of *Hof-* and *Kanzleistilus*, in which especially members of the legal profession express themselves with a looseness that cannot discipline itself. Gottsched intends to take away from it the dignity of a model that is still imitated. Against these wretched writers, he holds up the good foreign models, particularly such "unofficial" writers as Bussy-Rabutin and St-Évremond (both, incidentally, exemplars of basic "Senecanism").[47]

In § 7, he attacks the abuse of conjunctions not strictly necessary for the sense (*obwohl, jedoch, gleichwie, also; nachdem so; alldieweil, dahero; sintemal*, and *allermaßen*). This topic acquires its full meaning only when seen in the context of the French theory of *style coupé*, even though in Germany it had a special implication as part of the critique of *Kanzleistil*. Indeed, Gottsched goes beyond the recommendation of dropping superfluous conjunctions and particles, since he proposes not the loose but the cut style, with short simple sentences rather than complex periods (*einfache* rather than *zusammengesetzte Perioden*). His argument is that attention to detail can be closer and comprehension fuller when the mind does not have to keep several things together at the same time. When the thought is complex, the way to render it clearly and economically is not to produce a complex period, but to separate the elements and line them up in orderly succession (pp. 269–97). And he gives a lengthy example from Fléchier. His concept was a good point of departure for the reform of German style, but the way to go was very long indeed, and Gottsched himself was unable to follow such theories in his own oratorical practice. The remainder of the chapter analyzes and lists the figures.

In chapter xv he gives examples of bad style. Particularly noteworthy is the discussion of the *allzuweitläufige Schreibart*, failing in clear distinction of members, and therefore of thoughts (§ 22); § 23 then takes up the opposite, the *allzu kurze, . . . gezwungene Art*, that the Greeks called the Laconic (*die lakonische*). This style lacks all *Bindewörter*, omits some members or parts of speech, plays with riddles, thus demanding much reflection for understanding (p. 343). Tacitus and at times the two Plinys wrote in this manner, in Germany Gottfr. Polyk. Müller (cf. "Hist. Einleitung," § 29) and Lassenius. He censures only the "lakonische Kürze," not "die attische," he says. The example he gives from Lassenius is not so much obscure as it is overdone with extremely short, quick clauses (like what the French called *style haché*, rather than a style showing the extreme Taciteanism most often associated with the model of the Italian Malvezzi).

Chapter xvi (pp. 347–63) describes the good types of writing and their uses. The expressions *die gelassene, die sinnreiche, die bewegende Schreibart* appear in § 14, p. 357 (p. 406 in 1759 ed., reprt. 1975), and the three types are analyzed successively in §§ 14–17. The first was commonly called *natürliche Schreibart*; the three are rather improperly related by Gottsched to Cicero's terminology in *Orator*, chapter 29: "Is erit igitur eloquens . . . qui poterit parva summisse, modica temperate, magna graviter dicere." He also acknowledges another type of classification into Laconian, Attic, Rhodian, and Asiatic, somewhat corresponding to his own classification.

I have already mentioned as a typical case of Latin influence the issue of participial constructions, consisting of clauses hinging on a participle made "absolute" or "loose" by being undeclined and pre- or postpositioned. Gottsched disliked their use for heavy periodic purposes, but he had to admit that one like the following would be unobjectionable: *Sterbend ging er hin, lebend kam er wieder.*[48] However humanistic in origin, and of Latin, poetic flavor, a sentence of this kind would be more Senecan than Ciceronian. The Swiss **Haller** attacked Gottsched on this matter in his review of the latter's *Sprachkunst* for the *Göttinger Gelehrte Zeitung* of 1749. Although overstated, Gottsched's position was in line with the need to lighten up the German sentence and free it from the Baroque heritage. Later on, in his 19th *Literaturbrief*, 1. Theil of 1759,[49] **Lessing** notes with approval that in the new edition of the *Messias*, Klopstock had dropped a number of participles that had made his periods heavy and obscure, as in . . . *seit der Erschaffung / In der ersten von Gott ihm gegebenen Herrlichkeit glänzte*, which has become . . . *in der Herrlichkeit glänzte, die ihm der Donnerer anschuf*. But resistance had kept coming from many quarters, and another Swiss, J. J. **Breitinger**, *Critische Dichtkunst* (Zürich and Leipzig, 1740, 2 vols., vol. II, p. 150), defended participles for their emphatic value (*nachdrücklich*), as in *Die Diener liessen die Pferde, um den Bauch festgegürtet, an das Gestade hinunter*, rather than *Die Diener liessen die um die Bäuche wohlgegürteten Pferde an das Gestade hinunter*. Likewise, *Die Welt verehrte todt, wer lebend sie verheerte*, which he called a good case of ellipsis.[50]

The division of schools had become clear, but only the reactionary party (best represented by Gottsched's critic Dornblüth) was still clinging to a Ciceronian position; the true periodic and florid style was by now superseded and relegated to the literarily stale spheres of the

Kanzleistil. The other two major parties were advocating what could be described as varieties of Senecanism, the curt and the loose, or broadly Tacitean and *coupé*. An anonymous reviewer of Schönaich's *Hermann* described most effectively the division of these two schools in Germany in 1752 (*Göttinger Gelehrte Zeitung*) as follows: "Die eine sucht die Größe in starcken Bildern, erhabenen Gedanken und gewichtigen Beiwörtern. Die andere schätzt die Gedichte nach der Reinigkeit der Sprache, nach der Deutlichkeit des Vortrages und der Flüssigkeit der Schreibart."[51] In other words, the one is chiefly after the *sinnreich* made such by the figures of thought, whereas the other prizes above all purity, clarity, and plainness.

Yet the reactionary partisans and obdurate apologists of the chancery style do not deserve to be dismissed and simply thrown into oblivion. Indeed, not only was their cause, though backward-looking and essentially sterile, far from being a dead one (bureaucratese is immortal, and certainly less mortal in Germany than anywhere else), but some of their arguments threw light on features that were valid and acceptable even outside the domains of *Kanzleistil*. One example will suffice. The chancery style was signally fond of, and ridiculed for its addiction to, periphrasis and variation, including double negative for a positive as a device of diplomatic indirectness (*nicht nur . . . sondern auch*, *mir zweifelt nicht, daß* for *ich bin sicher*), obsequious politeness, tautological doublets (hendiadys), and above all *connectio verbalis* — that is, transitions made explicit through the heavy use of conjunctions and particles, whereas the *connectio realis* relied on the reader's intuition by making sure that the ideas clearly showed their own logical connection by themselves.[52] But one must not forget that some of these devices, and especially diplomatic indirectness, were also common to the courtly writers of the French salons in the seventeenth and eighteenth centuries, including the most elegant of them, from St-Simon to Crébillon fils.

At any rate, the most determined of Gottsched's adversaries in this line of thought was no other than the Benedictine **Father Augustin Dornblüth**, with his ponderous and bilious *Observationes oder gründliche Anmerckungen über die Art und Weise eine gute Übersetzung besonders in die teutsche Sprach zu machen* (Augsburg: Mattheus Rieger, 1755).[53] What makes this curious document important and even exemplary is that it contains one of the most systematic presentations in favor of a view that many observers, past and present, consider self-evident, namely, that the German language is the natural host for periodic sentence structures of the sort experienced in the chancery style. Seeing the matter from this *Stellungnahme*, Dornblüth considered Gottsched not a genuine German writer, but a disguised French stylist in a hybrid garb.

The first section of this work that reveals its pedantic author as a total devotee of the *Kanzleistil* even from its title is chapter 15, "De transitionibus et earum particulis" (pp. 190–205). It contains a full defense of the *connectio verbalis*, understood as the logical and necessary clothing of the *connectio realis* through the formal and methodic use of *transitiones*, conjunctions and particles. The context of the discussion is clearly, from the outset, a polemic against French *coupé* style and its conspicuous feature of doing away with most conjunctions. Since *coupé* style was the result of a long tradition of theoretical speculation that appealed for its authority far beyond mere grammar or school rhetoric, all the way to the foundations of Stoic logic, it is important to keep this background in mind to perceive the full scope of the argument at a stage when a man like Dornblüth assumes the defense of the opposite tradition — basically, the Ciceronian in the positive setting of German *Kanzleistil*.

Dornblüth begins (pp. 190–1):

As already discussed elsewhere, the French have undertaken to avoid equally all *transitiones* (God only knows through what obstinacy), so that in their books one often is held up a long time before being able to perceive the connection between something and the foregoing. . . . But the French have become so accustomed to this that they no longer notice the lack of clarity which results from the absence of *transitiones*. Such practices are unacceptable in German, because in this language we would end up with incoherent discourse, as one sees in the sermons of Mossheim, and all those who fashionably either translate directly from the French or try to imitate them.

Now the *regula claritatis*, he goes on, demands the maximum use of all the means at our disposal to achieve a direct, clear communication with the reader or listener (one can never be *too* clear), therefore French must be translated *ad sensum* and not literally, much more so because the German language demands *formam periodicam*. In other words, he wants no truck with those who prefer juxtaposition to intercalation.

THEORY OF SENTENCE STRUCTURE ☐ 27

The remainder of this chapter is a rambling, pedantic series of censures with regard to the allegedly incorrect use of conjunctions: The rules and the examples are often moot, inept, or even wrong (one must be advised that Dornblüth's writing is generally confused and unclear, besides being so frightfully archaic).

Chapters or "Anmerckungen" 16 and 20 deal with matters that we will have to consider in our section on Word Order. Chapter 21 then turns to the question of participles, under the title "Participia praeteriti sobrie applicanda; praesentis vero nunquam aut rarissime, nec nisi ex necessitate ponenda." Past participles, he asserts, are all right when not too heavy; present participles, however, are to be avoided.

Finally, chapter 43, "An stilum modernorum Saxonum sequi consuetum sit? Critica Grammaticae Gottschedii" (pp. 322–62), first considers whether it is advisable[54] to follow the linguistic and stylistic practices of the Saxons, and answers in the negative, then throws the last arrows against Gottsched's grammar. Page 354 refers to Gottsched's censure of the Laconic style, accusing him of practicing it himself. Dornblüth, in other words, is part of the Ciceronian party against Senecans of all hues.

Thereupon follows the final, explicit defense of the *Kanzleistil* (which he calls the *ganz-periodischer Kantzley-Stylus*, p. 355) against Gottsched's strictures in his *Redekunst* and *Sprachkunst*. A long quotation is given of one of the attacks, *Redekunst* p. 292, § 3, where the principal objection is that the practitioners of this contorted and unnatural style write routinely in the manner conventionally transmitted by their profession, thus betraying their lack of a humanistic, liberal education (lack of *freye Künste*, mere *Schlendrian*). Writing is for them not a literary activity but a mechanical means to exercise their trade: They are only professional bureaucrats, who would do well to take a trip to France and see how naturally a Bussy-Rabutin or a St-Évremond writes (pp. 356–7). All that Dornblüth can say in rebuttal is that Gottsched does not respect the differences among genres: There is a style for oratory, another for history, another for reasoning, and so on, and their differences must be reflected in the modes they choose for communication.[55]

One underlying idea that gives life to this otherwise uninspiring exercise is a serious one, and one that has both a long history and an important future. It is the patriotic, nationalistic idea that the superiority of the German language was founded on its being a manly and heroic language (*männlich*, *Heldensprache*) — and that periodicity was an essential ingredient of that quality. Even in his time Dornblüth was not alone in this opinion. If his allies were not to be found among such leading critics as Gottsched and Bodmer — at opposite ends in other respects but together in rejecting periodicity — one could find the defense of periodicity coupled with that of the *Heldensprache* in the Bavarian Catholic periodical *Parnassus Boicus oder Neu-eröffneter Musen-Berg* (1722–40), in an article that appeared in three installments in 1723–24. Personally, while rejecting the Saxon model, Dornblüth found his ideal criterion in the language of the *Reichskammergericht* at Speyer in the 1680s.[56]

In the later periods, a basic shift was consummated that moved the more vital discussions of such matters away from the discipline of rhetoric into that of linguistics. It is, therefore, not necessary for us to follow this late development text by text, and we shall proceed, when we pick up again the subject of sentence structure (in ch. 3, 1), with a sampling of typical theories down to the present. We will, in particular, note how the circle was ideally closed, as it were, when **Heinrich Bauer** (1833) logically associated sentence structure and word order in the same section of syntax under the heading of *Topik*, thus bringing again together, within grammar, the two concerns that had been together, within rhetoric, in the classical theory of *compositio* (Gr. *synthesis*). The separation had prevailed in the Middle Ages and down to the end of the eighteenth century. After Bauer it will again be possible, indeed natural, to treat the two subjects together, as we shall do.

CHAPTER 2

THE THEORY OF WORD ORDER FROM THE RENAISSANCE TO ADELUNG

1. Renaissance to Steinbach

And now, to the questions specifically concerning word order. To put, into proper perspective the main thrust of the following survey as well as to throw light on some of the assessments it contains, I must anticipate summarily the general conclusion of this study by saying that it is based on the hypotheses recently advanced by Theo Vennemann and his collaborator Renate Bartsch. Their ideas will be expounded and discussed in detail at the end of our historical presentation. It will suffice here to state that they propose to explain the German linguistic system by assuming that it presents a combination of two conflicting systems, basically SOV (Subject + Object + Verb), the original form still prevalent in subordinate clauses, and SVO, which started to replace it at some time but has so far been unable to move beyond the main clause. For the advantages it offers in complex analysis, the formula SVX (or TVX) is used occasionally in place of SVO, X meaning "objects and everything else," and T "topic" rather than merely "subject."

To begin our survey with a brief reference to the ancients, Dionysius of Halicarnassus confessed to have first espoused, and then rejected, the doctrine whereby the order of words would have been determined by nature in such a manner that substance (the noun) should precede accident (the verb).[1] But he had applied this principle of nominal priority in a rather radical and logically indiscriminate way, insofar as he had made no syntactic distinction between subject and object,[2] since his examples were of sentences with direct object first, then verb ("ăndra moi ĕnnepe, Moūsa," etc.). Henri Weil 1844, p. 5 fn. 1, accused Dionysius of having misunderstood his sources, but Jellinek disagrees. Thus, for Dionysius the adverb also should follow its verb, because the circumstance is secondary to the action (or passion).[3]

Priscian gave the example *fortis imperator fortiter pugnat* to show adverb before verb and adjective before noun.[4] On the other hand, the Lat. qualificative adjective normally followed its head noun; cf. *bonus vir*, but *civis romanus* (and also *vir bonus* for emphasis, see Quintilian). Hence *domus aurea*, then similarly *filius Caesaris* and *pulchrior amico* or *quam amicus eius*, according to Greenberg's "universal," whereby genitives and comparatives are harmonic with the NA (Noun + Adjective) or AN order as it prevails in a given language (for Greenberg's rules, see below). All this appeared to follow the classical (logical) rule still echoed by Alexander de Villadei and contradicted in that narrow case by Priscian. The classical rule was theoretically grounded on the philosophical consideration that what is necessary (the noun) must precede what is unnecessary or dispensable (the adjective). Hence the subject must precede the complement (and the verb itself, in the sense that a noun, but not a verb, can stand by itself and make some sense).

The rule happened to correspond *grosso modo* to the widely held grammatical principle of precedence of governing element over the governed, of the determined over the determinant, the qualified over the qualifier — a principle that later would sound both logical and natural to speakers of Romance languages. The facts of classical literary Latin that did not jibe with these patterns were explained as part of *ordo artificialis*, an artistic, rhetorical, stylistic choice rather than a grammatical or logical feature. But the matter did present a difficulty to observers accustomed to the movements of German, since this language appeared to reverse the Latin order part by part in the sequences adjective + noun, nominal compounds, and determinant → determinand; therefore it could not justify itself by invoking Latin precedent.

Generally, the axioms of noun before adjective and subject before predicate, pillars of SVO doctrine just as they had been the logical foundation of ancient syntax, were founded on such ontologically misplaced dicta as *prius est esse quam sic esse* and *prius est esse quam operari*.[5]

According to Thurot (pp. 87 ff.), the first medieval representation of word order is a Priscian manuscript of the eleventh century, but Jellinek considers much more relevant a treatise "Quomodo VII circumstantie rerum in legendo ordinande sint" (ca. 1000?), which is bound together in a Brussels manuscript with Notker's letters, the St. Gall rhetoric, and the *De partibus logicae*, all of these edited by Paul Piper, *Die Schriften Notkers*.

Rather typically, this "St. Gall treatise," to use Jellinek's designation, shows the medieval SVO order with the philosophical justification that the object must follow the verb because the *passio* must come after the *actio*: "prius semper actio et deinde passio. In verbo enim actio est, in obliquo casu fit passio."[6] "Et quia verba transitiva sunt, videamus unde et quo transeant. Scilicet a nominativo in obliquum, si activum verbum est, hoc est ab agente in patientem, ut *Varro docet Ciceronem*. Si autem passivum est, transitio fit de obliquo in nominativum, ut *Cicero docetur a Varrone*."

Some of the earliest grammatical texts containing German rules have been edited by Johannes Müller in 1882, starting with the *Exercitium puerorum grammaticale per dietas distributum* (Antwerp 1485, then Hagenau 1491), as well as the *Quadrivium Grammatices Johannis Coclaei Norici artium magistri Norimbergae nuper elucubratum*, of 1511.[7]

These two texts are of some interest insofar as they exemplify the absence of direct influx of Latin patterns at this date, as with Claius later, 1578, since the relative freedom in the position of the verb is not affected by the visible temptation of placing it last, even in dependent clauses, in imitation of the Latin phrases offered in the formal examples. One should keep in mind that the juxtaposed Latin examples appear to have remained inconsequential to the effect of verbal position when one thinks of the thesis that end-position was affected in a decisive way (starting in the following century) by the desire to imitate Latin style. Thus for 'precepit quod ego vocassem' we find *das ich solt haben gerufen*; 'cum vocatus sim vel fuerim' becomes *als ich bin oder gewest bin gerufen*; the only cases where one might read the impact of the Latin pattern are, somewhat perversely, two where the *Satzklammer* is consequently broken: 'Ego vocabor ab uno' gives *ich soll be-*

rufen werden von eym; 'tu vocaberis ab alio,' *du solt werden berufen von eym andern*. Even as late as 1578 we find in Claius (p. 87 of the reprinted edition) 'cum amatus sim vel fuerim' rendered with *so ich bin geliebet worden*.[8]

The background to German grammatical speculation through most of the seventeenth century (and including the pivotal figure of Schottelius) must be traced back, rather than to the contemporary French grammarians, to the two distinct yet sometimes convergent trends established by Melanchthon's humanistic Latin grammar (1525–6) and Ramus's logical reform. Ramist influence, in particular, was transmitted by **Wolfgang Ratke (Ratichius,** 1571–1635) and by his collaborator **Christoph Helwig (Helvicus,** 1581–1617), whose *Libri didactici grammaticae universalis, Latinae, Graecae, Hebraicae, Chaldaicae*, and the German version of it, *Sprachkunste*: I. *Allgemeine*, II. *Lateinische*, III. *Hebraische; teutsch geschrieben durch Weyland den . . . Herren Christophorum Helvicum . . .* , were published by his widow in 1619 (Giessen: Caspar Chemlin).[9] Helwig's universal grammar was carried on by **Heinrich Alsted** in the *Delineatio grammaticae germanicae*, part of his *Encyclopedia* in 7 tomes (Herborn, 1630).

These summary bibliographic indications shall suffice for the general ideological or theoretical orientation and background of late Renaissance and early Baroque grammatical activity in the German area. What concerns us directly are the empirical steps taken in detailed analysis by the following grammarians. The first that imposes himself to our attention is **Laurentius Albertus** with his *Teutsch Grammatick* of 1573.[10]

A complete description of German word order must rely on an articulate conception of hypotaxis. Since such a notion was lacking until the middle of the eighteenth century, we cannot expect a distinction of verbal position between main and secondary clauses, and consequently an assessment of inversion in main clauses (VS) when caused by anteposition of a secondary clause or of any clause-complement or adverb. Once this expectation has been disposed of, one must acknowledge Laurentius Albertus's unusual power of observation in detail. He is, though, unmethodical; he scatters his rules all over the text instead of packing them neatly under the heading of syntax. We will pick them up in the order in which he chose to give them.

We begin with the section of Morphology dedicated to the Verb. He notes that German allows no finite verb to go without expressed preceding subject (more precisely, *nomen vel pronomen*), even though Latin often omits it *per ellipsim* (p. 93). We could then say, in our own words, that normally the verb has second place. And he shrewdly adds that German is very particular about "construction" (*constructio* then being synonymous with word order), so much so, that it does not even allow impersonal verbs to appear without an anteposed nominative ("*articulus es, es gerewet* 'poenitet,' *es nutzt* 'refert,' *es pflegt* 'solet'"). In his words, "Adeo autem sollicita est lingua nostra de constructione, ut ne impersonalia quidem verba praecedentibus suis nominativis destituat" (p. 94). Further on (p. 97), having turned to *composita verba*, he notes that such *praepositiones* as *be-, ent-, un-, zer- et similes* can be called *inseparabiles*. The others, *auß, ein, in, wider, ab, zu et similes*, being separable, can come at the beginning of the verb or later, but not indifferently, since their position depends on the tense and mood. He gives no precise rule but points out that normally the *infinitivus* keeps them in front, unless poetic rhythm requires *anastrophe*, as in *treiben auß, denken für* for *fürdenken*.

Such compound verbs normally do not receive the *ge-* (of the participle): *Ich hab umgeben*, not *umgegeben* (p. 103). Yet some do admit the *ge-*, especially those composed with *an-* and *auß-*. It is to be noted that Laurentius Albertus does not practice the separation of separable particles in the finite tenses, although he recognizes that it can take place as the more common usage, *usitatius* (and he calls it, once again, an *anastrophe*: "*Ich anmaß*" or "*maß an, ich hab angemasset*"). He adds that he regards truly separable compounds as complete phrases made up of verbs and adverbs rather than as *composita verba*. Therefore the *ge-* (*augmentum*) is added because it is as if these verbs remained simple: *Ich bin hinweg gegangen*.

The auxiliary immediately precedes its participle in compound tenses: *Ich hab gefürchtet* (p. 104); but if accusative objects are present, they are positioned between the two: *Ich hab den Herren und seinen Zorn gefürchtet* (p. 105). It is in this way that Laurentius Albertus shows awareness of the German *Satzklammer*. In verse, to be sure, reigns the freedom of the Greeks and Romans, so that the accusatives sometimes follow: *Ich hab gefürchtet den Herren*. Pronouns habitually precede their verbs, but "in iuramentis et execrationibus, obtestationibus et interrogationibus, interiacent verbum *hab* et accusativum qui a praeterito (i.e., the participle) regitur hoc ordine: *Hab ich solchs gethan, so straff er mich* 'Si hoc ego feci, puniat me.'" That is to say, the subject (here a pronoun) lies between the finite verb and the object, this latter being followed by the participle. Yet the author misses here the true nature of this typically German hypothetical construction, which shall be correctly analyzed in the early eighteenth century. At any rate, the rule as stated is correct even though the example chosen is somewhat marginal: It is the rule of first place for the verb.

He then comes as close as anyone before 1750 to a recognition of the nature of hypotaxis when he reflects that in specifically listed types of *membra* that are suspended and incomplete, since they cannot form a complete sentence by themselves (and these we call dependent clauses), the verb goes to the end — but he is speaking only of the auxiliary *haben* (p. 105). This section and the preceding are referred to under stricture by Jellinek (II, p. 442), and the passage deserves full quotation (pp. 105–6):

In execrationibus, in causalibus et racionatiuis orationum membris, in interrogationibus, aposiopesibus, comminationibus, parenthesibus [note the borrowing of terminology from the rhetorical doctrine of figures, a well developed and influential field, in the absence of an elaborate, systematic grammatical terminology], et in iis membris, quae a Graecis et Latinis cola dicuntur [note here the classical term *kólon*, the closest thing to 'clause'], duobus punctis a Latinis signata [introduction of the medieval custom of designating syntactic divisions by relative punctuation marks], et quae suspendi ac tractim enunciari volunt [the "physiological" theory of sentence divisions], quia sententia adhuc imperfecta est, necessario enim aliquid subsequi debet, quam figuram Graeci ἀπαγγελίαν vocant, tum verbum *hab* in finem collocatur, *als* execrative . . . , ratiocinative, *dieweil er sich dann dessen angemasset hat* 'siquidem haec ausus fuit' . . . , *wann ers gethan* 'si fecit,' Aposiopesis est.[11]

An observation is in order here, since a curious implicit confluence is apparent of Albertus's comments with modern research. In an important comprehensive study on German word order, F. Maurer (1926) concluded the section on dependent clauses (p. 181) by proposing a project of research on medieval Latin and German grammarians designed to establish whether there could be an impact of theoretical and scholastic grammars on German word order. Maurer felt inclined to accept C. Biener's yet unproven axiom that such grammars were to be credited with helping the establishment of final position for the verb (p. 181). Albertus is certainly a good case in point. Furthermore and more specifically, Maurer found a difference between *haben* and *sein* in their relative frequency of end-position, the former being markedly less frequent (see pp. 164–8, with Maurer's hypothesis for explanation of this difference). It is therefore noteworthy that Albertus could concentrate *de facto* on recommending final position for *haben*, the very auxiliary that tended to resist the Latinizing trend. One must add that Albertus deviates from the last-position rule as soon as he goes beyond the auxiliary *haben*, as in the examples "*so ich lesen werden* oder *ich werde lesen* 'si legero'" (p. 107).

On p. 133 we read a workable and comprehensive definition of *coniunctio* as that which "casus nominum, modos et tempora verborum, membra sententiarum, et sententias orationum subinde connectit." As to the order of conjunctions, "quaedam . . . praeponuntur," whereas some "praeponi et postponi indifferenter volunt," like *aber* and *auch* (p. 136).

Turning then to *syntaxis* (pp. 137–49), he begins by pointing out that the adjective always precedes its noun, except in the vocative *Vatter unser*, and in verse. Further on (p. 143): the "nominativus gestum significans sequitur verbum: *er schlafft stehent, er starb sitzendt*." Finally, and most interestingly (pp. 148–9), he makes the rather strange remark (but in keeping with Priscian, *vide*) that adverbs mostly precede their verb: *Cicero hat am besten geredt* — an example that contradicts the rule, since what the adverb precedes is not the verb but the participle. Speaking of conjunctions, he offers a gem that will come back in Gottsched's grammar, but without realizing its value: *das* (= *daß*) is often omitted: *Ich wunscht es gescheh*. The impact on the position of the verb is neither mentioned nor shown in examples. And he closes with an equally precious tidbit on the "anastrophe" of certain prepositions: *Ein gantz Jar uber, Den gantzen tag durch auß*.[12]

In his grammar published in the same year as Albertus's, **Albert Ölinger**, *Unterricht der HochTeutschen Sprach* (1573),[13] although relying on Melanchthon's Rules, shows no awareness of the distinction between main and dependent clauses; yet he gives examples of *Satzklammer*, but with oscillation in order: See "*Ach* oder *Wollte Gott ich were* vel *seye gewesen*," but "*Oh* oder *Wolt Gott das ich geschrieben hette*" for optative perfect and pluperfect, and then again, for optative future, "*Wolt Gott das ich solte schreiben*," etc. (pp. 77, 78, 83). In the first two examples, the variation in order might reflect the difference between direct and indirect construction (i.e., without or with *daß*), as already noted by Laurentius Albertus, but the third example gives the finite verb in nonfinal position despite the presence of *daß*.[14] We should note also that Ölinger's practice does not conform with Maurer's findings on the relative frequency of end-position between *haben* and *sein*.

The *Grammatica* of **Johannes Claius** (1578)[15] shows, in the example *So ich hette geliebet*, the independence of end-position (which appears occasionally and unsystematically) from the subjunctive, whereas in the next century their concomitance appears to become a rule, even to the point of confusing the subjunctive with verbal end-position. Fleischmann (p. 332) aptly notes that Claius's already quoted example, *so ich bin geliebet worden* (p. 87 of the reprinted edition), may attest (though not unequivocally, I should add) to a usage that Gottsched deemed worthy of erection to the status of a rule, namely, that in a dependent clause the finite element of a three-element verbal form precedes the others.

Claius, like his predecessors, recognizes the peculiarity of German *Satzklammer*, and extends his observations on the matter not only to the participles and infinitives in compounded verbal forms, but also to the separable particles of compound verbs. He duly notes, however, that *be-*, *ge-*, *ver-*, *zer-* do not separate, since these *praepositiones* are characterized by their not bearing the verb's accent (p. 163). This crucial accentual principle will not be mentioned again in a rigorous way until the nineteenth century, as far as I have been able to ascertain. Aside from this rule, in attempting to identify the cases when the separation does not take place, Claius is, of course, unable to connect them with end-position (due to subordination). However, he aptly points out that this rule of non-separation not only does not obtain after certain conjunctions (and he notes that *Wolt Gott ich schriebe ab* becomes *Wolt Gott das ich abschriebe*, because of the introduction of *daß*), but is a consequence of (we would say) subordination since it is also found after relatives: *Der ich abschriebe* 'qui describo' (p. 77).[16]

Apparently leaning on Claius (the most successful grammarian of his time, who continued to be reprinted until the eleventh edition of 1720), **Stephan Ritter**, *Grammatica germanica nova* . . . (1616),[17] p. 151, assigns particle separation to present and imperfect of the indicative and to the imperative, but excludes it from the present and imperfect of optative and subjunctive (and, of course, the infinitive). Leaving aside the optative, which was a mere throwback to Greek grammar without foundation on morphological reality (a practice that remained common in all modern language grammars as it had been in Latin),[18] the reference to subjunctive reflects the enduring prejudice that it was the mood of subordination; as such, it normally came at the end, where separation of the particle will not apply.[19]

Christian Gueintz, *Deutscher Sprachlehre Entwurf* (1641),[20] displays no original point, but the same year saw the appearance of the first grammatical work of **Justus Georgius Schottelius**, the *Teutsche Sprachkunst*.[21] Schottel was one of the great scholars of his age, tutor to the sons of the Duke of Brunswick. His more important work, the *Ausführliche Arbeit von der Teutschen Haubt-Sprache*, appeared 22 years later (1663).[22] His theoretical orientation must be seen against the background of the confluence of Melanchthon's humanistic grammar and the universal grammar on logical grounds inspired by the Ramist reform and carried on by Ratke, Helwig, Finck, and Alsted. Accordingly, Schottel develops a sort of 'absolutist' notion of the German language based on a fundamental structure or system (*Grundrichtigkeit*), which he sees centered on the word rather than on the sentence, and which is as unchangeable as it is beyond the relativity of usage and dialects.[23]

Schottel remains a child of his time in the uncertainty with which he attempts to analyze the syntactic mechanisms of subordination and consequent ordering, although he is among the first to free the subjunctive both from the presence of conjunctions and from subordination itself, since he is, according to Fleischmann, pp. 335, 367, the first to give the subjunctive without accompanying introductory conjunctions in his paradigms, and in a position that indicates possible use in independent clauses.[24] Nevertheless, he does not show a clean break with the tradition, insofar as he still formally defines this mood as dependent on conjunctions. Furthermore, he precludes for himself the opportunity to link certain conjunctions with subordination, since he classifies the conjunctions simply by their semantic value. More seriously still, he displays the rhetorical bent of much of his time's speculation on linguistic matters when he analyzes the rule of the verb's end-position by referring it simply, under the pressure of the taste imposed by the *Kanzleistil*, to the particular predilection of the German language for ending a sentence with a significant verb, in a display of *Satzklammer* effect. Let us listen to him (*Ausführliche Arbeit*, p. 755):

Es lautet wol und schleust sich ordentlich in teutscher Sprache, wenn man die Meynungen also einfügen, und die Spruchrede (*periodum*) mit dem Hauptzeitworte (*illo verbo quò totus sensus respicit, seu quod primarium significandi locum in periodo obtinet*) schliessen oder endigen kan.

And the example is:

Wie ein Mensch in einem Bilde die Kunst, und nicht das Bild, in einer Pflantze die Frucht, und nicht die Pflantze liebet, also müssen wir in einem schönen Frauenzimmer nicht die Gestalt, sondern wo sie vorhanden, die Schönheit des Gemüthes, und in dem Gemüthe die Schönheit dessen, von dem sie herrühret, erheben und hoch halten.

The observation, based on the desire to revive in German the virtues of Latin periodicity, is logically right but grammatically wrong, because it is with dependent verbs (*erheben, hochhalten*) that the sentence of the example ends, not with principal ones, like the Latin "Ciceronian" period, despite Schottel's reference to "the verb that contains the primary meaning." He can so refer to it because he thinks of the logical sense of the sentence, not of its grammatical constitution, and therefore he disregards the auxiliary *müssen*. In terms of Latin syntax, we cannot say therefore that we have here a "period." The difficulty was, at any rate, that a precise description would have necessitated distinguishing between an independent clause, in which the more meaningful verb would come last, after its auxiliary or modal, and the dependent clause, in which the auxiliary or modal would come last.[25]

The *Ausführliche Arbeit* is an impressive achievement that strikes today's reader, even on first approach, by its topical and typographic organization. One cannot help but think of the author as the contemporary of Komenský and the court tutor of the Prince of Braunschweig.[26] Not only is Schottel well informed on his direct predecessors (he cites, for example, Laurentius Albertus, p. 21), but also on the foreign ones. In fact, he can be said to open in an authoritative manner the long and painstaking discourse with French grammarians and rhetoricians that will occupy German linguistic speculation for the next hundred years, thus making his country largely subservient to a position of reaction to whatever charges came out of the neighboring country. He begins by offering a quick rebuke of the French Claude Duret's statement that German is an unnecessarily and unnaturally complicated language: "On l'apprend difficilement et est encore plus fascheux à prononcer: de sorte que les enfants mêmes, qui sont naiz au pays, sont bien grandeletz avant qu'ils puissent bien former les mots et proférer les paroles." This is an interesting point that psychologists have continued to test even in our century; but Schottel counters without much ado: "Dieses letzte aber werden auch die Kinder bekennen, daß es misgesaget sey" (p. 21).

Constructio or syntax is covered in Book Three.[27] He starts right out with a warning not to indulge in the excesses of *Satzklammer*, thus opening the long campaign against the vices of *Kanzleistil* that will be joined by all the most sensible grammarians: "Nimiam distantiam nominis et verbi, periodum vinculantis, affectare, vitiosum est." In discussing the position of nominative pronouns (which, like nominative nouns, precede their verbs), he fails to note among the reasons for inversion the impact of an adverb at the head, or of a secondary clause preceding the main clause, as in the very example he gives: *Doch wie er wil, lebt niemand hier*; *Liebet ihr uns? So lieben wir euch wieder* (p. 742).

He notes the separation of auxiliaries from their infinitives, but he warns against allowing too great a distance between the two. The examples sound, once again, as a healthy condemnation of the incapsulated style. He notes that auxiliaries referring to several verbs need not be repeated: Coming at the close of a period, they cover all the preceding parallel verbs (p. 743, §§ 3–4). Similarly, infinitives covering several objects need not be repeated (§ 5).

In compound verbs, the preposition may have to be separated and moved to the right: "Von den gedoppelten Zeitwörteren ist in gemein zumerken, daß dieselbigen . . . zertheilet werden, also daß . . . muß das Vorwort folgen" (§ 11, p. 747). Putting this together with the feature already mentioned (§ 3), separation of auxiliaries, he concludes that German is unique in this, and that correct usage in such matters is the result of close application: "Denn solches komt einem Knaben oftmals schwer und seltsam vor: Wenn er aber der Hülfswörter und Vorwörter und dero Stellen und Fügungen berichtet ist, wird er sich richtig finden können." As one can see, Duret's intuitions on German children's linguistic troubles may have been brushed aside a bit too quickly, and seem to linger on in Schottel's mind. Although *um* and *ab* are separable, they normally would not be separated in this manner.

He is, of course, aware of the inseparable particles *be, er, ent, ver, zer* (p. 748). Furthermore, the separation may occur in exceptional cases and forms through poetic license: *Bey einem Berge sie um den Verrähter brachte* (=*umbrachte*); *Das Eisen bricht entzweg / ab sie den Pantzer streiffen* (=*abstreiffen*) (ibid.).

When dealing with the separation of separable particles, Schottel no longer refers to the difference among verbal moods, as some of his predecessors had done (like Claius and Ritter, who expanded on Ölinger's remark that the separation occurs in the present and imperfect of the indicative, by pointing out that it occurs in the imperative also, but not in the subjunctive). We know that it occurs in all moods (but with the infinitive and participle it is limited to the insertion of *zu* and *ge-*). The main point is that it does not occur when the verb is in a dependent clause, and Schottel is on the right track when he states that the separation does not occur when the verb is introduced by *so, wenn, daß, als, der* (the first and last in relative sense) (p. 748) — that is to say, when it is introduced, as we would put it, by a subordinating conjunction or pronoun. An intimation of the right orientation was in Claius when he said that the optative may or may not take *daß*, and exemplified: *Wolt Gott ich schriebe ab*, or *Wolt Gott daß ich abschriebe*. Better still, Claius himself pointed out that the relative pronoun also impeded the separation (78, 2 ff.: *Der du abschreibest*), whereas Schottel overlooked the relatives (relative and other subordinate clauses were not understood as being in the same syntactic range until close to the end of the eighteenth century, even in France, as we shall see).[28]

Concerning one unoriginal and particularly confused grammarian of this period, **Johann Girbert**, *Deütsche Grammatica oder Sprachkunst*, 1653,[29] I wish to call attention to a notion that occurs in several other grammarians, from the Renaissance to the Enlightenment, and that modern linguists keep criticizing without being able to analyze it correctly. I have offered a solution of the problem in my *Ars grammatica* (1970), to which I refer the reader for full details. The problem is as follows. Girbert assimilates some indicative and subjunctive forms while listing the forms of the indicative, thus: "*Futurum*, die künfftige, als: *Ich werde schlagen*; *Ich werde geschlagen werden*. Hierher gehöret noch eine Art der künfftigen Zeit, *Futurum perfectum* genannt, wird formirt durch *werde haben* oder *würde haben*. Als: *Wenn ich würde geschlagen haben*; *Nachdem er würde geschlagen haben.*" (*Deütsche Grammatica*, Tabula 37, 67, 69.) The auxiliary *würde* is, of course, a subjunctive form, and its presence within the indicative is due to the fact that traditionally in Latin the anterior future was regarded as belonging exclusively to the subjunctive, in which, of course, it would become difficult to distinguish it from the perfect tense.[30]

By this time German grammatical speculation was beginning to come under French influence. One of the French grammarians who found echoes abroad was Louis Le Laboureur with his *Avantages de la langue françoise sur la langue latine* (Paris: G. de Luyne, 1669). This book often referred to Cordemoy's claim of superiority for those languages whose normal word order follows the order in which children learn — and children were said to observe first the things (subjects), then their qualities, and finally their actions or effects. Jellinek, for one, finds not only absurd but contradictory Cordemoy's further claim that children observe the objects of actions (*les termes des actions*) after the actions themselves, since objects are things too, and this would establish a hierarchy among things that cannot be attributed to the child's mental operations.[31]

Isaac Vossius answered Le Laboureur in *De poematum cantu* 39ff., as did Daniel Georg Morhof, *Unterricht von der teutschen Sprache und Poesie* (Kiel: Reumann, 1682; Lübeck & Frankfurt: J. Wiedermeyer, 1700, 1702, 1718).[32] But the analysis started to shift from the logical to a formally linguistic level with Bernard Lamy, *La rhétorique* (1687), who seems to have been the first to note that French word order has in part a syntactic function in that it replaces the lost flectional endings.[33]

Condillac, the major figure of his century in the broad area of linguistic speculation, began by postulating that nouns appeared before verbs, since in gesture language, man first pointed to the objects of his desires and then named them; later he gave names to his desires. Hence the natural order is to place the object (grammatical object, that is) first, then the verb, for example, *fruit vouloir*.[34] This view, more than revising them, practically reversed Cordemoy's rationalistic inferences. Consequently, Condillac insisted that *Darium vicit Alexander* must not be regarded as an inversion, even in the mature stage of the language. For from the point of view of consciousness, either the three concepts are simultaneous, without order of hierarchy, or they appear in a sequence, in which case *Darium* may be the element that evokes the others or vice versa, indifferently. But from the point of view of mental conception, the only thing one may postulate is that what is bound together without mediation must be expressed together without mediation. From this follows that *Darium* + *vicit* is a unit just as *Alexander* + *vicit*: Consequently, it will be indifferent whether *Darium* or *Alexander* comes in first or third place. Yet, according to this schema *vicit Darium Alexander* would, indeed, be an inversion — or at least an "unnatural" sentence. What neither Condillac nor anyone else could envisage at that time was a VSO order, which extra-European, and some then unknown European languages, do display.[35]

In the meantime, the thesis of free order, hence of the superiority of Latin models, that sanctioned the freedom of inversion, was upheld chiefly by Batteux. Diderot rebutted Batteux on other accounts, but trod the same ground in upholding Condillac's view on the simultaneous coexistence of several conceptions in the mind. As we shall see later on in greater detail, the opposite thesis of linear and chronological succession of ideas in the prelinguistic stage of the mind, and its parallelism with word ordering, marked the metaphysical and psychological stand of the doctrine of analytical or direct order.

As proof of direct order being the natural one, Du Marsais and Beauzée held up the fact that in inverted sentences, when the first element is an oblique case, it postulates its governor, which must therefore be present in the mind on a prioritary basis.[36] Shrewdly, Jellinek strikes this theory down as a *petitio principii* that could easily be turned on its head. First of all, one equaled the relationship between *regens* and *regimen* to the relationship between cause and effect, thus inferring that the *regens* must come first because the cause precedes its effect. But, as Batteux countered promptly (*De la construction oratoire*, Paris, 1763, p. 90), if *arma virumque* at the beginning postulates the transitive verb *cano*, of which it is the object, so, conversely, the transitive *cano* placed first would presuppose an accusative object.[37] And he went on suggesting that Beauzée had not thought of Hebrew, which nevertheless he knew, in which the *regens* is inflected (hence presupposes foreknowledge of the *regimen*), whereas the *regimen* remains unchangeable. In other words, we have, in this manner of reasoning, a dead-end street.

Stieler 1691 seems to have been the first to dedicate a special section to word order in a grammar predominantly designed for Germans.[38] Wahn and Steinbach followed him in this regard and then, after Gottsched, Heynatz and Hemmer. Before Stieler, no treatment was presented in a coherent fashion and our conclusions must, as a rule, be based on scattered observations. Regarding the position of the verb, only singular cases were treated, such as the placing of auxiliaries and the *trennbare Komposita*. Confusion arose from the habit of looking on the nominal forms of the verb as real verbs in the compound tenses, although Albertus, as we have seen, clarified that participles "per se revera non verba sunt, sed participia, nec activae, sed passivae vocis" (p. 104). This lack of realization is all the more surprising in that Latin grammar had consistently taught the separation of participles as a distinct part of speech.

Among the few grammarians who handled word order in a coherent, methodical fashion one can find that a traditional group proceeded by ordering all the *circumstantiae*. The best example is Finck-Helwig, *Grammatica latina*, 1621, pp. 359 f.:

Denique grammaticus ordo in quavis oratione talis est: 1. Constructionem orditur Adverbium vocandi, hortandi, . . . similitudinis; et vim relativam habentia, *donec, quando, siquidem, postquam*: Conjunctio, Interjectio. 2. Vocativus, si adsit. 3. Verbum impersonale cum suo casu. 4. His deficientibus, Nominativus, aut quod vice Nominativi fungitur, primum locum occupat. 5. Nominativo subjungitur vox illi cohaerens: nempe Adjectivum, item Genitivus vel Ablativus. 6. Hinc Verbum personale finitum. 7. Inde Adverbia caetera. 8. Et casus, qui a Verbo reguntur, ubi casuum ordo servandus.[39] 9. Succedunt Infinitivi cum Accusativo a fronte. 10. Ablativi consequentiae:[40] Et praepositiones cum suis casibus, Gerundia.[41]

In treating the position of the pronominal subject, **Johann Bödiker**, *Grundsätze der deutschen Sprache*, 1690,[42] "41. Regel der Syntax," states that it follows the verb when the object (*casus verbi*) appears before the verb, but that it remains in front as normal when there appears *wenn, wie, als, nachdem, so fern, so bald, damit, daß, auf daß*, or, also, *der* or *welcher* (this goes beyond Schottel). Jellinek suggests that Bödiker was aware that this was not a characteristic of

44 □ THEORY OF WORD ORDER

the pronoun alone, but of the subject in general, because in dealing with order in questions Bödiker states that "so stehet das Pronomen und auch sonst der Casus Nominativus hinten."[43]

Kaspar Stieler, *Kurze Lehrschrift von der Hochteutschen Sprachkunst*, in the appendix to *Der teutschen Sprache Stammbaum und Fortwachs oder Teutscher Sprachschatz . . . gesamlet von dem Spaten* (Nürnberg: Johann Hoffmann, 1691), chapter 24, sections 3–11, begins by stating (§ 3)

daß man allewege, wo die Hülfswörter gebraucht werden, mit dem Nennworte [noun: *nominativus* in Latin text], und zwar mit Vorsetzung des Geschlechtsworts [article], samt dem, was darzu gehöret, oder doch mit dem Vornennworte [pronoun] eine Rede anfange, darauf das Hülfwort und die Abwandelungen [complements], so von dem Zeitworte regiret werden, nebst den Vorwörtern und ihren Nennwörtern setze, mit dem andern Teil des Zeitwortes aber die ganze Rede beschliesse; Ist dann auch ein Zuwort (particle, preposition) dabey zu gebrauchen, so muß es ganz nahe vor dem letztern Zeitworte stehen. . . . Worbey zu beobachten, daß die Hülfwörter: *ich habe, ich bin, ich werde*, von ihren vergangenen und künftigen Zeitwörtern abgerissen und stracks nach dem ersten Nennwort gesetzet werden. . . . Wenn ich aber in gegenwärtiger und gantzvergangener [*imperfecto*] Zeit rede; so folget das Zeitwort stracks nach dem Nennwort mit den Zahlendungen, so das Zeitwort erfordert, und gehet so dann das Zuwort nach.[44]

Then, in § 5: When the clause begins with *wie, weil, indem, nachdem, so bald, in maßen, sintemal*, the whole verb must go to the end. In § 8: When the clause begins with a preposition and its oblique case ("Zuwort und eine abfallende Zahlendung des Nennworts"), the nominative goes after the verb. Next, § 9 warns not to place too many members between verb and separable particle or between auxiliary and participle or infinitive. Finally, § 10 gives the rules on final position of modals *wollen, sollen, mögen*, etc. Examples: *Ich hatte dieses wol denken sollen; wofern er sich dieses hätte bereden lassen können.*

Like Schottel and Girbert before him, Stieler repeats the by then inveterate notion (derived from Latin grammar) that the subjunctive mood depends on the use of certain conjunctions (and that, therefore, it belongs in what came to be called dependent clauses), even while, as earlier practice often had it, the examples offered contradictory cases of subjunctives in independent clauses (cf. pp. 125, 127ff.). The subjunctive was accordingly also referred to as *die Fügweise*, and furthermore it was regarded as a mood that required verbal end-position. Thus end-position, use of the subjunctive mood, and dependence on certain conjunctions all went together: "Die Fügweise der Zeitwörter sparet allemal ihr ganzes Zeitwort auf die letzte: sonderlich wenn die Wörtlein *daß, wenn, so* (as a relative), *wofern,* sich dabey einfinden" (pp. 198f.). The notion of end-position after these conjunctions is reiterated even more explicitly on p. 199, where the pronouns *der, die, das, so,* and *welcher* are added to the list of conjunctions. Only Steinbach and Aichinger will begin to lay aside this error concerning the subjunctive.[45]

Johann Daniel Longolius, *Einleitung zu gründtlicher Erkäntniß einer ieden, insonderheit aber der Teutschen Sprache* (Budissin: David Richter, 1715), uses (for the first time?) the terms *Haupt-* and *Nebensatz*, although only, as Jellinek, II, p. 473 underlined, in a logical, not grammatical, sense: "*Periodus conditionalis* oder der bedingende Fürtrag, welcher einen Hauptsatz mit einem gewissen bedingenden Nebensazze proponiret" (pp. 644ff.). But he still does not separate the *unterordnende* or *untergliedernde Konjunctionen* from the *beiordnende* or *nebengliedernde,* and in complex sentences he takes for granted that the dependent clause will come first, not after the main clause or imbedded in it (as relatives usually are), so that in the first part of these complex sentences the verb is generally deferred until the end of the clause, whereas in the other part it is placed first (with "inversion" or front-shifting of the verb in the main clause): "In teutschen *Periodis compositis* wird insgemein im ersten Theile das Verbum biß auf die Letzte gesparet, im andern Theile aber vorne angesetzet" (Theil 3, ch. 10, § 4, p. 646). He also, most interestingly, discriminates between *direkte* and *indirekte Rede,* though imperfectly and unclearly (he calls them *periodus recitativa* and *relativa,* p. 100).[46]

In chapter 10 of Part 3 on German clauses or periods ("von den teutschen Satzen oder Periodis"), §§ 2-5, Longolius shows once again the systematic pattern of sequences inherited from medieval Latin syntax: (§ 3) In *simple* periods not of the interrogative kind, we have first the interjection with its vocative, then the nominative article and the nominative adjective preceded by its adverb and followed by its nominative noun, then the genitive with its epithets, then the auxiliary or simple verb, together with the accusative or dative pronoun, thereafter the dative noun with its qualifiers, next the negative and the adverb, or else its substitutes (*vicaria phrasis*) and interjection, followed by the accusative noun or demonstrative adjective, and finally the main verb (presumably if there was an auxiliary before) or its separated particle.[47]

Longolius speaks of *ordo naturalis*, which he has just expounded, but he adds that it is not universal but peculiar to some languages (he has just analyzed the German), and that it represents the usual arrangement, from which, however, the *künstlich* or artistic usage will depart by giving emphasis to any term that is thrown out of place. This is the *emphatica periodus* versus the *naturalis*.[48] This way of putting the matter may sound more reasonable than the appeal to the affective causes of inversion that will develop in the eighteenth century (thus preparing the ground for Romanticism), insofar as it more accurately applies to German, a language in which "inversions," even when optional, are more often than not of a "logical" nature in terms of what Condillac will define as *liaison des idées*. This shift is well expressed in the terminology of the next author, Wahn.

Hermann Wahn, *Kurtzgefassete Teutsche Grammatica* 1723,[49] speaks of *ordo naturalissimus* or *logicus*, and *naturalis* or *proprius*, which latter is the commonly used one, and distinguishes itself into *congruus* without transpositions and *elegans* with transpositions (*Versetzungen*). The essence of the *naturalissimus* (traditionally, *naturalis*) lies in that it always places the governing element before its referent (in German!).

Wahn offers an unusually correct specification of subordinating conjunctions by using denominations that hark back to Latin grammar: In the *congruus ordo* "die Conjunctiones der Uhrsach, des Schliessens, etc. oder die Adverbia des Ermahnens, Wünschens, Ruffens, Anzeigens, Verbietens, Vergleichens, Fragens, und alle andere Frag-Wörter, it. die relative oder Wörter, so sich worauff beziehen mit ihrem Zubehör."

Wahn deserves credit for clearly prescribing that the auxiliary must come last in clauses introduced by (subordinating) conjunctions or relatives; for example, *Weil du solches gethan hast*, etc.,[50] thus realizing the rule of end-position in subordination, with specific reference to the auxiliaries understood as main part of the verbal complex, whereas many, including Gottsched, will be very slow in recognizing end-position for the auxiliary, as we shall see.

Of particular importance is **Christian Ernst Steinbach** (1699–1741), *Kurtze und gründliche Anweisung zur deutschen Sprache* 1724.[51] He marks a turning point since the new speculation that started with him showed little impact of previous grammarians.[52] He divided *constructio* between *ordinaria* and *disposita*. The former has the sequence of: (1) Nominativus, (2) Verbum mobile, (3) Casus obliquus pronominis, (4) Casus obliquus nominis, (5) Adverbium, (6) Praepositio cum suo casu, (7) Verbum immobile. Items number 4, 5, and 6 can exchange places.

The *disposita* has two modes, according to whether the nominative appears after the verb or whether the *verbum mobile* goes to the end. "Constructio disposita est: I) Quando nominativus post verbum . . . ponitur; II) Quando verbum mobile in fine collocatur" (pp. 81–2). This is a good, clear beginning in the treatment of transformations or transpositions no more as stylistic devices in the *elegans*, artistic, inverted, or eloquent constructions, but as grammatical rules. The two constructions are, indeed, both grammatical, not one essentially grammatico-logical and the other essentially rhetorical (an inherited classical schema that did not *de facto* have much meaning for German). On the other hand, note that VO is regarded as normal to German, OV as a transposition. Furthermore, despite the positive features of the doctrine, it was in a sense a false start, since the clauses are characterized ambiguously either by the position of the subject or by that of the verb. Yet, soon thereafter Steinbach managed to hit upon the right formula by focusing on the position of the verb alone — a fundamental breakthrough not fully exploited until it was "rediscovered" in our own century. Here is the way he puts it. Referring to the above, II: "Quando verbum mobile in fine collocatur, hoc fit: (1) Post voces interrogativas *wer* quis, *welcher* qui, *wenn* quando, *wo* ubi, *wie* quomodo etc. quando non interrogant, et relativas" — in other words, after relative pronouns (and note the use of the old rhetorical paradigm traditionally listing *quis, quid, ubi, quibus auxiliis, cur, quomodo, quando*); "(2) Post conjunctiones . . . " (pp. 82–3), giving here only examples with *weil* and *als*. And after advising placement of the auxiliary after its participle, he aptly notes that it can occasionally be omitted at the end of the clause: "verba auxiliaria in fine ponenda saepius omittuntur" (p. 84). Aichinger 1754, § 409 p. 438 (see below) will begin to object to excesses in yielding to this contemporary fashion.

The ambiguity underscored above concerning the double focusing on the subject and on the verb as the central feature was really due to Steinbach's putting together a necessary phenomenon (verbal end-position) and an optional one (starting the clause with other than the subject) or, to put it differently, his referring to the necessary second position of the verb (in main clauses) as possibly entailing the postposition of the subject after the verb when the first position has been preempted by another element. He was incorrectly but understandably framing both phenomena, generally of a genuine linguistic nature in German, within the doctrine of inverted order or figurative syntax (the traditional *syntaxis figurata* or *ornata*, which he called *constructio disposita*), as a matter of artistic and stylistic choice, thus improperly assimilating verb position in dependent clauses to a question of ornamentation or choice.

Fleischmann (p. 347) knows of no other cases at this time but Steinbach's for the realization of the optional inversion, as it is still called, of the verb in a subordinate clause, when the verb can be placed either at the end (an "irregularity" brought about by *constructio disposita*), or in second place (according to the rules of the *constructio ordinaria*): "Post conjunctionem copulativam *und* etc., si praecesserit constructio disposita, eadem retineri vel in ordinariam mutari potest" (p. 84).

The value of Steinbach's paradigm was soon understood, and it formed the basis of a brief, polemically slanted essay, "Von der Wörter Ordnung überhaupt in der deutschen Sprache" that appeared in vol. I of the *Beyträge zu einer critischen Historie der deutschen Sprache, Poesie und Beredsamkeit*, hrsgn. von einigen Mitgliedern der Deutschen Gesellschaft in Leipzig (1732), pp. 175–82.[53]

The anonymous author begins by regretting that with all that has been written on the German language and grammar, nobody has ever said much on *Wortfügung*. He recalls Schottel's promise in his vol. I, p. 5 "*operis germanici oratoris*" to give in the third book a "systema artificiosae constructionis omnium germanicorum vocabulorum," but that he has not been able to find any such thing in that book. The book contains something pertaining to the subject, but in a fragmentary and inorganic way, so that one cannot regard the presentation as a coherent treatment of general principles. He names and takes to task for similar or worse failures Morhof, Bödiker, Körber, Steinbach, and Wahn (he overlooks Stieler).

So he begins by giving the order of ordinary clauses: Nominativus, finite verb, casus obliquus pronominis, casus obliquus nominis, adverbium, praepositio cum casu (and these last three, he says, "werden untermengt gesetzt"), "das unbewegliche *Verbum*, oder was zum *Verbo* gehört, als das *Supinum*, der *Infinitivus*, die *Praepositio verbi separabilis.*" This order is not negated by the possible insertion before or after the nominative of something that qualifies it — "so ihn erklärt" (p. 177). Before the nominative can be placed "bejahende und betheurende Nebenwörter" and also (coordinating) conjunctions, *Verbindungswörter*, or such (adverbs) as *nemlich, sondern, allein, aber, (denn)*, and also, at times, *zwar* (without causing inversion).

This is the normal order (*ordentliche Wortfügung*), which can then be disturbed (*versetzt*) when an element is displaced. This displacement happens in two ways: (1) Nominative goes after verb (when the inversion VS is brought about by one of the following):

1. Verb takes first place, in question clauses;
2. In conditional constructs ("in einer Rede, wo eine Bedingung ist") of the type: *Hätt'ich Bosheit im Gemüthe . . . / So verzieh' ich mich der Güte . . .* ;
3. When the first word is an element normally belonging in third or fourth place (i.e., an object, direct or indirect): *Splitter in des Nächsten Augen / Trift ein jeder leichtlich an*;
4. (p. 180) When the nominative is replaced by *es*: *Es hat die Welt bisher im Blut / Und einer Thränensee geschwommen*;
5. When a secondary clause precedes (I interpret in this way the author's "In der Redensart, wenn sich was auf das vorhergehende beziehet, welches man sonst *consequens* nennt"): *Ach feige, wollt ihr nicht des Nachbars Haus erretten, / So wird das eurige gewiß zu Grunde gehn* (Steinbach had here: "In *Nachsätzen*, in which the verb is sometimes preceded by *so* or some other particle").

2) The second way of abnormal order occurs when the verb is moved from second to last place:

1. In questions introduced by *wer? welcher? wenn? wo? wie?* (*Fragewörter*): *So geht es, wenn man dich / Den Himmel und auch sich / Aus tollem Wahn verkennet* (Gryphius). As the several examples show, the author makes here a strange confu-

sion between poetic inversion, question clauses, and indirect question as simply a case of subordinate clause. In other words, he bungles his source, Steinbach, who had phrased the matter correctly: "Post voces interrogativas . . . quando non interrogant." The real issue is that the verb goes to the end in secondary clauses by general rule, and this is, indeed, the only issue at stake in this "second way" of "inversion" or "disturbance" as shown by the following points:

2. After relative pronouns;
3. After (subordinating) conjunctions, *Verbindungswörter*, such as *als*, *nachdem*, *weil*, etc.

The author concludes (p. 182) by saying that, whereas Steinbach has used prose examples ("in ungebundener Rede"), he has chosen verse, but of the regular, orderly type, such as that of Gryphius and Günther. Should one look to such other poets as Lohenstein and Hoffmanswaldau, one would find in them innumerable faults against the right word order. It is therefore to be hoped, he says, that later grammarians interested in both verse and prose will study this sketch of his, improve on it and expand it, so that foreigners will no longer have reason to despise German authors.

A radical case of the typical concern with answering French charges is the work of **Johann Andreas Fabricius** (1696–1769), *Philosophische Oratorie, das ist: Vernünftige Anleitung zur . . . Beredsamkeit* (Leipzig: bey denen Cörnerischen Erben, 1724, 1739), pp. 497ff. We read there that "The normal arrangement (i.e., the traditional sequence answering piece by piece the scholastic questions *quis*, *quid*, *ubi*, *quibus auxiliis*, *cur*, *quomodo*, *quando*) cannot according to reason be otherwise, since it is also found in languages that bear some similarity to German, like English, Swedish, French, and others." Jellinek crisply interjects (II, p. 450) that the end-position of participles and infinitives, which Fabricius himself teaches, accords neither with reason nor with the Latin verse, and is not found in French or English.

2. *Gottsched to Bodmer*

We must now turn to one of the principal figures in eighteenth-century German literary criticism, **Johann Christoph Gottsched** (1700–66), the apostle of French Enlightenment, who also happened to be the editor of the first eight volumes (1732–44) of those *Beyträge* in the first volume of which had appeared the essay we have just examined. Gottsched's major shortcomings as a grammarian came from his having "irresponsibly ignored Steinbach's landmark performance," as Jellinek (II, p. 450) pointed out, which appears all the more surprising in that no other than Steinbach was the declared source of that essay. One must conclude that in this case Gottsched had not been a very attentive editor, and his carelessness was to cost him dearly in his later grammatical work. For Gottsched, grammar was nothing but a means to an end, and his contributions to this discipline were not typical of German speculation at this time, but were rather "an exception," as Jellinek pointed out in a deprecatory vein.

As we are about to see, Gottsched, as a grammarian, lacks a clear notion of dependent clause; he speaks only of separable particles and compound tenses, and still relies on verbal moods as the decisive factor in hypotaxis. Nor does he grasp the difference between finite verb and nominal forms of the verb with regard to their place in the sentence. On the other hand, owing to his prestige from other quarters, his grammatical work also enjoyed long and widespread fame, so that its historical importance remains great. At any rate, Gottsched's impact is a reflection of his having acted as the intermediary between France and Germany.

In his 1730 *Versuch einer critischen Dichtkunst*,[54] Gottsched discussed Du Cerceau's doctrine that the secret and essence of poetic style lies in the use of inversions, and denied it.[55] He had started the discussion of this point somewhat earlier by declaring that poetry must respect the word order that is natural to the language.[56] Most writers since Opitz, he asserts, have accepted this principle even in the face of some objections, such as those to be found in the preface of the Swiss Bodmer's translation of Milton.[57] Gottsched's rationalistic bent is so strong that he even denies the claim that Greek and Latin poets have used inversions extensively, since, he says, he has found no proof of this, and cites Aristotle, *Poetics*, chapter 23, for his strictures against such possible practices. Likewise, he gives examples of what Maro Grammaticus would have taxed as *synchysis*, completely mixed-up hyperbata, by showing reshuffled Virgilian lines which would have satisfied metrics but not logic, and would have been found totally unacceptable. In short, the ancient poets rarely had gone beyond what was acceptable to Roman and Greek ears in word order, just as the Germans have become accustomed to do.

Gottsched also recalled Father Claude Buffier's rejoinder to Du Cerceau in Buffier's new *Anleitung zur Poesie* (on which more later), but interjects that Du Cerceau did, indeed, have a point: The French poets do use a number of such inversions that their prose writers would find unendurable (p. 359). And later on Gottsched will give examples of similar practices in German verse. Yet he disagrees with Du Cerceau's attributing to inversions such a central and almost exclusive role, even to the point of denying poetic value to figurative, allegoric, metaphoric, or symbolic language ("die verblümten Redensarten für nichts Poetisches ansehen will"). Furthermore (p. 362), he prefers to warn against abuse of transpositions and, especially, the kind of lexical distortions that are unacceptable in German but might have been acceptable in Greek — if one listens to Aristotle's approval of lengthening and shortening of words (*Poetics*). Almost all poets up to Christian Weise, including Hoffmanswaldau, have used such devices and even written *brechen an, schlingen ein*, etc. (pp. 360–1).

In conclusion (pp. 374–9), Gottsched goes over his material to reiterate the principle that inversion is a beauty both in verse and prose, but only on condition that it be used with moderation. As to the order of indirect complements among themselves there are no rules; the ear alone is the judge (p. 375). The transposition of the basic parts of the clause must rest on reasons of euphony or, more important, expression of emotion or arousal of the listener's attention (*Affekt, Aufmerksamkeit*, pp. 375, 377). Examples of expressiveness: *Alle dein Bitten ist umsonst, ich werde es nimmermehr leiden*, or *du sollst den Tag nicht erleben . . .* undoubtedly carry less passion and vivacity (*feurig und lebhaft*) than *Umsonst ist alle dein Bitten! Nimmermehr werde ichs leiden! Den Tag sollst du nicht erleben!* (p. 375). Likewise, a word acquires emphasis (*Nachdruck*) through transposition: *Ich will dir zu Leibe sterben* would be less effective than *Dir zu Leibe will ich sterben*; Günther's *In den Wäldern will ich irren / Vor den Menschen will ich fliehn* is clearly better than the direct order (p. 376). But German poets will do well to keep firmly in mind the principle that their language will not tolerate the kind of grammatical violations that other languages are ready to welcome. We cannot emulate Milton: We can do in verse only what would be acceptable in prose, and only under the stress of emotion (p. 378). Nevertheless, it was precisely Milton that Bodmer and Klopstock soon would turn into an exalted model for bold transpositions, in clear revolt against Gottsched's specific "rationalism."

Gottsched was not satisfied with citing Buffier's rebuttal of Du Cerceau. He published his wife's translation of Buffier (if this identification of the translator is correct), with a wealth of learned annotations, in the eighth volume of his *Beyträge zur critischen Historie der deutschen Sprache, Poesie und Beredsamkeit* (Leipzig, 1742–4), pp. 420–64, under the title "Des Paters Buffier Abhandlung, daß alle Sprachen und Mundarten, die in der Welt geredet werden, in sich selbst eine gleiche Schönheit haben."[58] The historians of grammatical literature and students of Gottsched have failed to pay attention to this remarkable essay, nor do they appear to have attempted to trace its source, which happens to be the "VIIe Dissertation" (later: "Proposition"): "Que toutes les langues et les jargons qui se parlent au monde ont en soi une égale beauté," a section of Buffier's *Examen des préjugés vulgaires*.[59]

To understand the import of this text and place it in its proper perspective, we need to stop for an observation of a general nature. The rationalist tradition, especially in France, had posited the basic "realistic" principle of a necessary correspondence between words and thoughts. The train of linguistic expression must therefore follow the train of thought on somewhat parallel tracks. Consequently, those languages must be regarded as best ordered that reflect the logical march of ideas through their word order: The succession of the parts of the clause and sentence must be that of logical analysis. This was the position of those "partisans of the French language" who called themselves *métaphysiciens*, and whose triumph was sanctioned in 1784 by the prize-winning essay of Antoine de Rivarol on the reasons for the superiority of the French language — these reasons being essentially its analytical or direct order. The *métaphysiciens* were opposed by the *mécaniciens* (so styled after Abbé Noël Antoine Pluche's *La Mécanique des langues*, 1751), who extolled the virtues of Latin and all "inversions."

Modern linguistic science appeared to have neatly disposed of the prejudice concerning the correspondence between analytical order and the natural order of thinking when Saussure approached the question in his customary trenchant manner. Saussure's theoretical discussion of the way language organizes thought through the phonic material, in chapter iv of the Second Part, § 1, pp. 154-5 of his *Cours de linguistique générale* (1949), concluded that "When we prescind from its expression through language, our thinking is nothing but an amorphous and indistinct mass, . . . like a nebula. . . . There are no predetermined ideas, and nothing is distinct before the appearance of language." "Thinking, chaotic by its nature, is compelled to define itself by dividing itself into its constituents (*en se décomposant*)." (Translation mine: Cf. Rudolf Engler's "édition critique," Wiesbaden: Harrassowitz, 1968, I, Nos. 1821-24, 1829, pp. 252-53.) Saussure went on to relate this premise to his principles of sign, linearity, and arbitrariness. Nevertheless, the question has surfaced once again in the controversy between the Chomskyan transformationalists and the proponents of natural generative grammar; the former hold once more to a view of linguistic nuclei as being basically ordered in a linear way in the deep structure, whereas the latter object that the linear order belongs solely to the surface.[60]

In his 1968 monograph on *Saussure* (p. 54), Georges Mounin categorically proclaims that Saussure's concepts of arbitrariness and linearity were never formulated by any linguist before him. The facts are very different indeed. Both questions were the object of a lively and extended debate throughout the eighteenth century, and the German contribution, in particular, has not yet been picked up even by the best informed historians of linguistic ideas. Let us then take our point of departure from Frau Gottsched's translation of Buffier's dialogue.

To begin with, Buffier denies that thoughts present themselves in our mind linearly, i.e., in an order. He says unequivocally that (it is Theander who speaks to Timagenes, *Téandre* and *Timagène* in the original), as to Timagenes' opinion that "die Ordnung unserer Worte . . . der Ordnung der Gedanken in unserm Gemüthe gemäß seyn soll," his reply is: "so ist dieselbe nur ein sehr mäßiges Vorrecht, wofern es ja ein Vorrecht ist." Indeed, he goes on, his opinion is that "die Gedanken müssen unserm Gemüthe alle zugleich vorstellen, wenn sie einen Satz ausmachen sollen; sonst haben sie keinen gewissen Sinn. Daher aber begreifen die Lateiner alles was sie sagen, eben so geschwinde und deutlich," when they place the verb at the end. It all comes from habit, "Gewohnheit, und auf einem gewissen Schwung der Einbildungskraft." He finds proof of this in French itself, where an example from Boileau will show that the subject can quite effectively be placed at the very end of four alexandrines, right after its copula, so that one would see here that "Unordnung der Begriffe" for which Timagenes blames other languages (read: e.g., German).[61]

Timagenes objects that this is a case of poetic style, which profits from a bit of obscurity and limited license. Poetry, like oratory, especially of the sublime kind, must have something that sets it apart from the common manner of speaking. But the translator adds to Buffier's text a footnote (pp. 453–4) where she explains that this is nothing but another prejudice of Père Bouhours, which Buffier revives and plays up (for polemical reasons, in order to deny it, we should add). She rebuts further that there is nothing more preposterous than to presume that French always observes the natural order of thinking. Showing herself as well informed as Professor Gottsched, the translator adduces the opinion of "P. Cerceau" (Du Cerceau), who claimed inversion, *die blosse Versetzung der Wörter*, as the essence of French poetry, and adds that, in line with Du Cerceau's thinking, one could follow up Buffier's example from Boileau with innumerable others from La Motte, Rousseau, and La Grange (from whom, p. III.112, a lengthy quotation is added as a case in point). We have seen that in his *Dichtkunst* Gottsched had taken a somewhat more sober view of these same texts; yet even here the translator performs a cautious balancing act. Nor does she miss the opportunity to censure those many *neumodische Deutsche* (read: the Baroque poets, especially of the Second Silesian School) who seemed to agree with Du Cerceau's standard, since they did not feel that one could produce decent verse without subverting the order to the point where the thoughts "go the way of the crab," *den Krebsgang gehen*. We have here an example of the difficulty of divesting oneself of the thinking habits induced by French prejudice in such matters. The author concludes that the La Grange passage just quoted is made awkward by the inversions — whereas her own ordering of the elements is the really awkward version of it (same fn., p. 454).

In the Dialogue, to Timagenes' explanation that we have just seen, Theander promptly and ironically responds that he now understands how fairly the partisans of direct order defend their model language. They will admit that an exception (like in Boileau's given example) is a beauty in French but a fault in another language. This arbitrariness ends in hopeless, self-contradictory subjectivism, wherein one's own taste becomes the mysterious oracle of universal judgment. Make this so-called accord between words and concept the natural law of our prose, and it will follow that our poetry is unnatural, if we want to be consistent. But our poetry is equally natural, and we had better allow other languages to use in any style they wish those ornaments that we so successfully use in the noble style. Indeed, other languages have an advantage over ours in that they do naturally and easily what we do with art and effort (*Beyträge* VIII, p. 454, p. 400 of Buffier, 1843 ed.). The translator could not refrain from applauding at this point: One could hardly be more "philosophical," more "unprejudiced" than P. Buffier![62]

Incidentally, it may not be out of order to stress the inner coherence between Buffier's healthy relativism, as it were, and the first part of his Dialogue, where he went to great length to disprove a connection between sound and meaning in all languages, in pages of analysis that could be safely related to what Saussure will theorize as the principle of the *arbitraire du signe* (see, esp., pp. 383–4 of 1843 ed.).

At any rate, the common sense of this defense of German achieved indirectly yet effectively through the translation of a French text is evident, even though theoretically marred by the difficulty of casting off those very fetters that vitiated the adversary point. One remained subject to the temptation of speaking of exceptions and ornaments, thus remaining on the level of style rather than grammar. The translator, however, did not content herself with the technical arguments in favor of recognizing German peculiarities in linguistic habits: She saw her text as an opportunity to defend a growing national self-awareness moving in all directions (see, e.g., fn. p. 462, censuring French letters for containing far too much frivolity for a people so proud of its rational heritage, and so prompt to charge others with logical deficiencies).

It may seem somewhat paradoxical that Gottsched, the militant leader of the German Aufklärung and chief proponent of French rationalism in literature, was led to ally himself (here through his wife's translation of Buffier) with the theses that will soon become those of the *mécaniciens* versus the *métaphysiciens* (that is, of the critics of French direct order versus the partisans of French) on the matter of word order. His stance here was demanded by the very necessity of defending the "inverted" German language against the French charges of irrationality and disorderliness, even while he proposed to blunt the blow to his favorite cause of rationalism by restricting the freedom of inversion to the strict minimum.

If the stigma of irrationality and objective inadequacy was to be removed from the German language, the metaphysical postulate that based the direct order of language on the logical ordering of the thinking process and, underlying it, the linear development of our thoughts in the mind and deep consciousness, had to be destroyed. Buffier's welcome statements on the arbitrariness of word order, hence the right of every language to have its own conventions in this and other areas, were the best weapon for the purpose, so much more providential since they came from a Frenchman. So all languages were equal on principle no matter what their word order and the order of the elements in their sentences. Latin, German, or French were all based on mere surface habits, socially or culturally acquired.

Before we leave Buffier's essay, to realize its originality within the context of the author's thought we must take a look at his *Traité philosophique et pratique de poésie*, whose chapters 7 and 8 also deal with the question of inversions in implicit polemic with Du Cerceau's pretended discovery that the "stile poëtique grammatical . . . consistoit dans les transpositions.[63] The *stile poëtique grammatical*, a variation of the *stile grammatical* in general, which prescribes word order according to grammatical rules, is said to depart from the language and order of prose only slightly and occasionally, especially in French, and is distinguished from the *stile poëtique personnel*, which concerns what was traditionally called poetic license, to wit, individual departures from the norm and intensive uses of figures of speech.[64] He gives examples from Boileau, Racine, Corneille, Rousseau, and La Motte (translation of the *Iliad*), to show that the direct order can be just as effective in verse as the inverted order. Buffier calls the uninverted style "le genre naïf de notre poësie françoise," and regards transpositions as its greatest adversary (col. 434).

Buffier seems to have been the first to contrast the temporal linearity of language with the simultaneity of the thinking process, and we have just seen how this important statement, which is ideally related to Saussure's notion of linearity, found an early echo in Germany, with noteworthy adaptation to special national, polemical needs. The doctrine was soon to be expanded by Condillac, who stressed that feature of language that forces man to decompose into sequential order the initially unitary, picture- or painting-like experience of reality. This aspect of Condillac's doctrine has been fully explored recently by such specialists as Hans Aarsleff, but without tracing it further back and without mention of Buffier.[65]

In Condillac the concept of linearity became, like that of arbitrariness, a central and crucial one: "Si toutes les idées qui composent une pensée sont simultanées dans l'esprit, elles sont successives dans le discours: ce sont donc les langues qui nous fournissent les moyens d'analyser nos pensées."[66] The idea was forcefully restated by the President of the Berlin Academy from 1746, Pierre-Louis Moreau de Maupertuis (1698–1759), in his *Réflexions sur l'origine des langues et la signification des mots* published in Paris in 1748 in limited edition, then reprinted in the first volume of the Dresden edition of Maupertuis' *Oeuvres* of 1752. This work was based on Condillac's *Essai* of 1746, whose ideas it therefore carried into the circles of the Berlin Academy at this very early stage (if one does not count Gottsched's *Beyträge*).[67] Subsequently, Diderot, in his celebrated *Lettre sur les sourds et muets* of 1751, offered a statement on the matter that deserves our attention for its full articulation:

L'état de l'âme dans un instant indivisible fut représenté par une foule de termes que la précision du langage exigea, et qui distribuèrent une impression totale en parties; et parce que ces termes se prononçoient successivement et ne s'entendoient qu'à mesure qu'ils se prononçoient, on fut porté à croire que les affections de l'âme qu'ils représentoient avoient la même succession. Mais il n'en est rien. Autre chose est l'état de notre âme, autre chose le compte que nous en rendons, soit à nous-mêmes, soit aux autres, autre chose la sensation totale et instantanée de cet état, autre chose l'attention successive et débillée que nous sommes forcés d'y donner pour l'analyser, la manifester et nous faire entendre.[68]

Richard A. Ogle 1974 concludes from this passage that "language, then, imposes linearity and segmentation on the intrinsically unanalysed thought."[69] "Therefore language, far from following *la manière naturelle dans laquelle nous exprimons nos pensées*, must continually struggle to reconstruct the unity of thought" — a process that is explored in this other passage of Diderot:

Notre âme est un tableau mouvant d'après lequel nous peignons sans cesse: nous employons bien de temps à le rendre avec fidélité; mais il existe en entier et tout à la fois: l'esprit ne va pas à pas comptés comme l'expression. Le pinceau n'exécute qu'à la longue ce que l'oeil du peintre embrasse tout d'un coup. La formation des langues exigeoit la décomposition, mais *voir* un objet, le *juger* beau, éprouver une sensation agréable, désirer la possession, c'est l'état de l'âme dans un même instant. . . . (ibid.)

But before we leave Condillac I should like to add one more relevant text, which seems to have escaped the attention of his most careful readers, including Aarsleff. Chapters vi–ix of the *Art d'écrire* (Third part of his *Cours d'études*, which only appeared in 1775 but was composed for the Prince of Parma and completed not later than 1766 — Condillac returned to Paris in January 1767) discuss parataxis and hypotaxis, namely (see our Ch. I), the ways in which the *propositions principales, incidentes*, and *subordonnées* are to be ordered and tied together. It is an illuminating and pioneering analysis in many respects, and it ends with the refutation of Boileau's *dictum: Ce que l'on conçoit bien s'énonce clairement*. The argument is entirely in keeping with Condillac's systematic premises. One can think and conceive well and yet express oneself poorly. For it is one thing to conceive one's thoughts, and another to translate them into language. This is because, in the first operation, all our ideas present themselves to our mind at the same time, whereas in the latter they must show themselves successively. Consequently, we must learn the art of arranging our ideas, ordering them out of the chaos of simultaneous perception. It is the art of analyzing thought and understanding the *liaison* of its parts.[70]

Without mentioning Condillac in this regard, Ogle goes on to trace Du Marsais' treatment of the same motif.[71] In his famous article "Construction" of the *Encyclopédie*, Du Marsais, like Diderot, maintains that language does not reflect thought, but rather reconstructs it (p. 4). This is because each mental act of thinking, judging, imagining and so on, is both instantaneous and indivisible. It is only the need to communicate thought that forces us "de donner à nos pensées de l'étendue, pour ainsi dire, et des parties" (p. 6). Ogle, p. 67, points out that Du Marsais' basic second condition is that the basic type of meaning-bearing relation is the ordered pair "modified/modifier," in this order (p. 7 of same article "Construction").

Carrying the point even further, Nicolas Beauzée, *Grammaire générale ou exposition raisonnée des éléments nécessaires du langage*

60 □ THEORY OF WORD ORDER

(1767), "Préface," p. vi, maintained that the sounds of language "ne peuvent former qu'un tout sensible, successif, et divisible; ce qui paroit fort éloigné de pouvoir représenter la pensée, objet purement intellectuel et nécessairement indivisible. Mais la Logique, par le secours de l'abstraction, vient à bout d'analyser en quelque sorte cet acte indivisible de l'esprit: elle considère séparément les idées qui en sont l'objet; elle observe les diverses relations qu'elles ont entre elles. . . ." The indivisibility of the thinking process was founded on the psychology of Locke, whose theory of perception took the firmest roots in France through Condillac. Beauzée combines this tradition with the Cartesian postulate of a correspondence between language and thought, but he achieves this shrewd combination by breaking down the complex process that leads from sensation to linguistic expression and by seeing the perception stages as prerational, while the expression stages conform with logic.[72]

Thus, according to Beauzée (II, p. 469), the logical law of the scholastic philosophers *prius est esse quam sic esse*, which he invokes, demands that the subject should precede the predicate because the thing or the agent precedes its predication or action. Analogously, adjectives must follow their head nouns as qualities follow substances, and prepositions precede their referents just as all complements follow their governments, verbs or others, and dependent clauses follow the clauses they modify. Obviously, the principles of scholastic logic are here exploited to canonize the order modified → modifier that characterizes not universal grammar, but the syntax of SVO languages specifically, such as French.

We must now return to Gottsched and turn our attention to his grammar, *Grundlegung einer deutschen Sprachkunst* (Leipzig, 1748, 1762^5).[73] The section of syntax (called *Wortfügung*) opens with an "Erinnerung" in which a footnote expatiates on Buffier's statement that each nation's views on word order are relative and subjective, since they are conditioned by that nation's language. Indeed, in a pronouncement that almost sounds lifted out of the Sapir-Whorf theory, Gottsched concludes that "allein, sie irren alle, und bemerken nicht, daß ihnen ihre Art zu denken, zuerst durch ihre Muttersprache beygebracht worden" (p. 399 of 1762^5 ed.). The note refers to the dialogue by Buffier in *Beyträge* VIII for a critique of the contrary prejudice (*Vorurtheil*). But the critique of the French prejudice in favor of French direct order as universally valid is vitiated by the incapacity, once again, to use any other than the "logical" frame of thought used by the French *métaphysiciens*, since Gottsched here criticizes French for being less "natural" than German in saying *Je vous dis* instead of *Ich sage dir; Je ne le sais pas* (=*Ich nicht es weis nicht*) versus *Ich weis es nicht*, etc.

Chapter 4 concerns the ordering of verbs, "Von Fügung der Zeitwörter." After a long section on cases governed by verbs (pp. 444–71), we read the eight rules on order (pp. 471–6), covering separation of separable particles in compound verbs (*Trennung der absonderlichen Vorwörter in zusammengesetzten Zeitwörtern*). Rule 1 says: In the indicative present and imperfect (or perfect) tense, the particle goes to the end of the clause. Rule 2: But if the compound verb governs another verb, the particle will be placed before the latter, not after: *Sie fiengen [fingen] frühmorgens mit Sonnenaufgange an, zu schlagen*, not *zu schlagen an. Ich hebe morgen an, zu arbeiten*, not *zu arbeiten an*. 3: In other tenses and moods (*Gattungen und Arten*: he also means participles, which can be part of a passive construction), the particles remain in place, except that the *ge-* of the past participle and the *zu* with the infinitive will be inserted between the particle and the verb. 4: With inseparable particles, however (*unzertrennliche Vorsetzwörter*), the *ge-* is not used and the *zu* goes before (pp. 471–2). The next rule (p. 474) concerns auxiliaries (*Hülfswörter*, but he also means modals, since he puts in *sollen* alongside *werden*, *haben*, and *seyn*): They are separated from their verbs and so they come at the head in, we would say, main clauses, at the end in secondary clauses. But since Gottsched has neither the term *Nebensatz* nor the concept, his way of putting it is wrong on principle, since he still attributes the difference to a matter of verbal moods, which have nothing to do with it: "Die Hülfswörter werden insgemein von ihrem Zeitworte getrennet; so daß sie in der anzeigenden Art (= Indicative) vorne, in der verbindenden (= Subjunctive) aber hinten stehen." But he adds the remark that the verb will not go to the end if the conjunction *daß* is omitted. If the illustrious president of the most learned society of Leipzig had taken a bit more time to reflect on what he was saying, surely he would have realized that his own examples (not very good ones at that, but correct) contradicted his own theory, since they correctly showed subjunctives in cases of both forward and back position of the auxiliary. The examples are worth reporting: *Der Frieden zu Aachen* soll *nunmehr völlig zur Richtigkeit gekommen seyn* (indicative); *Es heißt, daß dieser Frieden keinen langen Bestand haben* werde, *daß bald ein neues Kriegesfeuer in Europa aufgehen* solle (subjunctives, whose only meaning is that of reported opinion). And then, *Es heißt: der Aachener Frieden* solle *nun völlig geschlossen seyn*: (*aber*) *es* werde *bald ein neues Kriegesfeuer angehen* (*in Europa aufgehen*) (subjunctives, as above).[74] All in all, this was an interesting effort to define hypotactic structures in a better way than the usual, which was simply to say: When the verb is preceded by the conjunctions *weil*, etc. Indeed, this is the definition to which later editions chose to return, as shown by the ninth and tenth editions of the French translation.[75]

The matter was, to be sure, not an easy one, since the following rule shows that Gottsched did not really grasp the nature of subordination, hence he could not really distinguish between kinds of clauses. He simply says (p. 474) that in German it does not sound wrong ("es klingt im Deutschen nicht unrecht") to end a saying (*Spruch*) or the whole sentence (*die völlige Meynung eines Satzes*) with the verb, but the examples he gives are of end-position of the verb that is simply justified by its being in a dependent clause: *Als gestern unsre Stadt, wie vormals Ninive,/ In Sack und Asche lag, und ihre Fasten hielte:/ Geschah es bey der Nacht, daß zwischen Ach und Weh,/ Das schon betrübte Volk ein neues Schrecken fühlte* (Kanitz). The misunderstanding is compounded by the following rule (p. 475), where the previous statement concerning the German taste for ending a sentence with a verb is tempered by the warning not to overdo it; and the example, again from Kanitz, is simply one in which no end-position is called for because the clauses are of the main type! The next rule warns against a similar abuse, *Übelstand*, that is typical of *Kanzleyschreibart*, namely to suspend the whole trend of the sentence by unnecessarily postposing the verb, in order to have it, perhaps even piled up with others, at the very end, after all the circumstantial secondary clauses. Example: "*Wir wollen dir hiemit, daß du solches höchsten Fleißes vermeidest, und dich unserm Willen gemäß bezeigest, nachdrücklich, und alles Ernstes anbefehlen.*" Another interesting example is taken from Goldast: "*Es ist billig, daß man den deutschen Landen und Provinzen ein Haupt, welches dieselben in sämmtlicher Liebe erhalten, zieren, beschützen, und die Unfurchtsamen, mit dem Zaume weltlicher Gewalt aufhalten möchte, ordnen sollte.*" Gottsched suggests that *ordnen sollte* should have followed immediately *ein Haupt*.[76] He is therefore speaking of subordinate constructs, and since he recommends placing the verbs as near as possible to their subjects, he means by subject the term of reference or topic, here an object complement. He expands this warning by insisting that it is for clarity's sake that, whenever possible, the verb belongs immediately next to its head noun, instead of being separated with prolonged relative clauses, etc. Confusion and obscurity follow from such "bureaucratic" practices, as in "Lünigs Reicharchive." Interestingly, he ends by adding that the opposite error may be equally objectionable, that of placing the verb too soon in front. One wonders what he might have meant, since he gives no examples, except perhaps the possibility, frequent in the archaic language, of not sending the verb to the end in dependent clauses. Indeed, he speaks of the old poets as being guilty of what he has in mind, "nebst Opitzen," he says, and, in the very end, "selbst die deutsche Bibel, nebst Luthers Schriften, sind hierinn nicht unsträflich" (p. 476).

As we have just seen, and as Fleischmann rightly underscores (p. 349), Gottsched's reasoning is still vitiated by the confusion caused by identifying end-position with the use of the subjunctive, an error that was traditional but that the better previous grammarians had already implicitly obviated. This error goes together with the traditional habit (by that time also outgrown by the better grammarians) of introducing subjunctive forms in verbal paradigms and diagrams with the conjunction *daß* (as the Italians used *che*, and the Latin grammarians, but rarely, *cum, si, ut*, or the equivalent).[77] Furthermore, he gives only examples of end-position with compound forms, as if the rule did not apply to all tenses. As Jellinek sternly warned, "Gottsched had irresponsibly ignored Steinbach" (II, p. 450).

Fleischmann (p. 350) singles out an eloquent example of Gottsched's occasional ineptness. This is the treatment of three-member verbal forms, or verbs accompanied by two auxiliaries, of which one, says Gottsched ill-advisedly, will be placed before and the other after the verb, thus: *ich versichere dich, daß ich dahin* würde *gekommen* seyn, *wenn ich nicht* wäre *abgehalten* worden (p. 495 § 8). In the subsequent abridgment *Kern der deutschen Sprachkunst* (Leipzig: B. Ch. Breitkopf, 1759[3]), which otherwise does nothing but summarize the *Grundlegung*, Gottsched felt compelled to correct himself, possibly under the

64 ☐ THEORY OF WORD ORDER

impact of Aichinger's statement of the case in his *Versuch einer teutschen Sprachlehre* (1753, 1754). After restating the rule in the erroneous form (p. 214), he puts forward his doubts: "Indessen ist diese Regel nicht allgemein: und bisweilen stehen sie [the two auxiliaries] nicht unrecht beyde hinten." Indeed, his previous examples had been (p. 142): *Das ich gelobet worden sey* and (p. 143) *Das ich gelobet worden wäre*, and this reflected contemporary practice.[78]

Aichinger had taken Gottsched explicitly to task on this matter, insisting that this way of anteposing the finite form was prescribed only when the infinitive of a verb that governs another infinitive is used in place of a past participle (he calls this a *supinum*) to form a *praeteritum*: "Es ist aber diese Vorsetzung des *verbi finiti* nur alsdann unumgänglich, wenn der *infinitivus* eines *verbi*, das einen blossen *infinitivum* regieret, nach § 413 an statt des *supini* gebrauchet wird, um das *praeteritum* auszumachen. Z.B. *ehe Gott seinen Sohn hat kommen lassen*." (*Versuch*, 1754, p. 548). In other words, only in the case of participles of modals having the infinitive form.[79]

As a witness to the undeservedly wide influence of Gottsched's grammar, and as a way of realizing how his shortcomings could be partly obviated by those who needed to put his rules to the best possible use, we may want to take a look at the very successful translation and adaptation of it for French users, *Le maître de la langue allemande*, 1754 . . . 1782[9].[80] Since Gottsched wrote so very little on word order, the French translation expanded this section, of crucial importance to foreign learners, by culling the basic pertinent rules from other grammarians, although without great improvement. Otherwise, Gottsched's text was generally reduced in length (from 700-odd pages to 500).

At the beginning of the Syntax, the translator, as a loyal Frenchman, omitted from the "Vorerinnerung" the note on Buffier and the relativity of each language system, with the critiques of French constructions. Further on, three of the five pages on Latin and Italian examples, and the allusion to Michaëlis, also were omitted, while a two-page list of differences between French and German was added.

The Syntax is the Third Part of the whole work; under the section "De la syntaxe des verbes" comes the treatment "Du nominatif avec le verbe personnel." Chapter 4, section 1, third rule states that the nominative follows the verb when, in conditional constructs, one omits, as one often does, *wenn, dafern, wofern*: *Schläft er, so wirds besser mit ihm*, 's'il dort, il se rétablira'; the same obtains in polite constructions such as *Geruhen Eure Majestät nur zu befehlen: so* etc., 'Qu'il plaise a V.M. d'ordonner'; *Belieben Sie mir doch das zu geben*, 'Ayez la bonté de me donner cela' etc. (this is, however, a case of imperative construction). The same text and examples were in the German original (p. 445, 5th ed.)

The section "De la syntaxe des verbes composés" refers to the second Part, Morphology, chapter 6, under "verbes composés" pp. 241–52 (*Zusammengesetzte Zeitwörter*, pp. 358–65 of German original, 5th ed.), where separable and inseparable prepositions were listed and treated. The inseparable ones are: *after* (*afterreden* 'médire'), *be, durch, emp, ent, er, ge, hinter, mis, ver, verab, veran, verum, voll, über, um, unter, ur, beur, verur, wider, wieder, zer. Durch, voll, über, um*, and *unter* are separable in some verbs. *Durch, veran, beur, wider*, and *wieder* were not in the German original, fifth edition.

Similarly, some verbs compounded with other than a preposition are separable, others are not (cf. separable *wahrnehmen, wahrsagen, kund thun*, giving *ich nehme wahr* etc., versus inseparable *antworten, kurzweilen, radbrechen, liebkosen*, etc.). Inseparable parts not only do not separate in the conjugation, but also they do not admit the *ge-* of the participle (except *gemisbraucht* and *geurkundet*) and *zu* of the infinitive. Then, pages 334–6, section 7 (ch. 4 of Part 3), Rule 1: The separable preposition goes to the end with verbs in finite tenses, unless the verb is introduced by the conjunction *als, da, wann, nachdem, weil, obwohl, sobald, sintemal, daß, damit*, or other such. In these cases the preposition remains with the verb.

When, however, the verb governs an infinitive, the separated particle will be placed before the infinitive: *Rufet ihn her, sich zu verantworten*, 'appeller-le pour se défendre'; *Nimm deinen Bruder mit zum Tanzen* (Second Rule). The preceding list of conjunctions is of interest because it appeared in the translation but not in the original.

Rule 4 contains an interesting observation on German dislike for participial constructions (present participle) especially at the beginning of the sentence — a construct that had become obsolete, with only *anlagend, betreffend*, and *während* (= *während daß*, obviously conjunctionalized) remaining, and even these preferably replaced by concrete finite constructs (an example of German aversion to hypotaxis):

66 □ THEORY OF WORD ORDER

Anlagend or *Was seinen Lebenswandel anlaget, so können wir folgendes sagen*; *Betreffend* or *Was das Geld anbetrifft, so ich Euch schuldig bin* 'Quant à l'argent que je vous dois.' Likewise (Rule 5) a finite verb replaces the past participle, which, contrary to French, German no longer uses to start a sentence, except poetically. To say *Épouvanté par tes paroles* or *Satisfait de ta proposition*, one would say, not *Erschrecket durch deine Worte* or *Vergnügt* etc., but *Da du mich durch deine Worte erschrecket hast, so* etc. and *Indem ich mich über deinen Antrag sehr vergnügt [fühle* or *habe], so.* . . .

Chapter 6 deals with the syntax of auxiliaries.[81] Rule 2: When a "conditional conjunction" (*Bedingungsformel: wann, wenn, dafern, wofern, im Falle,* etc.) precedes the auxiliary, this goes to the end after its (governed) verb; when the conjunction is suppressed, the auxiliary comes at the very beginning: *Wenn du das überlegen wolltest* or *Wolltest du das überlegen, (so würde er wieder dein Freund werden).*[82] Likewise, of course, in questions.

We have seen how methodically and programmatically Gottsched had criticized the *Kanzleistil*. When **Augustin Dornblüth** counterattacked in his *Observationes oder gründliche Anmerckungen über die Art und Weise eine gute Übersetzung besonders in die teutsche Sprach zu machen* (Augsburg: Mattheus Rieger, 1755), he had something specific to say on the matter of word order in chapter 20 dealing with separable particles ("In verbis compositis, quae separari debent, praepositio eorum in fine ponenda. Secus in particulis compositis" — pp. 228–9), and especially in chapter 16, entitled "Verbum constructionem concludat, Gerundia in fine vitanda, et quemadmodum pariter Substantiva, Adjectiva et Adverbia ante Verbum concludens in fine ponenda" (pp. 206–17).

In this chapter 16, he gives a full defense of incapsulation, dealing specifically with end-position of the verb. "Im teutschen müsse das *Verbum* welches die *Construction* binden mus, (wan es *sine Verbo auxiliari* stehet) oder aber die *Verba auxiliaria* die das Haupt-*Verbum conjungi*ren (ausgenomen *in sensu Interrogationis vel Positionis*) gemeiniglich zu letst gesetzt und die *Construction* darmit geschlossen werden; welches sehr gut und bindig lautet" (p. 206).[83]

This is the SOV ideal still alive in its full anachronistic force, even though only mentally, and disregarding that in the main clauses the principle was definitely out of the question. Therefore he found

Luther's *der du bist im Himmel* (in the *Vater unser*) "*contra naturalem verborum ordinem*," not archaic, but un-German. *Qui es in coelis* was the pattern, and Dornblüth takes to task the German translators of the Bible, both Lutheran and Catholic, for having allowed the Vulgate to determine their German word order, as in the following further examples: *Geheiliget werde dein Nam* for *Dein Nam werde geheiliget*; *Zukome uns dein Reich* for *Dein Reich kome uns zu*; *Herr, ich bin nicht würdig, daß du eingehest unter mein Tach* from *non sum dignus ut intres sub tectum meum* (this last being a clear case of *Nebensatz*) pp. 206–7).

The first paragraph of this same chapter 16 contains, again in the author's rather awkward terminology, an interesting assessment of why modern writers were betraying the nature of the German language. Whereas we summarily identify the German tendency toward periodicity, including its two key features of hypotactic complexity and suspense through *Rücksendung* of the verb and *Satzklammer*, with the influence of Latin models, Dornblüth blames the violation of *Rücksendung* rules on the habit of translating from French *and* Latin. What he has in mind, however, is not the classical, Ciceronian Latin, which he champions, but Scriptural Latin, the Vulgate tradition, which of course showed such a striking affinity with Romance word order that a classical philologist has even suggested it as a major source for the drift from Latin SOV to Romance SVO.[84] The verb at the end, to Dornblüth's Germanic ears, sounds *sehr gut und bindig*, and it sounds so good precisely because it binds and ties together the whole period (p. 206). He therefore censures both Lutheran and Catholic versions of the Bible for what has since become, regrettably, a mechanical, passive routine, which must be corrected in order to restore German to its true nature.

Returning to Gottsched, his favorite target and whipping boy, Dornblüth chides him for condemning *incisa* or *Einschiebsel* (Gottsched's grammar, p. 104 fn.), to wit, for wanting relative clauses placed outside the principal clause (outside the "brackets"). Dornblüth wants them inside, so that the "Ciceronian" periodicity will be accomplished in the ending of the period with the main verb (p. 209). And yet, Dornblüth avers, Gottsched himself warns against placing the main verb too soon, as Luther and the poets up to Opitz used to do. It is just another case of Gottsched not practicing his golden rules (p. 210).

Dornblüth's pedantry reaches another peak of sorts where he insists (p. 211) that periods must end with the main statement, and dependent clauses introduced by *um . . . zu* must therefore go before, not after. Curiously enough, he calls these clauses *gerundia* (probably because of Latin equivalent constructs), whereas they are plain infinitives + *zu*. At any rate, he prefers to replace them with finite moods introduced by *damit*.

As far as his own style is concerned, what most German philosophers were doing with French (mixing it pitilessly with their language), Dornblüth, an arch-conservative, does with Latin, producing such linguistically composite monstrosities as the following, where the upshot is at least better by its clarity than many of his purer sentences, but the cause of the German language fares none the better for it:

Wan ein *Verbum compositum secundum exigentiam sensus* gleich *circa initium* zu setzen ist; mus die *Particula praeposita* darvon abgesondert und erst *in fine Constructionis* gesetzt werden.

After Gottsched, **Carl Friedrich Aichinger**, *Versuch einer teutschen Sprachlehre* (Frankfurt-Leipzig, J.P. Kraus, 1753 and Wien: P. Kraus, 1754), showed how a higher progressive stage could be reached by grasping the main types of syntactic phenomena and raising the question of a suitable methodological organization.[85] For Aichinger the main point is that of the placing of three key elements: (1) Nominativus oder das SUBJECTUM, (2) Verbum finitum, (3) Casus verbi. Three orders ensue: 1.2.3.; 1.3.2.; 2.1.3.; respectively labeled as *ordo indicativus* or *absolutus*, *relativus*, and *interrogativus* (1754, p. 541).

This schema, which exerted a deserved influence in later years, presents for the first time a clear identification of the basic patterns that we would now represent as SVO, SOV, and (inverted) VSO. One will also note the somewhat surprising absence of the obvious variation OVS (or, in a more refined symbolism: XVS); it will fall to Aichinger's follower Hemmer (see below) to fill in this fourth basic pattern.

Christian Friedrich Hempel, *Erleichterte Hoch-Teutsche Sprachlehre*, 1754,[86] lies confusedly and self-contradictorily between Gottsched and Aichinger, principally on such matters as the position of auxiliaries. More interesting is **Heinrich Braun**, *Anleitung zur deutschen Sprachkunst*, 1765,[87] a school textbook, where, as still with Hempel and Gottsched, the subjunctives are introduced by *daß* in the paradigms, and carry end-position (pp. 392ff. of 1765 ed.). But he no longer identifies end-position with the subjunctive, recognizing that certain (subordinating) conjunctions can likewise send the indicative to the end (p. 555). He also recognizes the true meaning of the choice between indicative and subjunctive in the indirect discourse without introductory conjunction, alternately expressing certainty or doubt (or, we would rather say, alleged or reported opinion); *Ich weis, du bist krank*; *Ich höre, dieser Mann sey gelehrt* (pp. 557f.).

We have come across several references to the question of inversion. Even though it developed as a topic of rhetorical or stylistic choices rather than grammatical rule characterization, it directly affected the understanding of the nature and function of basic sentence structures. We must, then, take a step backward and return to Gottsched's 1730 *Dichtkunst* as our starting point for a more detailed investigation of this typical controversy that flared up in the course of the century, with the potential of a disruptive crisis within the pervasive rationalism of the Enlightenment.

As we have seen, in his *Critische Dichtkunt* of 1730, Part I, ch. 9, Gottsched had echoed Du Cerceau in the admission, with caveats, of word displacement from the order of prose for the sake of expressing emphasis or emotion in poetry.[88] Admittedly, such inversions add vigor. Generally, however, displacement is to be avoided, even in verse. Christian Weise had gone further in cautioning against inversions, objecting that even rhyme or scansion cannot justify *die Stube dein, ich bin gewesen da, ich zu dem Freunde gekommen bin* . . . (pp. 214–5). The climate of enlightened rationalism was decidedly against Du Cerceau's insights: Separation of prefix from infinitive, postposition of epithet, proleptic pleonastic repetition of the article (*die Weisheit, die machet*), and free positioning of the verb in main clauses were ruled out by Neukirch;[89] Morhof had allowed some freedom in word order for the sake of emphasis or euphony;[90] Kohler, *Deutliche und gründliche Einleitung*, 1734, was peremptory; "Von der Construction, die in Prosa gebräuchlich, hat man, so viel möglich, nicht leichtlich und ohne Noth abzuweichen."[91] The structure of prose, in other words, remains the basis for the structure of poetry.[92] This was part of the process of regularization and normalization from which New High German derived.

Johann Jakob Breitinger (1701–76), vol. II, p. 463 of *Critische Dicht-*

kunst (Zürich & Leipzig, 1740), boldly rejected this advocacy of prose construction in verse and proclaimed that the origin of poetic inversions is in the *Sprache der Leidenschaften* (II, p. 354): "Die Leidenschaften haben eine eigene Sprache und eine ganz besondere Art des Ausdruckes. . . . [Diese] Eigenschaft . . . besteht darinnen, daß sie in der Anordnung ihres Vortrags, in der Verbindung und Zusammensetzung der Wörter und Redensarten . . . sich an kein grammatisches Gesetze, oder logicalische Ordnung . . . bindet."[93] This point was to be taken up by Herder, but not without direct inspiration from Condillac and Batteux.

Inversions were sanctioned as an ingredient of the *coupé* style that **Johann Jakob Bodmer**, *Critische Betrachtungen über die poetischen Gemählde der Dichter* (1741), recommended even for poetry to express emotion: "Die Leidenschaft redet mit unterbrochnen Worten, und schlägt in ihren Sätzen keine Achtung auf ihre Zusammenfügung" (p. 323); "Muntern Köpfen von einer feuerreichen Einbildungskraft wird es nicht schwer fallen, sich auf besagte Weise zu erhitzen, und einen gewissen Affect an sich zu nehmen; und alsdann dörfen sie sich nur der Führung desselben überlassen, und das schreiben, was derselbe ihnen in die Gedancken giebt" (pp. 342–3).[94]

With Bodmer, Milton became the *fons et origo* of the proposed new epic style in a curious and paradoxical coupling of his example with the newly discovered virtues of medieval German poetic diction. See Bodmer's preface to his 1732 translation of *Paradise Lost* — the anonymously published *Johann Miltons Verlust des Paradieses, ein Helden-Gedicht* (Zürich, 1732) —, his *Critische Abhandlung von dem Wunderbaren* (Zürich, 1740), his essay on Milton's language in the *Sammlung critischer Schriften*, III. Stück (1742), pp. 75–133, and finally his preface to the second volume of his *Sammlung von Minnesingern* (Zürich, 1759), especially p. iii.[95] Against, specifically, Christian Weise's advocacy of prose structure in verse, Bodmer praises the medieval poetic usage of sending a monosyllabic word, which completes the sense of a line, to the next line, an especially strong case of enjambment; he recommends the avoidance of normal word order, to be achieved with interpolations even of considerable length (1759), and poetic inversion in the broadest sense ("Versetzung der Wörter aus der prosaischen Fügung," 1742, p. 98). This is to be compared with Addison's praise of Milton's diction in his essays in *The Spectator*, especially no. 285, 26 January 1712: "Under this head may be reckoned the placing the adjective after the substantive, the transposition of words, . . . with several other foreign modes of speech which this poet has naturalized, to give his verse the greater sound, and throw it out of prose." What for Addison was foreign (= Latin?) became archaic for Bodmer, who proposed both the use of other German dialects, specifically Alemannic (his region), and Middle High German turns of phrases.[96] "Milton" says Bodmer, "has availed himself of several means to distinguish his diction from that of prose: he imitates foreign tongues, brings back to light old vigorous terms, coins new ones, alters the order of words, finds unusual metaphors, and runs his lines onto one another" (1732). Addison had assessed the epic language as "both perspicuous and sublime" by recalling implicitly Aristotle's enumeration of aids to the high poetic style: metaphor, idioms from other dialects, shortened or lengthened forms, obsolescent terms. Bodmer elaborates the point in 1742, showing how Milton followed Aristotle. Bodmer admired features in the English language that he likened to analogues in Middle High German, such as the monosyllabic verbs, the sloughing off of flectional endings, and the freedom of word order. This bold new perspective was tantamount to reversing the process that had led to the regularization of New High German.

Friedrich Gottlieb Klopstock (1724–1803) was inspired for his *Messias* by Bodmer's Milton translation, and Bodmer reacted with enthusiasm to the first three published cantos (1748). Klopstock revised it several times until the definitive edition of 1799–1800.[97] For example, *Flügel der rauschenden Cherubim* and *in den Tiefen der Erde* of 1748 became in 1799 *rauschender Cherubim Flügel* and *in der Erd' Abgründen*, with archaic anteposition of genitive, corresponding to determinant → determinand order as part of basic SOV order.

Klopstock's 1758 "Von der Sprache der Poesie" in the journal *Der nordische Aufseher*[98] suggested that the most forceful elements in an imaginative perception (*Vorstellung*) must be placed in a manner that will play on both phonetics and semantics: "Die Regel der zu verändernden Wortfügung ist die: Wir müssen die Gegenstände, die in einer Vorstellung am meisten rühren, zuerst zeigen." In another essay[99] he noted: "Unvermuthetes, scheinbare Unordnung, schnelles Abbrechen des Gedankens, erregte Erwartung, alles dieß setzt die Seele in eine Bewegung, die sie für die Eindrücke empfänglicher macht."[100] This echoed Breitinger's genetic tracing of poetic inversions to the *Sprache der Affekte*.[101]

Most comprehensively, in the essay "Von der Wortfolge,"[102] also of 1799 like the preceding, Klopstock stressed the multiple advantages of German in its departing from the customary order. This order is dictated by semantic association or correspondence between phrase composition and thinking process, hence by the need to achieve the quickest and most economical form of expression (*das Schneller*, *Geschwindigkeit*, avoidance of *Zeitverlust*, p. 274). But poetic inversions have four valid principles or causes (*Grundsätze* or *Ursachen*): "(1) Der Dichter will den Ausdruck der Leidenschaft verstärken; (2) etwas erwarten lassen; (3) Unvermuthetes sagen; (4) mehr Wohlklang oder leichtere und freyere Wendungen der Periode bekommen" (p. 280). Since their order was free, the ancients achieved mostly rhythmic effects (*Numerus*) through their inversions, whereas the Germans achieve chiefly emphasis and suspense (pp. 276–7). In a passage that is ideally reminiscent of Du Cerceau (p. 276), he concluded that "das Abweichen ist ihm [to the poet] also nicht etwa bloß erlaubt, sondern es ist Pflicht." Inversion, then, is caused by emotional tension, surprise, and euphony. To summarize it in Blackall's words: "Emotion causes first things to come first; tension and surprise lead to the delaying of some important part of the sentence which in 'cold prose' would come earlier. Poetry must 'etwas erwarten lassen.'"[103]

The philosopher **Johann Georg Hamann** (1730–88) was a key intermediary between the French *grammairiens-philosophes* and Herder.[104] In an essay on French word order he contrasted the rigidity of French with the freedom of Latin to employ inversion to the best advantage. Considerations of regularity should not render void the stylistic potential inherent in inversions. As to German, "die deutsche Sprache ist ihrer Natur nach vor andern dieser Inversionen fähig. . . ." In this essay, Hamann draws on the comparison between French and Latin order in Pluche, *La mécanique des langues* (Paris, 1751), which had mentioned the almost total lack of inversion in French. Diderot had further distinguished between natural and artificial order in the introduction to his *Lettre sur les sourds et muets*, also of 1751. Furthermore, in this text of 1761–2 (it is a section of his *Kreuzzüge des Philologen*, 1762), Hamann took to task the habit of French schools to reduce the beauty and forcefulness of Latin periods by parsing them for the sake of simplification and clarification, turning them into direct construction (*construiren*). It was a clear, if implicit, thrust against Du Marsais' 1722 *Exposition d'une méthode raisonnée pour apprendre la langue latine*,[105] and Hamann (ed. Nadler, p. 130) quoted explicitly the Italian Francesco Algarotti, "*Oeuvres* VII, p. 304," on the loss of phonetic values as well as psychological impact such methods entailed.

Algarotti's 1757 "Essay on the French language" was an extended indictment of French established ideas on language and style, and it was to be expected that Germans would lend a sympathetic ear to such an authority from another country, more so since Algarotti was doing little more than expanding, with approval, the ideas of Fénelon, *Lettre à l'Académie françoise*, which he quoted *in extenso*, with detailed references to the defense of freedom of construction, boldness of transpositions, and the poetic and expressive use of inversions.[106] What makes Algarotti's position particularly significant is that he made a clear distinction between the "nature" of the French language, which made it so inherently lively and effective, and what "legislation" had done to it, by putting it in chains — chiefly through the autocratic prejudices of the French Academy, an instrument of Richelieu's will.

Most important for us is that in the text in question Hamann is among the first to connect explicitly the capacity to invert the order with the presence of functional flectional endings: Greater flection leads to greater syntactic mobility (ed. Nadler, pp. 131–2). French *needs* direct order because of its drastic limitations in declension.[107]

Hamann's drawing on Pluche would seem to place him in the camp of the *mécaniciens* against the *métaphysiciens*. **Johann Gottfried Herder** (1744–1803) picked up from there and dedicated to inversion two sections of the first collection of his *Fragmente über die neuere deutsche Literatur* (1766–7).[108] Herder speaks of *kühne Inversionen* in the second phase of the evolution of the language, after the wild phase and before the rational phase.[109] In the rational phase inversions were dropped for the sake of logical clarity (an idea that reminds us of Vico) and to avoid ambiguity (but Herder does not attribute this ambiguity to the sloughing off of case endings or any specific phonetic change). Like most of the preceding critics, Herder speaks of stylistic choices rather than necessary grammatical drift. And the inversions such critics have in mind consist mostly of XVS patterns in main clauses.

A regulated word order is inadequate to express strong emotions.[110] Hamann had already made the point,[111] just as Diderot had stated: "Nous avons gagné, à n'avoir point d'inversions, de la netteté, de la clarté, de la précision, . . . nous y avons perdu de la chaleur, de l'éloquence et de l'énergie."[112]

For Herder, direct order is the language of philosophy and reason, inversion the language of nature, of the senses, and of sentiments, the language of the heart, of passions, and of aroused interest. In short, inversions are the soul of poetry.[113] German and languages close to nature gain advantages from their aptitude for inversions. Herder derived from Diderot via Rousseau, from Rapin and Condillac and Batteux, but in advocating head position of the object — which Condillac simply justified in primitive languages, "as representing gesture toward the object affected,"[114] and which was much more practicable in modern German than in French — he went beyond the *mécaniciens*. His attitude was in fact a development of Breitinger, who in the end harked back to Addison.[115]

When language evolved from the primitive wild stage to a state befitting the newly found orderliness of social and political organization, it became a poetic and sensual medium, rich in the features that distinguish poetry from prose, these features including fresh inversions and simplicity in the use of connecting particles (p. 157). The formula *einfache Partikeln* evoked long-standing debates in France and England, with conclusive reference to the devices commonly associated with the Senecan and Tacitean style, showing looseness rather than periodicity, avoiding pleonastic and less than functional conjunctions, and allowing the imagination to fill in the logical junctures instead of making them explicit in the form of coordinating or subordinating conjunctions. Indeed, later on Herder does turn to the specific terms of the stylistic controversies and, in Fragment 10 (ed. Suphan, pp. 182–6), he proclaims Tacitus "the historian for Germans, even in his style, rather than Livy." For his style is more emphatic (*nachdrucksvolle Schreibart*, p. 185). Tacitus, then, is not only above Livy, but even above Seneca and Pliny, who, with their pointes, their epigrammatic traits, and their wit, are more becoming to the French (p. 186).

Herder discusses these questions in the spirit of his general stand on philosophical and literary matters, in the wake of Hamann's speculation and in line with Bodmer's and Breitinger's polemics against Gottsched's intellectualism. His *Sturm und Drang* position in regard to the main tenets of the Enlightenment, his appeal to the individual originality of each national tradition in its popular roots, allow him to defend the right of Germans to have their own forms of expression without having to defer to a pretended French canon. His enthusiasm for poetry above prose, and imagination above or alongside reason, makes him uphold the value of inversion as the form of poetic and eloquent expressiveness: Vividness of representation demands that the objects be called to our attention from the vantage point (*Augenpunkt*) from which we actually experience them and react to them with sensibility and emotion (*Empfindung, Affect, Aufmerksamkeit*, p. 191). This is the origin of inversions. A philosophical language will reduce them to a minimum, since it reduces experience to mere concept, but modern German has managed to be both eminently philosophical and exquisitely poetical.

In language reminiscent of Locke, Vico, and Condillac (and indirectly echoing Hamann) he writes of the speech of a people that is still in the sensual stage of its development as essentially irregular and dislocated (*unregelmäßig und voll Veränderungen*, p. 192), hence full of inversions deriving from sensorial attention to the objects just as they strike our imagination (*sinnliche Aufmerksamkeit, wie die Gegenstände ins Auge fallen*). Language is not yet "grammatical," still in a state of actual "chaos" (p. 192). When writing was introduced, communication had to prescind from gesture and tone, which in the spoken expression had been part of the message. Hence a logical order had to be introduced into the sentence for the sake of intelligibility, but Greek and Latin nevertheless managed to preserve much freedom of construction that the modern languages have finally lost to progress (p. 193). One can see that Herder makes no allowance for the linguistic relationship between freedom of order and functionality of inflection. Yet he sees fixed order as a result of historical progress, although the prize will have to go, under these circumstances, to a language that, like German, can still combine the advantages of the poetic stage with those of the philosophical, a high degree of order as well as freedom. Such a language will be able both to follow the train of disembodied conceptual ideas and to render sensorial impressions in their full vividness. The two need coexist in mutual tension: Our sense of logic will strive to eliminate inversions or any dislocation, "since only the simple is clear, and any inversion allows at least the possibility of ambiguity" (p. 194).

The main Fragment on Inversions follows (No. 13, pp. 194-7). In treating the modern languages, Herder invokes Diderot's judgment to the effect that French has been put in the chains of rules by the grammarians. Indeed, the closer a language is to its origins, the freer, the livelier, hence the richer is the power of inversion. The philosophical or "metaphysical" regularity of French (in the context of the polemic between *métaphysiciens* and *mécaniciens*) is responsible for the weakness of poetic language in that country. Avowedly, the writer who through the power of the imagination aims to arouse attention, sensibility, and even passion, needs inversions. The order of imagination is definitely not the order of cold reason.[116]

In conclusion, German has developed a philosophic spirit without renouncing its freedom. The equation: Philosophy = French language is no longer to be accepted on German soil, and in this regard the German language can be proclaimed to offer advantages over French (p. 197).

In the conclusion to the first series of Fragments, "Beschluß, über das Ideal der Sprache," pp. 229-40, Herder turns more specifically to a relatively close analysis of the order of parts in the clause, leaving behind the ideological generalities of the polemic on inversion. Then, for the only time, he seems to come to a realization of the relationship of dependence between fixed order and weakness or absence of inflection. After quoting his text once again, namely the *Literaturbriefe* (here Theil 17, first ed., pp. 180-8),[117] on the desirability of modalities of word order flexible enough to accommodate the speaker's occasional special goals, he comes to the principle of adopting that order which will avoid ambiguity in the syntactic relationships (p. 234 — as the *Literaturbrief* puts it: "Die Worte so ordnen, daß sie bei aller möglichen Kürze keine doppelte Beziehung der Abhängigkeit leiden"). Here Herder relates this possible ambiguity to the limitation of flection, for example, when a language has similar nominatives and accusatives. This is the case with French, which therefore must offset this deficiency through a fixed order whereby one can tell the subject from the object by their position. But the rambling and dragging periods of the German official style (*der schleppende Periode*) sin by a second type of ambiguity applying to languages that achieve flection by the addition of particles (presumably when the semantic and morphological function of some such particles remains unclear); whereas the neo-Latin writers equally fail because they stuff their sentences with all kinds of random inversions without sensitivity for the laws of Roman writing, which left nothing uncertain and indeterminate.

Herder then asks, through Lessing's words, the question that was to lead to the famous 1782–84 contest of the Berlin Academy and to Rivarol's prize-winning categorical hymn to the virtues of French. What, asks Herder, has entitled the French to call their language the language of reason? He gives three reasons: A certain regularity in the order of construction; the early achievement of a linguistic and stylistic refinement that made their language apt to cater to a polite society, including women; finally, a happy mediocrity or golden mean (p. 236). This last achievement has been justly stressed, he recalls, by Prémontval (*Préservatif contre la corruption de la langue française*, a periodic essay of 1759–64, Part 1), although Herder does not conceal the need to qualify that praise.[118] Herder concludes that he is ready to grant the French language the prize for intelligibility (*Verstand* vs. *Vernunft*) (p. 237).

His old enthusiasm on the matter partly rekindled by Herder's forceful intervention, J. J. **Bodmer**, *Die Grundsätze der deutschen Sprache* (1768),[119] returned with renewed attention to inversions. In this way he took his place as the most influential adversary of Gottsched's French-oriented rationalism. More interesting for us, he derives from the abbé Gabriel Girard the concept of members of clause, or "phrases" (*Satzglieder*). He also knows the concept of *Nebensatz*. Accordingly, he contributes to the strengthening of the logical analysis of the sentence. Instead of noun or *nominativ* he speaks of *Hauptsache* (= subject), *verbum* becomes *Beymessung* (= predicate), *casus verbi* becomes *Gegenstand* (= object), and *Umstand*, meaning "phrase" or complement in the narrowest sense, replaces *adverbium* and *praepositition mit ihrem Kasus*.[120]

Bodmer reflects pretty closely the modern word order.[121] He says that "Der verbundene, untergeordnete Redesatz verweiset das Zeitwort und sein Hülfswort völlig an das Ende" (p. 98), and uses the alternative term *Untersatz* ("*Denn* hatte vormals den Sinn, den itzt *weil* hat, und dienete zum Untersatze. Man sagte: *Denn die Stunde gekommen war*" — p. 101).[122] He takes a major step toward recognition of the true nature of subordination with respect to word order and as a function of the use of conjunctions. True enough, one wonders exactly what he means when he says that "Conjunctions have no power to determine the verb's forward or backward position in the clause," yet, he continues, "since some of them introduce the clause, while others subordinate it and link it to the remainder, it follows naturally that in the former case the verb is placed forward, in the latter at the end."[123]

Thus, whereas Steinbach 1724, followed by Aichinger 1754, first respectively recommended and prescribed absolute end-position after what we call subordinating conjunctions, Bodmer 1768 (but preceded by **Johann Bernhard Basedow**, *Neue Lehrart und Uebung in der Regelmäßigkeit der teutschen Sprache*, 1759) is the first to grasp the distinction between main and secondary clauses, with its impact on verbal position. This progress in theoretical awareness parallels the practical progressive weakening of the *Nachtrag* (afterthought and delayed complements after the verb in secondary clauses) in the written language.[124]

Except in questions, Bodmer states, the indicative (*einfache anfängliche Form*) must be preceded by another part of discourse (*Redeglied*). It cannot come first: "Das erste an der Spitze darf es nicht seyn." This is a reasonably efficient formulation, perhaps the first, of Clemens Biener's "second place rule." Examples: *Die Mutter flicht gewiß einen Zweig*; *Gewiß flicht die Mutter*; *so flicht die Mutter*. Although Bodmer tends to explain the "inversion" on grounds of affect or emphasis whenever possible, it is obvious that the examples he gives are not all of the expressive kind. *So* at the beginning is simply a ligature to the preceding (*liaison des idées*). He calls such words as *so* here *Expletife* or *Fortsetzungswörtchen*.[125]

The *Versetzungsgabe* of German endows it with great flexibility in deciding what element to place first. But Bodmer does regard the direct order as the norm, *allgemeine Wortstellung*, which suffices to a calm and settled state of mind, "bey stillem und gesetztem Gemüthe." When a different element from the subject is placed first, its unusual position there makes it a focal point of special attention (*Augenpunkt*), which is demanded by the speaker's emotion or state of mind. The examples, which Bodmer calls "sufficiently well known," come from

Herder's *Fragmente*. When inversions are not called for by the need to express *den Affekt*, and when they would cause ambiguity (*Zweideutigkeit*), they ought to be avoided.

The first of **Jakob Hemmer**'s three works, the *Sprachlehre* of 1775, the *Rechtschreibung* of 1776, and the *Sprachkunst* of 1780, may be the most interesting for us.[126] The material appears chiefly in the "Eingang" of the "Wortfügung" and the Third Abschnitt "Von der Sazordnung, welche die Zeitwörter fodern." Under *Sazordnung* we read of the three *Hauptteile des Satzes*, namely: (1) *Das Vorderglied*, which indicates the thing of which something is said; (2) *Zeitwort* (finite); (3) *Hinterglied*, signifying the thing said about something else. The terms may come from Aichinger, according to Jellinek,[127] and with this nomenclature Hemmer carries forward Aichinger's valid reduction of the chief elements to three even while he makes four orders possible: *Gott ist gerecht*; *weil Gott gerecht ist*; *Ist Gott gerecht?*; *Gerecht ist Gott*. In other words, as already pointed out, Hemmer goes one step further than Aichinger by his important addition of the fourth order OVS (XVS). But another considerable step forward from Aichinger lies in the point that *Hinterglied* as a basic form covers all the cases governed by the verb (hence the fourth order should more exactly be represented as XVS), whereas Aichinger construed the *casus verbi* (third main element) in the strict sense, as no more than the formal object, so that he had to treat separately the position of the nominal verbal forms, the prepositional complements, and the predicative adjectives or nominal predicates.[128] Besides, Hemmer also might appear to have put to some good use the theoretical schema of the three parts of the logical judgment that Hempel had hastily and uncritically superimposed on Aichinger's nomenclature, and that could have no practical effect on later grammatical speculation, since Hempel remained content simply to state that the nominative must represent conceptually the subject, the finite verb the copula, and the *Casus Verbi* the predicate.[129] On the other hand, Hemmer's realization of subordination is vague and still traditional: In the Third Abschnitt "Von der Sazordnung," he rules that normally the verb comes immediately after the nominative, but that it is thrown all the way to the end of the clause: (1) After all *relative Für- und Nebenwörter*, and (2) after certain other words, which he lists (the usual list of *als*, *bis*, etc.).

3. Adelung

The last chapter of the *Grundregeln der Teutschen Sprache* (1778) by Friedrich Carl Fulda (1724–88)[130] represents the introducion of a far-reaching general principle by a master of pithy, concentrated description. The principle is that of precedence or anteposition of the qualifier before the qualified (*die Vorausstellung des Bestimmenden vor das Bestimmte*). Some specific rules are: adjective before the substantive, adverb before the adjective, and in Old German, the genitive before its head (*im Altdeutschen der Genitiv vor dem regierenden Wort*). Let us note in passing that Fulda has a keen historical sense and a sharp taste for Old German. He finds that "bei den Minnesingern erreicht die grammatische Einfalt, Kraft und Regelmäsigkeit der teutschen Sprache ihre höchste Stufe."[131] Jellinek regards him as a forerunner of the historical interest of the nineteenth century and the first historical grammarian of New High German.

On the ground of his general rule Fulda gives a curious explanation of *Rücksendung*: An infinitive or participle goes to the end because, unlike a finite mood, it does not qualify the complements but is qualified by them. These latter must, therefore, precede it. The finite verb does nothing but actuate a name, the noun-subject: "Einen andern Namen in Wirkung setzt"; "da ferner ein Verbum an sich nur ein 'Name,' d.h. eine Substanz-oder Eigenschaftsbezeichnung, ist" (II, 5) — a function that does not pertain to the infinitive or participle. Elsewhere, however, Fulda (II, 220; similarly II, 26) treats infinitives and participles as modifiers with regard to the auxiliaries. Nor is this the end of Fulda's difficulties with his principle. Another exception or anomaly is the position of the subject before the verb, since he regards the former as the governing agent (*regierendes Wort*), and yet it is the one that remains qualified by the verb, according to the preceding characterization. All in all, the attempt to subsume every element under the same characterization ends in a messy jumble. The difficulties of his not having coherently thought his definitions through cause him to alter the meaning of *Bestimmung* as he goes on, so that he ends up with two contradictory meanings for the concept. Particles and nouns, in particular, distinguish themselves in the *Betonung*: The former are less stressed. *Hilfsworte*, including *Hilfsverba*, are in this sense qualifiers of the proper verb, hence the infinitive and participle, which they "serve" (*dienen*) as all modifiers "serve" their heads or governors. Likewise, less stressed personal pronouns serve the following verb. But this rule, once again, contradicts the notion that precisely such pronouns "govern" as subjects, and that, on the other hand, infinitives and participles are modifiers of the auxiliary, which rules them (II, 23, 25 f., 153 f., 219 f.). Jellinek adds that the notion of *regieren* or "governing" was a development of medieval grammar, that of *dienen* of the Hebrew theory of *litterae serviles*, and he denies the possibility that Fulda would have borrowed from Donatus' (*Grammatici latini*, ed. H. Keil, IV, 390, 22) and Priscian's (*Gr. L.* III, 39, 11) "*clam* praepositio casibus servit ambobus," "monosyllabae praepositiones tam accusativo quam ablativo servientes."[132] Fulda's unfortunately misapplied doctrine of *minderbetonte* particles does raise an interesting point that can be applied to their aptitude to displace stronger elements in a way apparently similar to their showing up even before the verb as objects (direct or indirect) in French, Spanish, and Italian: Consider this example from Contemporary German, where the subject is forced to wait long after the verb by the pronoun *sich*: *Auf persönliche Einladung des Staats-Chefs . . . hält sich nach einer Meldung der Agentur Agerpres . . . der Generalsekretär seit Samstag in Bukarest auf.* Somewhat similarly, in the following example ambiguity arises from the forward position of *es*, which is due to its atonic nature, but which makes it impossible to tell — except from the sense — whether it is subject or object: *Der Inhalt ist, wie es die Form der Veröffentlichung bedingt, ein sehr mannigfaltiger.*

As we shall see, Fulda's principle was carried forward by Adelung, and is akin to Henri Weil's 1844 characterization of languages as belonging to the type with "ascending" or "descending order." But since it basically corresponds to the patterns of consistent SOV languages, it runs into difficulties when applied to a mixed state such as that of New High German. Thus the pattern *die für die Milchversorgung verantwortliche Behörde* conforms with the modifier → modified order that characterizes SOV languages ("ascending order"), whereas *das Haus des Vaters* does not, just as the pattern Subject + Complements + Infinitive / Participle + Auxiliary conforms, whereas S+Aux+X+V does not. More crucially, a difficulty arises in that the "operators" follow the finite verb in main clauses, whereas they precede it in secondary clauses. Fulda attempts to resolve this difficulty by offering, in a series of visible somersaults, his contradictory definitions of rection and function, but it is precisely the difference in ordering between main and dependent clauses that must be disposed of first.[133]

In any event, we may assume that Fulda's law was a direct response to a clear solicitation coming from the authoritative text of Du Marsais (d. 1756, article "Construction" in the *Encyclopédie*, tome IV, 1754, pp. 73-92), which, in turn, rested on a combination of Cartesian rationalism and Lockean empiricism.[134] In short, Du Marsais had affirmed that "dans toutes les langues du monde il n'y a qu'une même manière nécessaire pour former un sens avec les mots: c'est l'ordre successif des relations qui se trouvent entre les mots, dont les uns sont énoncés comme devant être modifiés ou déterminés, et les autres comme modifiants ou déterminants" (p. 7). He meant that the right order is modified → modifier, this being the universal law that established the canonical form of all syntactic relations, including, beyond noun and adjective, also subject and predicate.[135] It was to Fulda's credit to have boldly affirmed that rule as central and general but only after having, of course, reversed it to fit it to the nature of German.

Fulda's basic rule, for better and for worse, exerted a considerable impact on later grammarians, beginning with **Johann Christoph Adelung** (1732-1806), who made it the cornerstone of his own system. I shall now proceed to give a detailed analysis of Adelung's work because it represents the conclusive thought of his century in the most articulate and mature form. Such a detailed exposition is also made necessary by the difficulty of following Jellinek's sharp critique of it without knowing the details of a particularly involved text. With Adelung, the accumulation of observed material reached the point where almost all that was relevant was now available: All that was needed was the capacity to organize, synthesize, and, possibly, explain. These final tasks were beyond Adelung's power, try as he might — and he did try very hard. His general law was a brave attempt to do all three tasks, but it would have been operative only if he had applied it to the indirect construction (SOV) as the original one for German. Not being aware of this functional hypothesis, he unavoidably became entangled in endless contradiction because he applied it in reverse, to the SVO order of the main clause or direct construction, which he, a son of his century and of French rationalism, regarded as the natural and normal order.

Since the two German orders belong to two different language types, the same rule could not describe both.

In both of Adelung's main works, the *Deutsche Sprachlehre* of 1781 . . . 1816 (hereafter *DS*) and the *Umständliches Lehrgebäude* of 1782 (hereafter *UL*),[136] the chapter "Von der Wortfolge" (second chapter of 4. Abschnitt in Bd. 2 of *UL*, precisely titled there "Von der Wortfolge oder der Ordnung") is in three sections: (1) General, (2) According to the state of mind of the speaker, (3) On Inversion or departure from the usual order for the sake of emphasis.[137]

In Adelung, Fulda's contradictions become exasperated. "This central law [the *Grundgesetz* that the determinant precedes the determinand] means then nothing else than that the less determined always precedes the more determined, indeed, this is so according to the precise degree of determination, so that a whole sentence or clause is a true ladder (*Steigerung*), where the speaker proceeds to ever sharper determinations, until the chain of his conceptions reaches its fullness at the end of the clause" (*UL* II, 505; also 506). Of course, he stumbled right away into the curious fact that, if every concept carries its determinants in front, the verb, instead, carries them behind, and so does the subject. The inherited nomenclature had transmitted the characterization of the predicate as the modifier of the subject, and of the complements as modifiers of the verb — thus viewing both subject and verb as needing determination in this sense. But something else is meant when one states that *Haus* is more determined than *das* and *groß*, so that these words must precede it, *das große Haus* (*UL* II, 508). So, as Jellinek remarks, Adelung introduces the double meaning whereby the term becomes now active, now passive: The oppositions are then conceived as now *unbestimmt* → *bestimmend* (as with subject → predicate and verb → complements), now *unbestimmt* → *bestimmt* (e.g., adjective → noun).[138]

Much of this came out of Fulda's contradictory description of the auxiliaries' function. Sometimes the participle and infinitive are *Bestimmungen* of the auxiliary; at other times we hear, instead, that the auxiliary is the qualifier, just as the article qualifies its noun. Jellinek goes on in his detailed analysis of the ramifications of this impasse (pp. 461–2), but it is a rather unproductive area that we can leave aside after these sketchy bits. Suffice it to mention in closing that the whole matter

84 □ THEORY OF WORD ORDER

comes to a head of sorts in the unhappy realization that the "preposition-adverb" (*Präpositionaladverb*) of compound verbs has the same relationship to the verb whether it is joined to it or separated, and yet in the two cases the word order differs. Jellinek concludes with the appropriate appreciation that Adelung's doctrine contained an element of value. This lay in the stressing of the *Einschachtelungssystem* that had become typical of the written language, whereby the incapsulation or *Einschaltung* of a sequence of determinants between the article and the substantive (what today is called *die erweiterte Attributgruppe*, or extended attribute), or of the complements between either auxiliary and verb or verb and preposition (*Satzklammer*), created a closed circle, the closest thing to the classical "period" to be seen among modern languages.

Since Adelung, despite his familiarity with the concept of *Nebensatz*, does not use the term with reference to word order, he assimilates the *indirekte Rede* with or without *daß* to the *natürliche Wortfolge*. He characterizes *Rücksendung* as a violation of natural order (*Abweichung*). He then reintroduces Aichinger's three orders and calls the 1.3.2. order (SOV), Aichinger's *zurücksendende Ordnung*, "*verbindende Wortfolge*" (introduced by conjunctions) — which is somewhat equivalent to using the notion of *Nebensatz*. The Inversion covers all other possibilities.

Fleischmann's assessment is of interest chiefly insofar as he points out that Adelung was the first to provide a "complete" list of subordinating conjunctions, with the sole exception of *während*, which, however, appeared in this function only shortly before Adelung's work.[139]

I. Let us now try to follow step by step the text of *UL* II, pp. 503–65 (the *DS* was a scholastic summation of the theory more elaborately expounded here: Word order, for example, was reduced from over 60 pages to 23). (P. 503) The *Wortfolge* or *stricto sensu Redesatz* = *Ordo constructionis* can be either *gewöhnliche*, divided into three species according to the *Gemüthstand des Sprechenden*, or (504) *abweichende*, which departs from the former for the sake of *Nachdruck* 'emphasis.' We express both sensations and conceptions, *Empfindungen* and *Vorstellungen*. Because of the merely perceptual manner, *rohesinnliche Art*, by which man has arrived at rational knowledge and speech, we cannot think a matter with all its qualifications clearly all at once, let alone express it; therefore we must analyze it (*auflösen*) into a mass of individual *Vorstellungen* and *Begriffe*, and then resynthesize them into thoughts (*diese wieder in Gedanken zusammen setzen*) and express them in the way in which they now appear at this stage. (504–5) The difference in kind between ideas must be reflected by a word order that follows the order and hierarchy of the ideas themselves (e.g., hierarchy of things and qualities and their relationships).

The basic law of ordering being so necessary, it therefore must be simple and deeply imbedded in man's unconscious, since it operates darkly (*dunkel*) through his sensuous perceptions and without clear consciousness, *ohne klares und deutliches Bewußtsein* — in other words, automatically. Then follows the definition of the law of *Unbestimmteres → Bestimmteres*. This law is universal, "so natürlich und angemessen, daß man es ursprünglich in allen Sprachen annehmen kann." It is only in the later development of the individual positive languages that one finds all sorts of *Abweichungen* (the same term he will use for the "inversions"), that is, departures from this basic law. Clearly, Adelung has reversed Du Marsais' law, and ends up being as arbitrary as his French counterpart on the level of universal grammar.

The basic features of German sentences are: Every sentence (*Rede*) is made up of two elements, a thing or thought of which something is said (the *Subjekt*) and what is said of it (the *Prädikat*). The task of the sentence is to determine the subject (*bestimmen*), which with regard to the sentence is its most undetermined part and least clear ("der unbestimmteste und dunkelste Begriff"). Likewise, the verb is by and in itself a most undetermined concept, which is then determined by what follows it. When a word governs another (*regieret*), the rule is that it will precede it ("das regierende dem regierten vorgesetzt wird"), since *Rektion* is a true *Bestimmung*. Yet there are cases, such as the genitives (*Gottes Sohn*), where the same basic law demands "das regierte voran zu setzen" (507). The contradiction here could hardly be more obvious: Adelung will accommodate the law to the facts of the language. Later on (p. 529, § 783) the contradiction occurs again in a different context. The *Bestimmungen* of an infinitive must precede it: *Ich befahl ihm diesen Morgen in allem Ernste, mir so gleich aus den Augen zu gehen*. This is because it is, as an infinitive, not a self-sufficient, free-standing part (*Unselbständiges*). The qualifiers of the finite verb, instead, *follow* it (like what follows *befahl* in the example). Of course, Adelung seems to be making an effort to ignore that this variance has nothing to do with the moods, since in the *Nebensatz* all complements would keep the same position if the verb were in a finite mood. Added to this difficulty is the initial unsettling realization that the whole sentence is made of *Bestimmungen* respectively of the subject and of the verb that, as such, follow both instead of preceding them (505, repeated on 506).

Rather than through the a priori postulation of a unilinear law covering all features of the sentence, the correct way to proceed should have been to describe the order of different groups according to the basic language type (a method which, of course, was not available before non-European languages could be analyzed, as first done on a basis of universal grammar by Weil). Indeed, Adelung does attempt to pursue this more promising course, not by focussing on the mutual arrangement of syntactic groups in a systematic manner, but at least by assessing the internal order of syntactic groups, starting with the sequences of pronouns — adjectives: *alle diese deine drey schönen Häuser* (510) is the proper regular sequence, moving from the *schwächer* to the *schärfer* qualifiers. To anticipate, it is a curious fact that his principle led him to interpret verbal roots ("main verbs"), infinitives, and participles as "adverbs" of their auxiliaries or modals, and separable particles as "adverbs" of their verbs. This interpretation, strange as it may sound in the context of traditional grammar, corresponds *de facto* to some modern theory of roots as operators on their modifiers (conjugational markers or auxiliaries) and noun-phrases as operators on their pre- or post-positional markers.[140]

A preposition conditions its head noun, therefore it must precede it (512). Of course, only modern linguistic typology has been in a position to show that the operator → operand order postulates post-positions rather than pre-positions. Post-positions combine with their head nouns through agglutination, thus becoming suffixes. Part of the drift to operand → operator (from XV to VX) is the shift to analytical prepositions. But Adelung could have reflected further on the lingering presence of the former XV feature in the form of postposed prepositions (*nach*, *zufolge*, etc.), especially in pronominal compounds (*warum*, *davon*, *darüber*, *wovon*, *wohin*, etc.). He does not seem to have realized the importance of these latter cases, but he treats the former as exceptions later on (p. 514 § 768.2): The following always come after their nouns: *halben, halber, entgegen, zuwider*; and at times also *gegenüber, ungeachtet, wegen, nach, durch,* and *zufolge* (for which he refers back to the pertinent sections in the morphology, §§ 506–26). And speaking of prepositions, the (for German) correct rule he states here contradicts once again, in part, what he had said (p. 507) about the governing element having to precede the governed: *Diese große uns vor Augen schwebende Gefahr* is supposed to exemplify the rule whereby a preposition and its case-noun precede their term of reference ("wenn ein Bestimmungswort . . . eine Präposition mit ihrem Casu bey sich hat").

Words indicating a state (*Beschaffenheitswörter*) are an exception insofar as they precede their qualifiers when these latter consist of an infinitive with *zu* or a preposition with its case: *Geneigt wohl zu thun, gütig gegen jedermann*; but in the latter case the reverse is also possible: *Gegen jedermann gütig* (516).

The indirect object (dative) precedes the direct (accusative), no doubt because it is a weaker qualifier: *Ich gab meinem Freunde einen Rath* (517). Only pronouns are an exception. The specific cases are treated separately: *Gib es deinem Bruder* but *gib uns einen guten Rath* (in other words, the pronoun will come first, whether accusative or dative). If both cases are pronouns, the accusative generally will come first: *Schicke ihn uns*, although personal pronouns tend to come first: *Sage mir es* (518–9).

Prepositional complements come after the direct ones (520). At this point we witness a rather confused attempt to regulate the sequence of complements, without realization that such rules contradict once again the basic law inasmuch as the prepositional complements are obviously weaker, hence should leave the later and more emphatic places to the others. At any rate, if the preposition denotes a circumstance of place or time, it and its noun will often come first: *Die reitzendste Aussicht erfüllete an diesem Tage unser Auge*, probably because, he says, it makes a weaker complement than the direct ones (but so was the last phrase in this other example: *Die reitzendste Aussicht erfüllet unser Auge mit dem sanftesten Vergnügen* — would then this be the case to invoke Beauzée's law?).[141]

Adelung now turns to the place of adverbs (*Adverbien* or *Beschaf-*

fenheitswörter): They come last, being the strongest qualifiers — *der Wind wehet heute überaus heftig*; *ich sehe dich heute hier nicht gern*; *er reisete vorgestern früh von hier wieder weg* (note the exact order of every member, which recapitulates the rules specified before) (522). The last example introduces the question of the separable particles (*trennbare Partikel* in *zusammen gesetzte Verba*). As I have already noted, Adelung declares them to be nothing but adverbs and as such the strongest qualifiers, hence to be put at the end, just where participles or infinitives of compound tenses would go. The distance from the main verb should, however, not be too great, for clarity's sake (523).

In the First Part, § 434f., he had distinguished between *ächte* and *unächte Zusammensetzungen*. In the former the particle is inseparable, in the latter, it follows the basic law of word order by preceding the infinitive and the particle, and by following the finite verb (*verbum finitum*): *Ich gehe schnell*. It was, however, not a new idea: He had lifted it from Funk, and even Aichinger (p. 356) already was inclined to interpret separable prepositions as adverbs. (Indeed, we have seen this idea even in Laurentius Albertus.) Adelung at last closes this discussion with the not exceedingly bright remark that it would have been better if one had not acquired the habit of writing such particles together with the verb as one word (524).

Going back to the matter of participles and infinitives in compound tenses, he proudly reasserts his discovery of their true nature (nothing but adverbs) in a strong polemic against his predecessors, who insisted on the participle being the true verb, which forced them into painful somersaults when it came to explaining their variable positions (525). But this idea that the auxiliary is the *eigentliches Zeitwort* was, at least with regard to word order, not new at all, since, as Jellinek rightly points out, many grammarians since Stieler and including Fulda, one of Adelung's major sources, had held just that. After taking Adelung to task for this boasting out of place, Jellinek, in a lively aside, scolds him for downright "perfidiousness" in lumping Gottsched together with the grammarians of his and later time, since Gottsched was no example — he was an exception among his betters.[142]

When three infinitives follow one another, euphony (*Wohlklange*) prefers that the one that should come last be placed first, thus: *Ich habe dir die Sache wollen verfertigen helfen* instead of *verfertigen helfen wollen* (note that he regards this *wollen* as an infinitive rather than a participle) (528). He returns to this later on (552–3), while dealing with the *verbindende Wortfolge*, and there he specifies that when the verb consists of an auxiliary + infinitive + participle the "inversion" is often practiced but unnecessary, because euphony does not demand it except when infinitive and participle have the same ending. Thus *wenn ich es werde durchgesehen haben* is better than . . . *durchgesehen haben werde*, but *weil er sich die Sache so vorgestellet haben muß* is better than . . . *muß vorgestellt haben*.

The discussion of these multiple separations concludes with an appeal to the principle of Clarity (*Deutlichkeit*), which demands that the extreme terms (of the *Satzklammer*) be sometimes brought nearer together: Instead of saying *Die Sonne ging am frühen Himmel über bethaute Hügel, welche ihr Haupt in ferner Thäler streckten, mit majestätischem Glanze auf*, we shall say: *Die Sonne ging mit majestätischem Glanze am . . . über . . . auf, welche* etc. (529). This good practice is regularly violated by the practitioners of the *Reichs- und Kanzelley-Styl*, with resulting obscurity and loss of breath in the speaker. The echo of Gottsched is easy to perceive.

Inadequate understanding of the impact of subordination brings Adelung to a curious slip at the end of his treatment of where to place the negation (531). He says it must precede the precise term it covers, and exemplifies: *Ich verlange nie, daß du verlieren sollst* versus *ich verlange, daß du nie verlieren sollst*, without perceiving that the rule is negated by the examples since the order of the two is contrarywise: *Nie* precedes its term of reference in the second example because it is a dependent clause, whereas it *follows* its term in the first, a main clause.

II. We now come to the Second Abschnitt (532), on the impact of the state of mind (*Gemüthstellung des Redenden*) on word order. This section is said to concern departures from the normal and natural order of thoughts and words (*gewöhnlicher und natürlicher Gang der Vorstellungen und der Rede*) — whose general basic law had been discussed in the previous section — when they are due to the desire to express the speaker's state of mind. This rule will also include changes of order that are called for by the presence of certain conjunctions (*Conjunctionen*) (533). Such an inclusion, we are compelled to observe, cannot fail to surprise by its relative lack of logic, and indeed the apparent disorderliness in the organization of the material is compounded by the division of this section into three parts, dealing respectively with (1) The natural order — which seems to throw us back to the first section, and indeed it covers the same ground, only adding new twists and arguments, always with reference to cases that do *not* involve the specific expression of the state of mind in such a way as to necessitate changes of order; (2) the interrogation (*fragende Wortfolge*); and (3) subordination (called simply *verbindende Wortfolge*, conjunctive or joining order'). It is in order to note here that for the types of verbal placement, Adelung displays a generic reliance on Bodmer, specifically in the appeal to the speaker's point of view or state of mind to explain and justify the "abnormal" placement, even such as that of the verb at the head in questions.[143]

1. The natural order (and the term is only a convenient label, whose implications, Adelung implies, would be questionable if taken literally) refers first and foremost to the narrative (or expository or declarative), the descriptive, and the didactic discourse (*erzählende, beschreibende und unterrichtende Rede*), as long as they involve simple sentences (*einfach*) without any subordination (*Verbindung*) (534). There are two ways, according to whether one simply states, implying a vouchsafed truthfulness, or reports one's own or others' feelings or opinions as such. This latter way is called *die relative Rede*. He goes on with further subdivisions that need not detain us here, since what he really means is the distinction between direct and indirect discourse, rather ineptly treated with the usual complications and repetitions due to his inability to reduce the subject matter to the simplest possible terms. To say "I told him he was a fool," German can have *Ich sprach zu ihm, du bist ein Thor* or *Ich sprach zu ihm, er sey ein Thor* (with the subjunctive), or *daß er ein Thor sey* (535).

Now the question arises: Why do certain conjunctions entail a change in order? (537). What was the obscure (= subconscious, see pp. 504–5) cause that moved the Germans to adopt such a course? Here and again later on, Adelung will candidly confess that he does not know. Of course, his question was wrong from the beginning. For, coming as he did before the birth of comparative philology, he could not know that the phenomenon he had in mind may not have existed. The change may have occurred the other way around, since the original construction was probably the very one that German preserved only after these conjunctions, whereas what Adelung and his predecessors called the normal and natural construction was the new development, the real "departure," coming perhaps at the beginning of *Althochdeutsch* as part of the shift from SOV to SVO. Adelung feels compelled to conclude that, as it appears, the finite verb in the *Nebensätze* (a term he lacks) was felt to be the strongest determinant of the clause, and as such it had to be pushed to the extreme right. Thus its own determinants had to precede it according to the basic law, whereas in other cases (i.e., in the *Hauptsätze*) they would follow it. This tortuous way of arguing shows how useless his argument on reasons for serialization has become, since it can be bent to explain anything (538).

The moment when Adelung should have introduced the concept of subordination and coordination, but did not, comes where he realizes that not all conjunctions affect the order. Some of those that do not (the coordinating conjunctions) present, of course, no problem. They are such as *und, weder, oder, entweder, allein, nähmlich, aber, sondern, zwar, vielmehr, doch, dennoch, denn, hingegen* and *hergegen*. Others, however, are problematic, because they are subordinating, and of these Adelung mentions only some very transparent cases, such as *daß* and *wenn*, but without further ado (537–8).

2. *Fragende Wortfolge*. Adelung rather arbitrarily places under this heading all inversions of the subject (after the verb) (539). Once again, Jellinek appropriately takes our author to task on this and related points on two accounts.[144] First, Adelung confuses the subjective factors conditioning affective style and the necessary grammatical displacement due to subordination. He is thus forced to treat the displacement of the verb to the end due to the presence of certain conjunctions as a case of *Gemüthstellung des Sprechenden*, which obviously it is not. Second, he incorrectly separates the treatment of inversion by emphasis (*Nachdruck*, in the Third Abschnitt) from the treatment of state of mind. Jellinek does not elaborate this point, but I assume he means that it was inconsistent to treat some cases of adverb in first place, with shifting of the subject to third place, among the varieties of *fragende Wortfolge*, as one will see presently, and others among the varieties of *Nachdruck*. Furthermore, Jellinek points out, if in actual questions the verb comes first because it deserves the most attention, this will apply to any concept that is placed first, sending the subject to third place with a resulting "inversion,"[145] so that the difference be-

tween state of mind (or affective language) and emphasis becomes arbitrary and vague. It is confusing to operate at one time with *Affekt* or *veränderter Gemüthsstand*, and at another with *Nachdruck*. The problem with Adelung really was, we might conclude, that he was a muddling thinker.

In any event, the *fragende Wortfolge* obtains: (1) When the imperative mood is used to express command or exhortation, with a pronoun as subject (540); (2) In direct questions (541); (3) In exclamations (542); (4) In optative sentences (expressing desire) with the verb in the past tense: *Hätte ich es doch nicht gethan!* (543); (5) In *es*-clauses; *Es kommt jemand* (a rather debatable classification); (6) When *wenn, so, da, obgleich, obschon*, or *da doch* are omitted — or the first particle of the compound ones, as *ob* in obgleich: *kommt er, so ist es gut; bin ich gleich arm, so bin ich doch tugendhaft* for *ob ich gleich arm bin* (544) — in other words, as we might put it, in hypothetic or concessive constructions without conjunction in the protasis. (This last point concerns an important peculiarity of German that obviously belongs not here but, once again, in the treatment of subordination.) (7) Again improperly phrased is the inclusion here of *Nachsätze* as main clauses coming after a conditional clause and introduced by *da* or *so*: As the examples show (*wo ich bin, da will er auch seyn; wenn es drey schlägt, so will ich kommen*), these are cases of "inversion" of the subject after the verb when the first place is preempted by a complement, an adverb, or a dependent clause (again we see the consequences of unclear envisioning of hypotactic structures). The VS order would obtain even without the presence of the *da* or *so* particles, which are not strictly necessary. Furthermore, the two examples are not categorically or typologically equivalent, since *da* is functional through its locative emphatic meaning, whereas *so* is more or less pleonastic. (8) Finally, the rule obtains in all other cases of inversion of the subject caused by anteposition of anything else, thus with the adverbs of order *erstens, erstlich, zweytens*, etc., *also*, some pronouns like *ein solch* (*einen solchen Mann hab ich nie gesehen*), etc. The reason is that such words want to attract all the attention to themselves (*Aufmerksamkeit*). The verb must come immediately next because they must remain as close as possible to it as their immediate *Bestimmung* (544).

3. *Verbindende Wortfolge* (Indirect Construction). Adelung fails to establish a clear connection between this phenomenon of *Rücksen*-

dung des Verbs and the *Gemüthstellung*, since he has confessed above that he does not know why verbs move to the extreme right when certain conjunctions intervene. Now he adds (545) that the same happens after all relative pronouns, that is, not only *der, welcher, wer, was, wo,* but also all their compounds, *weswegen, wobey, (von wannen), woher, wohin, womit,* etc. (549). Interestingly enough, he censures here the use of the compounds of *da* and *dar* as if they were relative pronouns requiring indirect construction, whereas they are nothing but *determinatif oder demonstrativo-relativ,"* nonsubordinating conjunctions generally demanding inversion of the subject, not indirect construction of the verb: *Daher ist es denn geschehen,* not *daher es denn geschehen ist; dabey blieb es denn,* not *dabey es denn blieb* (550). It was a sound piece of advice that Adelung himself did not properly observe; see his "Da es . . . nichts . . . voraus hat, als die Abstammung von einem Verbo, daher ihm auch der Nebenbegriff der Zeit anklebt; so findet es . . . seine Stelle da, wo. . . ." (526); and "So auch der Infinitiv, . . . daher er auch mit demselben einerley Stelle hat" (527). This is a telling instance of the peculiarly German ambiguity and fluctuation in the syntactic import of conjunctions and pronouns, to which we shall have to return when discussing contemporary theory on reasons for *Rücksendung* as a substitute for the weakness of morphological markers of subordination.

Indirect questions introduced by interrogative adverbs and pronouns, *warum, was, was für, wie, wo,* etc., trigger the indirect construction. A predicative attribute (a direct determinant of the question word) will come immediately after the introductory particle: *er weiß selbst nicht, wie gut er es haben wird* (*gut* determines *wie* as a localized *Bestimmung*) (550). The order of the successive *Bestimmungen* is regulated: example *Wenn er es dir gewähren wird* or *Wenn der Himmel es dir gewähren wird* shows Conjunction + Subject + Object + Indirect Object + Infinitive or Participle + Finite Verb or Auxiliary (551).

Turning once again (553) to a critique of the *Kanzelley-* and *Curial-Styl* (especially, he says, in the *Oberdeutschen Provinzen*), he warns against excessive embedding of clauses inside one another: under the *Rücksendung* rule full-fledged clauses must be kept as sequences of successive units (thus the principle of Natural Serialization should also define individual clauses as natural constituents, not to be incapsulated into one another as if they were incidental phrases or clauses, *Zwisch-*

ensätze, 554).[146] The confusion derives from the fact that by such practices sequences of clauses are treated as if they were a single clause with a series of inserts within it (554). He will return to the "false beauties" of the bureaucratic style, especially of the "Upper Provinces," in the section on *Nachdruk* (561) with the examples: *Daß Ew. Wohlgeb. mit diesem Schreiben beschwerlich zu fallen, ich mir die Freyheit nehme; und damit er, daß man ihm wohl gerathen, durch den Ausgang erfahre.* The specific objection here is to the embedding of a clause between the conjunction (*daß* and *damit*) and the verb of another.

III. Inversion for the sake of Emphasis (*Nachdruck*) (554).

German displays a peculiar freedom in the frequent use of *Inversion* or *Versetzung* — this freedom resting on the presence of declensions, so that the nominative remains recognizable even when removed from first place (555). Adelung proceeds to list one by one all the elements that can occupy first place, that is to say all the grammatical parts of speech as well as the logical parts of the clause (558). When he comes to the complements (which he keeps calling *Umstand, oder eine Präposition mit ihrem Casu*) he makes a curious slip with the example *Wenn von ihrem Genusse unsere ganze Seele erfüllet ist*. Since this is a *Spannsatz* or *Nebensatz*, and Adelung adds no warning to this effect, it does not belong here: Its subject is not postponed to the verb but only to the complement. He then comes to impersonals governing the dative, capable of several inversions: *Es grauet mir davor, mir grauet es davor, davor grauet es mir*, and without *es, mir grauet davor, davor grauet mir*.

Further on, he includes cases of what we would call anaphoric or rather proleptic subjects (or objects), when the inversion lies in a pronoun that picks up the subject (or object) again, repeating it (common in French and Italian as *reprise* or *ripresa*: *Cet homme je le connais bien, Quell'uomo lo conosco bene): Die ewige Nacht, was ist sie sonst, als ein zorniger Blick von dir!* (559). An interesting development of this possibility belongs to the higher literary style (*die höhere Schreibart*), when the repetition of the subject through a pronoun is called for by the desire to insert another element between the subject and the verb (this being a clear case of emphasis): *Die Freude des verjüngten Jahres, überall blickt sie hervor* (560). But most such cases, as in the former examples, involve no inversion.

At this juncture a subtle point is introduced that, within its narrow boundaries, is meant to test the spirit of the basic law. We hear that when the dative is moved to the right of the accusative, it acquires special force because the later places are stronger (as Adelung puts it, stronger *Bestimmungen* stay closer to the verb in the *verbindende Wortfolge*, farther from it in the *natürliche* or *fragende*). The examples of datives in emphatic position are: *Ich gebe den Rath dir; laß diesen einzigen Trost der leidenden Unschuld; der Milch aus dem Felsen und Wein sich erschuf* (559). Jellinek, II, p. 464, criticizes this and counters that Hemmer (see Jellinek, II, 456), in his Third Abschnitt "Von der Satzordnung, welche die Zeitwörter fodern" (Adelung's source), had better understood the impact of end-position. Hemmer had theorized that when several prepositional complements come together, the most important, that is to say, the one that is most relevant for the verb, goes to the right: ". . . so stehet die vornehmste davon, d.i. diejenige hinten, die das Zeitwort am nächsten angehet"; thus, in *Ich habe mich mit einem Messer in den Finger geschnitten, mit einem Messer* is the mere circumstance, less important, and to this it owes its position. Indeed, we can add, to say *Ich schnitt mich in den Finger mit einem Messer* would be unidiomatic. Since *in den Finger* is the more important complement, it must go to the right in any case.

Inversions are only justified by the need for emphasis, otherwise they are to be avoided (561). He gives examples of unfunctional inversions. In particular, he dislikes separable particles in first position, as in *Fort ist er schon gegangen, Weg wäre er gereiset!* (562). On principle, inversions should be avoided when they cause obscurity or ambiguity (*Dunkelheit, Zweideutigkeit*), as when the accusative is unrecognizable as such (*unkennlicher Casus*): One must keep in mind that it is declension that gives German its freedom to invert. We can note here two things: (1) that the term inversion, which had been transmitted through the grammatical and rhetorical speculation as a party-label, has practically been restricted in German to the shifting of the subject from first to third place, as it should be; and (2) that Adelung clearly realized the connection between inversion and declension as well as the overall linguistic rule of achieving clarity or avoiding ambiguity (cf. Vennemann's Disambiguation Principle). The first law in any language is the highest possible intelligibility (*höchste mögliche Verständlichkeit*), to which elegance, brevity, and even grammatical correctness are subordinated ("welchem Schönheit, Kürze und . . . selbst die grammatische Richtigkeit untergeordnet sind''). In the normal word order the morphological similarity between nominative and accusative (singular feminine and neuter, all plural) is of little consequence because position itself shows the logical function (563). But this similarity may rule out inversion. Thus, for example, *Der Vögel Schaar durchschnitt die jovialische Luft* may not be inverted (563).

A typical development of German grammatical analysis that still lingers today and that may appear confusing is first seen in Adelung, where he distinguishes between *wahres* (*logisches*) and *künstliches* (*grammatisches*) *Subjekt*. The latter is the result of inversion, which sends forward part of the predicate: For example, *heiter* in *heiter war der Tag* (or, we could add, a complement, as with *gestern* in *gestern sah ich ihn*).[147]

Adelung's *Sprachlehre* also contains his contribution to the critique of the bureaucratic style (§ 808, p. 443): It is against the nature of the language to insert the *Nachsatz* between the *Vordersatz* and its conjunction: . . . *daß Ew. Wohlgeb. mit diesem Schreiben beschwerlich zu fallen, ich mir die Freyheit nehme; und damit er, daß man ihm wohl gerathen, durch den Ausgang erfahre.*[148]

In conclusion, Adelung's exceedingly tortuous way of reasoning produced such a complicated system that it could have been of no practical value to teach the language to a foreigner. He makes us realize the pragmatic advantages of such previous treatments that, as even those of the sixteenth-century grammarians, professedly were addressed to foreigners also. This forced the authors to achieve a level of simplification and clarity that brought them *de facto* closer to a scientific correctness than several of their more sophisticated successors. On the other hand, Adelung shows to an eminent degree the "scientific" trend of his rationalistic century in that he never ceases to strive toward a full explanation of the inner principles lying behind and beneath the phenomena of the language.

CHAPTER **3**

MODERN THEORY AND ITS NINETEENTH-CENTURY BACKGROUND

1. Herling, Bauer, and Becker

As already announced above (Chapter 1), for the period after 1800 we shall proceed by mere sampling of typical theories. Furthermore, we shall treat sentence structure concomitantly with word order, since with S. H. A. Herling 1821 and H. Bauer 1833 the two became logically associated in the same section of syntax called *Topik*, thus ideally closing the circle, as it were, that had begun in antiquity with the two sets of phenomena being subsumed under the classical theory of *compositio* (Gr. *synthesis*). A basic shift, however, has occurred, in that the classical composition was part of rhetoric, whereas with *Topik* we are now entirely within grammar proper (syntax).

At the beginning of the nineteenth century, the Romantic penchant for philosophizing spills over into grammatical speculation. One after another the new grammarians indulge in extensive and, at times, involved and inconclusive discussions of general or specific causes of linguistic phenomena, which they often treat as if they were parallel expressions of logical processes. This observation does not apply, to be sure, to the terse and sober style of S. H. A. **Herling**, whose essay "Ueber die Topik der deutschen Sprache," *Abhandlungen des frankfurtischen Gelehrtenvereines für deutsche Sprache*, Third Stück (Frankfurt/M.: Franz Varrentrapp, 1821), 296–362 presents the first authoritative case of systematic amalgamation of word order with sentence structure. Herling adopted for the purpose the preexistent term *Topik*, which indeed was also found in an unsigned paper of the same volume of the Frankfurt *Abhandlungen*, "Anhang einer deutschen Bezeichnung sprachlehrlicher Kunstausdrücke," p. 19, in precisely that sense of "Wort- und Satzfolgelehre," and was there articulated into a logical and an expressive subdivision ("Constructionslehre, von der vorstellungsgemäßen, natürlichen Wort- und Satzfolge" and "Inversionslehre, von der darstellungsgemäßen, veränderten Wort- und Satzfolge"). This section of *Syntaxe* or *Satzlehre* was, in turn, distinguished from the plain *Construction*, itself subdivided into *Congruenz* and *Rection*. Herling did follow this general schema in his own landmark exposition and naturally took over that useful term of *Topik* or theory of "places," which obviously echoed a long rhetorico-logical Aristotelian tradition (it had been revived also in the original context of Kant's *transzendentale Topik*).

Herling started out by asserting that clauses are divided into *Haupt*- and *Nebensätze* — these latter being nothing but representations (or expansions) of parts of discourse or of the clause, hence not independent. Only main clauses are syntactically independent. One must keep firmly in mind the difference between logical and grammatical analysis. According to the latter, syntactic connections extend no further than the period or sentence, whereas the logical structure of a discourse can extend to the whole context. Hence two independent clauses, in particular, can be tied together lògically but not, of course, syntactically: *Er wird kommen, darum bleibe ich zu Hause.*

Die Sätze werden eingetheilt in Haupt- und Nebensätze. Die Nebensätze stellen nämlich nur Satz- oder Sprachtheile des Hauptsatzes dar und sind demnach unselbständig. . . . In logischer Hinsicht, in welcher die Eintheilung der Sätze eine ganz andere ist, kann von zwei Sätzen, die beide in syntaktischer Hinsicht selbständig und daher Haupsätze sind, der eine nur z.B. die Ursache des andern enthalten. . . . Die logische Verknüpfung der Sätze kann sich über eine ganze Abhandlung erstrecken, die syntaktische nur über das Gebiet einer Periode. (P. 296: See § 35 p. 316)

Here lay the main thrust of that system that is expanded upon in the body of the essay (cf., e.g., pp. 315–6), and that, according to Delbrück (*Grundlagen*, pp. 71–2), was to be taken over by J. C. A. Heyse (*Aus-*

führliches Lehrbuch der deutschen Sprache, 2 Bde., Hannover, 1838), and thus transmitted down until at least G. O. Curme 1905, 1922. "Das Herlingsche System ist am besten von Heyse dargestellt worden, von wo es weiter übernommen worden ist, unter anderem auch von Curme." Delbrück attributed the success of this system to its practicality, but insisted that, as its followers realized as early as Heyse, it did not imply a scientific explanation of the actual historical genesis of syntactic structures. Its value was simply that of establishing descriptive analogies and logical correspondences. Delbrück himself was a partisan of the thesis that hypotaxis developed from parataxis, and pointed out that although a detailed historical reconstruction of such processes was practically impossible, Herling's system left out the types of clause that correspond not to the complementary elements of the clause but to its essential elements, as some subjective *daß*-clauses correspond to actual subjects, and some relative clauses to the nominal predicate.

Herling carries on his discussion by going over the traditional rubrics of natural order, first in the main clause (where the subject can be inverted), then in the dependent one (where the verb is transposed to the end). He uses and discusses Adelung's basic principle at length, but he is clearly aware of those inner contradictions that were to be so painstakingly censured by Jellinek (see, especially, pp. 302–3, § 12).

In discussing *Nebensätze*, pp. 315–7, Herling maintains that, although both main and secondary clauses can be classified logically or semantically as *concessiv, causal*, and so forth, only the latter can be formally (morphologically) classified in the following types, and only these: *Substantivsätze* when they replace a noun (hence these can be *Subject-, Object-, Genitiv-*, or *Dativsätze*); *Adjectivsätze*; or *Adverbialsätze*. For example: *Der Bothe, welcher gestern ankam, verkündete mir, als er mich sah, daß mein Vetter gestorben sey* is equivalent to *Der angekommene* (adjective) *Bothe verkündigte mir so eben* (adverb) *den Tod* (noun) *meines Vetters*.

Turning to *Inversion* (p. 324), he implicitly rejects Adelung's rubric of *Fragende Wortfolge* by observing that it is not characteristic of interrogation, since it is shared by the topical form of the *Nachsatz* (*Da er mich bat, befolgte ich seine Vorschrift*) as well as by the imperative construct (*Imperativ* — p. 326). Once again he applies his distinction between accidents of the essential elements of the clause, *wesentliche*

Theile, and the complements, *Nebenbestimmungen*, in terms of *Hauptinversionen* and *Nebeninversionen*. Among the latter he includes cases of what we call *Nachtrag* or 'afterthoughts' (postposed complements).

The section on *Satzfolge* begins with the definition: "Die Verbindung der Sätze ist entweder eine unterordnende oder bloss beiordnende (coordinirende) Verbindung" (p. 342). Two *Nebensätze* can be connected to each other either through coordination or subordination. The remainder analyzes the various structural options. The last two chapters examine the "elliptic" connection of clauses, *Zusammenziehung der Sätze*, in the form of members of single clauses, either through coordination or subordination (p. 357: *Sie waren, wie wir alle, sehr erfreut darüber; er ist, weil gut, auch des Lobes werth* as examples of the latter), and finally the nature of the syntactically loose parenthetic clauses (*Parenthese*, pp. 361-2).

Adelung's ineptly formulated basic principle had repercussions through the years, despite its inner contradictions, including the one between the *bestimmend* → *bestimmt* movement and the reverse process of the basic elements: subject → predicate and predicate → complements, where one has a sort of *bestimmt* → *bestimmend* movement. Thus **Heinrich Bauer** 1833,[1] after recalling that Bernhardt had stated outright the basic rule of *das Bestimmende vor dem Bestimmten* (Bauer, V, p. 4, *re* Bernhardt p. 297, § 283), restates the principle (*Grundsatz*) at the outset of his chapter on *Wortfolge*, which can be taken as the clearest, most informed, and most systematic discussion of the whole matter down to, and including, the more authoritative but somewhat fuzzier and inconclusive K. F. Becker. Bauer (to be followed in this by Becker) reintroduces the term *Topik* as the general term for *Wortstellung* and *Wortfolge* taken together with *Folge der Sätze*, since it means "Lehre vom Ort."[2] Word order and sentence structure — at least insofar as this latter is understood as ordering of the parts of the sentence — therefore are arranged as consecutive sections of the same division of syntax. Incidentally, *Satz* is still used somewhat indiscriminately to mean both sentence and clause, whereas *Periode* carries a heavy stylistic or rhetorical connotation. "The sequence of words and clauses generally depends on the sequence of ideas (*Vorstellungen*), concepts (*Begriffe*), and thoughts (*Gedanken*). But since this sequence is not the same with all peoples, consequently the order of their words also varies" (p. 1). Here we have a clear statement of the "relativity of languages" as understood in the tradition of Condillac-Michaëlis as well as in the Sapir-Whorf thesis.

As to the order of clauses and all other parts of the sentence, we find a conspicuous case of confusion with the classical notion of the "period" when Bauer states that the basic principle of the German language, "which the first speakers and writers must have felt only darkly" (an echo of Adelung), has been to proceed "from the (logically) less important and less *bestimmt* to the more important and determined, whereby the attention of the listener or reader is not only kept in suspense, but also increased up to the end of the sentence." "There ensues . . . a *gradatio*, a *klimax*" (p. 2).

Bauer takes Bürger (*Rhetorik*) to task for his terminology (p. 5), insofar as he refers to the normal arrangement as *philosophisch*, to the inverted one as *poetisch* or *oratorisch*, corresponding to the *ästhetische Wortfolge*. Nevertheless Bürger confirms the success of Adelung's principles by upholding that normally the process goes from the least to the most determined, and that inversion works by drawing attention to an element by putting it out of its place (= before). Here again one might wonder what it is that gives first positions (or earlier positions) greater importance, if we accept the basic principle whereby positions normally become progressively more important, at least in the sense that they are more determined, and more determinant toward the subject or clause — this being the other contradiction.

Bauer then turns to the eighteenth-century context of comparative criticism of German word order, which was traditionally compared with the clarity, simplicity, and rationality of French. He retorts that those very virtues of French can be regarded as a disadvantage with respect to the freedom of German, and he adds the interesting information that the better French writers, who have also familiarized themselves with the German language, have begun to recognize this, and consequently attempted — with limited success — to break through the fetters of French grammar (p. 6). Indeed so it was, after Rousseau and Chateaubriand, and in line with Condillac's teachings. For the purpose of a fair assessment of German word order, he adduces two judgments by German critics, one from the eighteenth century and the other a contemporary, who concern themselves more appropriately with periodic structure but could have been speaking of clause structure as well, namely, Abbé Jerusalem, Letter to the Duchess of Braunschweig "Über die deutsche Sprache" (Berlin, 1781), and Kolbe, *Wortreichtum* (1806, 1818–20), Theil 2.[3]

Jerusalem avers that French construction is undoubtedly easier and more uniform. German embedded clauses or incidentals (he speaks of *eingeschobene Zwischensätze und Parenthesen*), accumulated *Beiwörter*, postponed prepositions, and infinitives separated from their auxiliaries and modals (to be precise, he speaks rather of governing verbs placed at the end away from their referents, *Hauptwörter*) do make a long period particularly difficult (Bauer, pp. 6–7). But so are the periods of Cicero, and if it is true that the fixed order of the French sentence makes the sentence clear and easy, it is equally true that the best writers endure uneasily these chains that their grammarians have imposed on them, just as those Frenchmen who have acquired some knowledge of German recognize the advantages of German's greater freedom. For what it loses in ease, it gains in strength. Principal and secondary ideas are directly tied together through parenthetic or incidental construction, while the principal idea fulfills itself with energy by having its verb at the end as the conclusive element of the thinking process. Jerusalem concludes with the "pre-Romantic" warning that grammar cannot give rules for the correct use of these advantages, since correct expression is a matter of feeling (*Gefühl*). When foreigners complain about the awkwardness of German sentences such criticism is due, more often than not, rather to lack of feeling in the writer than to an objective handicap of the language (pp. 6–7).

As to Kolbe, he offers a Romantic appreciation of the inverted-affective style, which he declares to be the poetic one. *Das Bestimmte* goes before *das Bestimmende*, the effect before the cause, as a means to arouse expectation through gradually progressive, ascending movement (*stufenweis fortschreitende Steigerung*), until the *Hauptwort* comes at the end, binding the sentence into a whole, like a keystone in a suspended arch (*schwebende Bogen*) (p. 8). The style is therefore the opposite of the French manner, which by regularly putting the governing before the governed easily satisfies the demands of the ordering intellect. Objections are justified not by the pattern per se, since it is common to Greek and, even more, Latin, but by the possibility that it may tire us by appearing too repetitive. The example is *Er hat, was er beweisen wollte, wirklich bewiesen*, declared to be more effective than *Er hat wirklich bewiesen, was er beweisen wollte* (pp. 7–9).

Bauer believes that Kolbe is referring to sentence structure rather than word order, to wit, to the order of clauses rather than clause-elements, as the example would seem to show, and therefore criticizes him for calling this "inverted" construction *gewöhnlich (fast überall)*. But Kolbe raises the interesting question that modern linguistics has revealed to be at the root of the consistent end-verb order (TXV), that in consistent SOV languages, like Turkish or even better Hittite (see Lehmann's studies below), not only does the clause construct as SOV, but the whole sentence will have the dependent clauses, including all objectives and relatives, before the main clause.

Nevertheless, despite Bauer's brave and perhaps misplaced efforts to save him, Kolbe mishandles his case, all but spoiling it through a terminology that goes counter to the established one and becomes counterproductive within an otherwise meaningful context. It would have made better sense to speak of the "periodic" features of the German progressive and ascending sentence as containing a movement *bestimmend → bestimmt*, not vice versa.

In the Second Abtheilung, on "Wortfolge der Theile eines Satzes," pp. 24–34, Bauer quotes several recent authorities on inversion, from Herder to Herling, and ends by summarizing Adelung, with his criticisms. In his *Fragmente* Herder had pointed to emphasis, feeling, and emotion (*Aufmerksamkeit, Empfindung, Affekt*) as the sources of *Inversion* through the display of the subjective point of view of the observer, acting on the related point of view of the hearer (p. 28). Kolbe, Heinsius, and others had stressed the freedom of German from the French rule of placing the subject first (thus pointing in the direction of interpreting German as an eminently "impressive" language, as some twentieth-century linguists eventually have stressed, for example. Andreas Blinkenberg, and Albert Dauzat).[4] Bauer concludes that any part of the clause can obtain special emphasis by being placed either first or, he interestingly adds, last, and he specifies this manner of being last as, quoting Herling, "außerhalb der Gränzen des Satzes" (pp. 27 and 31) — which is what a modern linguist would call being outside the *Satzklammer* or "outside the brackets." An example is (p. 31) *Ich theilte ihm mit das theuerste Geheimniß meines Lebens* (in *Hauptsatz*)

— *da ich ihm mittheilte dies wichtige Geheimniß*. Equally interestingly, this sort of inversion does not affect the logical relationships but, according to Herling, only the rhythm.

Bauer quotes other predecessors who methodically and explicitly distinguish *Hauptsätze* and *Nebensätze* with the respective difference in the order of basic clause constituents: So do both Bernhardt, "l.c. p. 296 and 303," and Lorberg, "l.c. p. 57 *nach* Wittmer" (p. 32). He agrees with those who, like Bernhardt (305–8), recognize the presence of inversion in *Nebensätze* also, whereas Becker (p. 370) maintained that in such clauses the construction is not susceptible of inversion.[5]

Of Adelung, Bauer summarizes the seven causes of inversion (pp. 30–1) and carries forward his campaign against their abuse by proscribing inversions that serve no purpose of emphasis, clarity, vivacity, or euphony. He does not hesitate to accuse the poets of overdoing their privilege of transposing words as poetic license (including the unusual placing of *trennbare Partikeln*) for the sake of meter or rhyme, and we may assume that the list of illustrious sinners could have started, in Bauer's mind, with Klopstock. At any rate, he denies that such practices contribute much beauty to style (pp. 33–4).

Then comes a paragraph (§ 829, p. 34) that contains in a nutshell the most essential features of Bauer's system, and that practically undermines all the efforts to defend the advantages of German over French by giving in on the point that had been the core of the French *métaphysiciens'* theory. The SVO pattern (more precisely, here, S + copula + *Prädikat*, broadly taken) is declared to be the natural, original order of the expository, descriptive, and didactic sentence (*natürliche, ursprüngliche, erzählende, beschreibende, unterrichtende*), because thus are the perceptions delivered in the order in which they appear to reason (*Verstand*) in independent clause statements, since the subject comes first and the predicate, which is the most determined (*das Bestimmteste*) and important element (*das Wichtigste*), at the close. Bauer thus solves, or hopes to solve, the impasse of Adelung's contradictory basic law, by reducing it to a principle that regards not the "verb" but the "predicate" as the most determined, therefore last, part. He too could not know, of course, that this was not the original order of German, and that therefore it contained nothing particularly "natural" or "rational" in an absolute sense. Furthermore, the impasse still was unsolved insofar as in the sequence SVO (more basic than Subject + Copula + Predicate), the rule did not explain why VO should be preferred over OV, V and O constituting the predicate when taken together.

Bauer's exposition carries on with a detailed and reasoned analysis of all particulars, and when it comes to the traditional (Adelung's) *verbindende Wortfolge*, which still remains so named, the usual list of subordinating conjunctions appears, but now with the clear specification that we are dealing with *Nebensätze* (p. 43).

When he turns to the *syntaxe de la période*, Bauer begins (p. 61) with Herling's representation, which even to modern researchers (cf. Sandmann, Forsgren) appears to be the first systematic use of coordination and subordination. Clauses in the sentence are assimilated to parts of the clause, and as such are said to be either *coordiniert* if they function as mutually identical parts or complements, or *subordiniert* if they are like parts that are governed by others (Herling l.c. Theil 2, p. 34). Even what we would call subordination of second degree is envisaged (p. 61), when a *Nebensatz* (later on, also *abhängiger Satz*: See p. 82) is *untergeordnet* to another *Nebensatz* rather than *beiordnet* to it.

In the introduction to this Fifth Abschnitt on composition of the complex sentence, Bauer enters the interesting hypothesis, confirmed by modern linguists, that "primitive" languages used to juxtapose grammatically independent clauses without morphological markers of their logical interrelationships (pp. 59–60). Thus *er ist glücklich, er hat das große Loos gewonnen* (p. 61) is made of two clauses logically but not formally tied together (*verbunden*). We could add that the very fact that this construction is still possible, indeed frequent, is a sign of the persistent paratactic nature of German. Thus, Bauer adds, the development of conjunctions (*Bindewörter*) to express the logical ties between propositions is a mark of advanced evolution in a language. Greek had a rich system of conjunctions, whereas Hebrew, "eine der ärmsten und ungebildetsten Sprachen," made use of few conjunctions, almost only of *and*. German, we could now add in our turn, is a language in between, since its conjunctions have developed late and not fully. This puts in an interesting new light the eighteenth-century French polemic on *style coupé*, which demanded the elimination of conjunctions to make the syntactic periodic relationships intuitive rather than formal, in reaction against the "Ciceronian" abuse of conjunctions to give a false impression of logical complexity when there was very little or none.

Finally (p. 230, § 893), Bauer comes to the theory of sentence structure, *Lehre vom Periodenbau*, and states at the outset that this matter does not properly belong to *Grammatik*. It belongs in part to linguistics taken in its broadest sense (*Sprachlehre im weiten Sinn*), and precisely to *Rhetorik*, in part to *Logik*. We find here, therefore, the inherited nomenclature of classical times, when sentence structure was never covered in any sense by grammar but only by rhetoric (while word order was treated in both). Bauer consequently will limit himself to nothing more than an overview of the most essential aspects of the question (pp. 231–46). In fact, rhetorical material, in the traditional sense, is widely scattered all over this fifth volume of his grammar, and in the later Sixth Abschnitt (pp. 266–94) he even goes into figures of speech and tropes, as classical grammar had regularly done.

Karl Ferdinand Becker 1837[6] begins by recalling the distinction between the grammatical form of the sentence with its *Satzverhältnisse* (II, p. 423, § 280), whose organic expression is in the flection and prepositions, and its logical form, whose expression is in the word order and accent: This latter form is the sign (*bezeichnet*) that represents the reciprocal arrangement and ordering of the concepts as well as the unity of the thought in the sentence and of the concept in each relation. There is "inversion" when word order gives only the logical form of the sentence in opposition to and independently of its grammatical form (*umgekehrte Wortfolge* or *Inversion*, p. 425).

The laws of *Topik* demand that the mutual hierarchy of the complements (*die Unterordnung der Glieder*) be marked by the postposition of that of two members which carries more logical value (p. 428). This seems to imply qualifier → qualified order. Later on it becomes clear (p. 431) that the "logical" order refers to the inversion of grammatical order, with the examples *es tobt der Sturm* instead of *der Sturm tobt*, *der Sohn meines Bruders* versus *meines Bruders Sohn* (operator → operand), *Rache sucht er* versus *er sucht Rache*.

Becker's impact on later generations rests in good part on his attempt to found a comprehensive science of linguistic phenomena by reducing them, on a level of universal philosophical grammar, to some basic principles that are at times of a logical, at other times of a metaphysical nature. Starting from the premise that what is needed is a system that rests not on the morphological facts but on the relations between the concepts being expressed ("die Verhältnisse der Begriffe und ihrer Beziehungen und nicht die Formen des Ausdrucks"), he arrived at a general theory of sentence elements.[7] He thus identified three basic types or manners of sentence relations: the predicative, the attributive, and the objective, "das prädikative, das attributive, und das objektive Verhältnis." The first of these is constituted by the relationship between Subject and Predicate, the original constituents, *Ur-Satzgliedern*, each one of these being able to subdivide itself into further elements in contrastive mutual organic relation, as well as to produce out of itself further, secondary constituents, conceived as *Ergänzungen* or *Erweiterungen* and equivalent to our complements. Consequently, the analysis of the sentence works with four main concepts: the Subject, the Predicate, the Object, and the Attribute. As to the arrangement of the parts, Becker never tires of insisting that word order and 'accent,' *Betonung*, cannot be separated: This latter is the 'foundation,' *Grund*, of the former. Both are the organic expression of the logical form of the thinking process: "So ist die Betonung der eigentlich organische Ausdruck der logischen Form . . . innerlich ist sie [i.e. die Wortstellung] eigentlich mit ihr [der Betonung] Eins und Dasselbe" (*Organism* 1827, pp. 586f.). Becker's metaphysics is obviously idealistic. His theses remained canonical for a long time, despite the opposition of such respected masters as K. W. Ludwig Heyse 1856.[8]

Becker is generally regarded as a landmark in the transition to modern methods of grammatical analysis. The later, step-by-step development of our subject need not detain us here. For new, original contributions one has to wait until the last decades of the century. We shall turn to events occurring during the last one hundred years.

While covering this area, we shall have an opportunity to observe a remarkable coherence and continuity despite the different nomenclatures and ideological frames of reference. Similarly, one will sense that some problems are resolved while others are simply restated in the midst of the very same difficulties that, *mutatis mutandis*, had caused their earlier proponents to fail. In the meantime, even though we shall hear so many familiar bells ringing repeatedly in our ears, some of the old issues will have been brushed aside, tacitly or quite explicitly, as pseudo-problems undeserving of our serious attention.

2. *Behaghel and Delbrück*

The theoretical framework of Becker's achievements becomes particularly interesting in the light of modern developments in our field, and it provides a good starting point for some general considerations that are now in order regarding the main shifts of the subject in our own century. One reason that we may find the specific topic of our inquiry of especial interest is the light it throws on the broad evolution not only of linguistic science but also of general speculation on communication aids (to use a recent frame of reference, semiotic theory, including applications to the literary code).

Traditional grammar had been conceived as study of forms without much concern for their broad arrangement (I have shown in *CTC* how little attention syntax had received, comparatively speaking). Until the beginning of the Prague School in the 1920s, syntactic analysis had been based either on morphology or on logic, this latter providing the only available approach to function and meaning — with some incipient effort to introduce psychological insights.

Semantic syntax began to receive its due with the Prague School, while the American brand of structuralism continued to rest essentially on morphology. The last decades of linguistic speculation have seen a proliferation of ideological and methodological options, which can be subsumed under the headings of the leading schools and their principal variations.

For what concerns our subject in a most direct way, after the prolonged debate on major hypotheses formulated by nineteenth-century Comparative Philology concerning the specific nature and evolution of German sentence structure (Behaghel and Delbrück), various brands of "Structuralism" have advanced what amounts in fact to opposite proposals. The Prague School (Mathesius, Firbas, finally Beneš) has aimed at a psychologically tinted appreciation of the communicative content of the sentence and its parts, whereas the morphologically slanted types of structuralism have tended to focus once again on the formal characteristics of the sentence (Drach, Glinz, Boost). A distinguishing feature of German Structuralism, however, as contrasted with its American counterpart, has been to keep firmly in mind the "organic" postulates implied in the original definition of structure in the sense advocated by the psychology of *Gestalt* — as we shall see especially with regard to Boost. This kept these grammarians remarkably close to the semantic and relational ("functional") concerns that, in a different direction, also characterized the Prague School.

The German applications (especially Bierwisch) of Transformational-Generative Grammar, as well as its application to the question of the German sentence by non-German linguists of this persuasion, have further emphasized syntax and semantics in an effort to explore the underlying reasons for the phenomena observable on the surface. This approach has led finally to the formulation of typological hypotheses that attempt to classify both surface and deep-level rules of German within the family of languages according to broad language universals.

2a. THE BEHAGHEL THESIS

Surveying the modern linguistic speculation, Fleischmann (pp. 33–4) finds that (1) **Otto Behaghel** 1892 first related verbal end-position to the impact of Latin. **Clemens Biener** 1922, 1922a, 1926, 1959, in the wake of Behaghel's theory, first stressed the importance of German school grammars as a qualification of Behaghel's excessive reliance on Latin grammars, since the medieval, Renaissance, and Baroque Latin grammars did not appear explicitly to prescribe verbal end-position.[9]

2) **Berthold Delbrück** 1911 and 1920 and, at first independently, **Wunderlich** 1892, 1894, then **Wunderlich-Reis** 1924–5, proposed the end-position as a norm for Proto-Germanic.

Fleischmann does not mention a theory that has been much debated over the years and still finds some partisans, though sufficient evidence to support it in all details is admittedly lacking. I refer to the thesis espoused by **Konrad Burdach** and others to the effect that the imperial court at Prague around Charles IV's Chancellor Johannes von Neumarkt exerted, from the 1360s well into the Renaissance, a humanistic influence on the use of both Latin and German in various chancelleries.[10] This thesis adds one historical dimension to that of Behaghel and need not detain us here because its acceptability would only reinforce rather than directly affect the meaning and outcome of the latter.

Let us then take a close look at the main points advanced by Behaghel and Delbrück. It will be necessary, however, to start somewhat earlier than Fleischmann does, especially for the Delbrück thesis.

The most relevant and original opinions at the beginning of modern Germanic philology are clearly represented and summarized by the following landmarks of scholarly opinion. **John Ries**, *Die Stellung von Subject und Prädicatsverbum im Hêliand: Ein Beitrag zur germanischen Wortstellungslehre* (Strassburg: Karl J. Trübner, 1880), claimed that the original position of the verb was at the end of all clauses, and that the increasing differentiation between main and secondary clauses in Old German had gradually led to a crystallization of the differential treatment of the verb, with second position in the main clauses and last position in the secondary ones becoming the rule (see, e.g., p. 107). In contrast, **Karl Tomanetz**, *Die Relativsätze bei den althochdeutschen Übersetzern des 8. und 9. Jahrhunderts* (Wien: Carl Gerold's Sohn, 1879), and **Oskar Erdmann**, *Grundzüge der deutschen Syntax nach ihrer geschichtlichen Entwicklung*, I, 2 (Stuttgart: Cotta, 1886), pp. 181 ff., especially 193 fn. and 195, both affirmed that second position was original and that the shift of the verb to last place in subordinate clauses was a late Germanic development.[11] **Jacob Wackernagel** 1892 provided new support for Ries's thesis by showing that, whereas the original construction in Proto-Indo-European was verb-final, at a relatively early stage a fundamental law governing accent caused a leftward movement of the verb to second position in main clauses only. This view, although with somewhat different arguments, was restated not only by John Ries, *Die Wortstellung im Beowulf* (Halle/S.: M. Niemeyer, 1907), but especially by Delbrück, who adapted and developed it further (cf. Ries 1907, especially pp. 29–31).

One third thesis, that of free word order for Proto-Germanic and Indo-European, was advanced by **Wilhelm Braune** 1894,[12] and was later espoused by such eminent scholars as **Hermann Hirt** and **Antoine Meillet**.[13] Clearly, most inflected languages can afford a high degree of freedom; therefore this thesis has its merits. Nevertheless, we will not be concerned with the details of its development since it has not proved to be as productive as others with regard to the specific issues of German.

The thesis of Tomanetz 1879 and Erdmann 1886 was carried forward by **Otto Behaghel** in a most original and influential way. Behaghel first stated this view in 1892 and then expounded it, after a succession of further exploratory papers, in its most extended form in his *Deutsche Syntax* of 1923–32.[14]

The original norm for German independent clauses, claims Behaghel, was to assign second position to the verb — hence SVO (cf. *Deutsche Syntax*, IV, p. 11). The decisive impact of humanistic Latin, from the Renaissance on, caused the shifting of the verb to the right. This shift did not extend to main clauses, however, and even with regard to dependent clauses Behaghel insisted that "the decisive mark of the German dependent clause is not the end-position of the verb, but the *Nicht-Zweitstellung*, the position after the second place. Whether anything else follows the verb or not is essentially indifferent" ("Zur Stellung," 1929, p. 277). Behaghel's thesis was carried on by Maurer and Biener, as we are about to see, and in its simplified form the Behaghel-Maurer-Biener thesis is still echoed widely in standard manuals, as in **Adolf Bach**, *Geschichte der deutschen Sprache* (Heidelberg: Quelle u. Meyer, 1970^9), p. 286, § 142: "From Latin influence came the rule that the verb goes to the end of the dependent clause. . . . In the sixteenth-seventeenth centuries even in the main clause the Latin word order is not seldom imitated."[15]

Clemens Biener 1926 elaborated on this notion of *Nichtzweitstellung*, which he also labeled *Distanzstellung*, and which reveals the presence in the clause of a *Nachtrag* (pp. 230, 255 f.).[16] The definition of *Nachtrag* depends on the word order type that one chooses as a point of reference for the clause in question. Basically, it is something that occurs to the right of and outside the "braces" (outside the *Satzklammer*), either for emphasis, as anticipatory tie-up with the following clause or even sentence, or as an afterthought. One appropriate rendering is *Ausklammerung* or "exbraciation" (cf. Vennemann).[17]

Biener (1926, pp. 255 f.) accordingly proposed the following two points: (1) The *Distanz-* and *Endstellung*, both already well established as characteristic features of Proto-Germanic (*Urgermanisch*), carry on uninterruptedly to the present day in formal dependent clauses (*eingeleitete Nebensätze*); (2) of these two possibilities the latter will prevail, aided by Latin influx and later on by that of the school grammars of the seventeenth and eighteenth centuries, which only recognize end-position. Yet it never succeeded in stamping out the *Nachtrag* altogether.

The strongest objections to this hypothesis of Latin influence may be those raised by Fleischmann, who begins by pointing out the ambiguous nature of Latin patterns, which, therefore, could not be presumed to have exerted a clearly determining pressure in a unilateral sense, that is, toward end-position. Latin writers, he points out, including Cicero and Tacitus, did not place verbs last to an overwhelming degree, although they always did so more often in dependent clauses (p. 44). According to a 1922 dissertation by B. J. Porten,[18] Cicero gave middle position to the verb in 41.22% of cases in main clauses but only in 30.54% in dependent clauses. In this respect there is, then, some analogy between the developments of Latin and German.[19] More important, Fleischmann points out that: (1) The humanistic Latin grammars produced in Germany, including the very influential *Grammatices latinae elementa* by Philip Melanchthon (Augustae Vindelicorum, 1570), ch. "De periodis," do not appear to prescribe verbal end-position explicitly, and indeed they tend to cling in practice to the medieval didactic habit of placing the verb soon after the noun, as Melanchthon does (Fleischmann, p. 49); (2) furthermore, didactic and literary documents offering side by side Latin texts and corresponding vernacular translations do not show influence on German word order. The most typical case seems to be that of Luther's bilingual *Tischrede*, where, as Birgit Stolt's research indicates, the Latin example did not carry over into German usage, since in German dependent clauses end-position prevails even in the face of second position in the corresponding Latin sentences (Fleischmann, p. 63).[20]

To be sure, the Behaghel-Biener thesis, despite its wide acceptance, presents a serious theoretical difficulty. We may assume, as we will show we must further on, that German, alongside English, underwent between 800 and 1200 A.D. a process of drifting from SOV to SVO order, and then remained in an ambivalent position by not completing that process, until a stable settlement was eventually found on the basis of a clearly differentiated assignment of SVO order to main clauses and SOV to dependent ones. It is, however, difficult to accept the notion that this settlement was due to the impact of an alien model, that of classical Latin, even though Latin itself contained only a limited behavioral differentiation between main and dependent clauses with regard to verbal position.

On the other hand, objectors to the possibility of a real Latin impact tend to go overboard when they insist, as Fleischmann does (p. 50), that Latin was ever-present even in the centuries preceding the spread of SOV habits then taking place. What this objection overlooks is the radical difference between medieval Latin (itself basically SVO) and classical Latin. Classical Latin, with its dominant SOV pattern, was the powerful new influence after 1500, even if the didactic texts did not explicitly underline this particular aspect, since this aspect was so conspicuous to any elementary schoolboy as to be taken for granted. That the dialects do not show the crystallization of end-position strengthens the plausibility of Latin influence, since this learned influence operated precisely on the educated level of the national language, first written and then spoken (we shall see below the use made by Maurer of the comparative study of dialects). Indeed, as Biener added in qualifying Behaghel's thesis, more than to the Latin grammars it is to the German grammars that we must look in our search for clear influences on the national language. Under the influence of Latin and Latin grammar, the new German grammars exerted a very effective action of standardization and normalization of practical usage. In conclusion, the school grammars brought about the shrinking of the stylistic freedom in the use of *Nachtrag*, in favor of grammatical uniformity and regularity, by imposing a generalized use of verb end-position in dependent clauses — as even Fleischmann is prepared to admit (pp. 60, 63). The problem is simply one of deciding whether to regard exbraciation as a genuinely German habit, reinforced by the drift toward SVO order in Middle High German — this was Behaghel's view — or to consider it a step toward SVO that was temporarily halted. In either case, its influence would have been reduced by the Latin impact and by the regularization demanded by the search for national patterns, although it later resumed its march forward, as witnessed in Contemporary German. This to and fro movement of the *Nachtrag* is thus symbolic of the movement of the German language, caught between the ups and downs of its natural SOV pattern, now in general retreat, then in partial counterattack, then again in a general state of weakening.

The possibility of a decisive impact from Latin on the educated use of the vernacular may appear more plausible when one keeps in mind that only 10% of printed books in Germany were in German in 1518, and only 30% in 1570, the remainder being in Latin, and that Latin still held 28% as late as 1740 and 14% in 1770.[21] Should one consider only works of learning and disregard fictional literature, the percentage of Latin obviously would be even higher.

Latin traditionally has been regarded as a typical case of free word order. In the major study on this subject, a three volume work of 1922–49, the leading French classicist Jacques Marouzeau proceeded to reassess a centuries-long tradition by denying the possibility of analyzing word order, at least for Latin, on the basis of whole clauses.[22] Only meaningful syntactic units could be an object of scientific study (noun + adjective, subject + verb, verb + object, etc.). What interests us now is that he, still quite traditionally, kept referring to Latin as a language characterized by free word order, using the expression *langue à construction libre* that had been sanctioned by Henri Weil 1844. He added, however, that if this order is free, it is not indifferent. Indeed, while he acknowledged no place of honor in the clause as a whole, he admitted that the verb is the only part of speech that has a locative preference (for the end). Speaking of syntactic units, the norm would be for the qualitative adjective to precede, *bonus hospes*, for the determinative to follow, *homo romanus*. As to the stylistic variations within an order that is free yet not indifferent, it had customarily been pointed out that first position or relative anteposition could produce emphasis, semantic and emotive: Thus the difference among *amat pater filium, filium pater amat*, and *pater filium amat* lies in stressing the act of loving, the object of this love, or nothing in particular. If a general conclusion is warranted, it must be that Latin word order was inherently and originally, as shown by the last option, SOV.

Biener 1922 had put forward the question: Why has the position of the German verb become what it is? In his 1926 paper he discussed two recent books that had propounded a comprehensive answer to his question, and especially the learned volume by **Friedrich Maurer**, 1926.[23] Through a statistical analysis of small samples from numerous sources, Maurer establishes the following general points: (1) In the simple independent clause (*einfacher Hauptsatz*) the verb is assigned second place as early as in Ulfila, and the earliest West-Germanic texts show a broad expansion of this rule; (2) first position is also documented in the early epoch for the declarative clause (*Behauptungssatz; gerader, direkter Aussagesatz*), but it is limited to logically joined clauses (*logisch angeschlossene Sätze*), and the frequency of this position fluctuates; (3) in coordinated main clauses (*coordiniert angeschlossene Hauptsätze*) first position and the normal second position of the verb vie equally with one another. The question of dependent clauses is more complex.

Maurer operates like a professional skeptic, questioning all previous assumptions and prevailing opinions. Syntacticians were, and have continued to be, of the opinion that Proto-Germanic, Old High German, and Middle High German showed a clear preference for end-position of the finite verb in dependent clauses. Maurer holds, instead, that in all three periods the documents do not warrant such conclusions and show a mixed situation. This presence of alternatives holds true, he says, also in the area of all the dialects, but it is here that Maurer believes the answers can be found to the basic question: Why and where did the current *Schriftsprache* choices prevail? (One must keep in mind that the bulk of Maurer's study addresses itself specifically to the question of the relative position of nonfinite verb to the finite verb or auxiliary in subordinate clauses.)

Methodologically speaking he holds that one must proceed pragmatically by analyzing documents rather than by speculating first on basic principles, as done by Elise Richter and John Ries. It will turn out that some choices have been influenced by those rhythmic laws that Ries and especially Behaghel have stressed. He therefore has little use, also, for the dispersively analytical method of **Rudolf Blümel** 1909 and 1914.[24] He believes, rather, that one must concentrate on basic types, which will be end- or not-end-position of finite verb in dependent clauses; end- or front-position of finite verb in main clauses of the declarative type (*unabhängige Aussagesatz*) — second position being, of course, the remaining basic alternative.

The geographic study of dialects (through the Atlas) seems to show a definite impact of sentence rhythm or intonation (esp. p. 72). No clear evidence exists, Maurer concludes, that end-position in *Nebensätze* was winning out anywhere before the fourteenth century. As to the critical formative period 1300–1600, he denies that the chronological scrutiny of sources can give results: Eike von Repkow, Konrad von Megenberg, and Ulrich Stromer's *Chronik* already show prevailing end-position in the fourteenth century, whereas Sender and Knebel in their Chronicles, as well as Luther, still offer, as late as the sixteenth century, massive cases of anteposition of the finite verb (p. 84). This is an example of the apparently zig-zagging history of German word order.

Maurer (pp. 162 ff.) offers his own findings, conducted on ca. 100 texts for this period, to corroborate the thesis of the influence of Latin on the literary language. Eike von Repkow, Johannes von Neumarkt, and Heinrich von Mügeln are Bohemian humanists who, together with their Swabian humanistic counterparts, adopt end-position predominantly or fully (in dependent clauses), in contrast with their nonhumanistic predecessors, contemporaries, and successors from the same two, noncontiguous regions, and likewise presumably in contrast with the prevailing usage in their own regional dialects — which even today do not adhere to the end-position rule. Humanistic education thus must have been the cause for this new usage (p. 163). Specifically, however, a *qui dixit* can correspond in a translation to a *der hat gesagt* or *der gesagt hat*, but a *quod dictum est* tended rather regularly to become *das gesagt ist*. With regard to this choice of examples one must keep in mind that, as Maurer points out (pp. 163f.), many writers of Middle High German "continue to place the auxiliary *haben* very often before the nominal form of the verb even while *sein* has already acquired last position within a broad circle of writers."[25]

In the remainder of his valuable albeit somewhat contentious monograph, Maurer, though accepting on the whole C. Biener's assertion that already in the tenth century main clauses had firmly assigned second place to the verb, gives a rich exemplification of the lingering, though dying, practices of first and last position (or later-than-second).

Behaghel gave broader circulation to his notion of *Nichtzweitstellung* by revising the *Satzlehre* section of the authoritative Hermann Paul, *Mittelhochdeutsche Grammatik*, twelfth through nineteenth editions (1924–66). Instead of speaking of end-position of the verb in dependent clauses introduced by a pronoun (mainly relative, I presume: *Fürwort*) or conjunction (subordinating, that is: *Bindewort*), this manual phrases the rule thus: Generally the verb acquires *Nichtzweitstellung*, a place after the second member of the clause. In other words, the verb loses its right to appear in second place; whether it appears actually at the end or somewhere between the second and last position depends on the length of the phrases that modify the verb ("hängt im allgemeinen ab von der Länge der Satzglieder, die das Zeitwort bestimmen"). Phrases longer than the verb usually follow it, while shorter ones precede it. This is given as a case of Behaghel's famous Law of the Growing Members (*Gesetz der wachsenden Glieder*), although Paul's manual introduces the further qualification that "necessary" modifiers are less amenable to postpositioning than unnecessary ones.[26] We have here, therefore, a signal case of impact of style and intonation (an aspect of phonetics) on grammar.

2b. THE DELBRÜCK THESIS

Back in 1894 the Danish linguist **Otto Jespersen** had advanced the philosophically challenging view that fixed or analytical order, that is, Subject-Verb-Object (SVO), was the cause, not the effect of the loss of cases, because it marks a progressive stage with regard to the more primitive flectional system, so that Chinese, for one, is not a primitive language, but one equally advanced as French and English — all these languages having in common a dependence of semantics on syntax, and Chinese and English, in particular, having a grammar in which there is practically no morphology, because these languages are all syntax. This hypothesis flies in the face of the genetic pattern so firmly postulated by Saussure and later confirmed and developed by structuralist speculation as well as positive philological observation. But what is relevant to us here is Jespersen's motivation. What he was aiming at was a radical revision of the Romantic theory of the Schlegels, as modified by Franz Bopp, whereby the primeval state of language was to be represented as one of isolated monosyllabic roots arranged according to a fixed pattern of order, which later would have given way to agglutination and finally to a flectional system with free order, showing relationships by case endings instead of by arrangement of sequence — a transition from a prevalently syntactic system to a prevalently morphologic one. The modern languages, with their minimal case system and relatively fixed order would, in this view, represent a decadent regression, a relative state of corruption. Jespersen claimed, on the contrary, that the real progress of language lies in its having evolved in precisely the opposite way. In his schema of genetic transformations Latin is, therefore, an "early" linguistic state, and German is less "advanced" than Chinese, French, or English. Flection and word order are apparently related aspects, probably in the sense that a natural development toward fixed arrangement has made useless, and eventually eliminated, the case endings.

Jespersen's provocative essay was only a preliminary step to clear the ground of the Romantic ideological historiographic schema. An objective, scientific approach based on observable facts and free of polemical intents was still to come.

In 1903 the study *Zur Entwicklung der romanischen Wortstellung* by the Viennese Romance philologist Elise Richter first placed in detailed scientific terms the question of the origin of Romance word order, holding that the loss of cases was the cause for the establishment of analytical order, rather than its effect, as Jespersen had held. We are about to see how Elise Richter's hypothesis has proved to be in harmony with much of recent linguistic theory.

The relationship between sentence order and case system presented, on the other hand, quite different problems for the Germanic languages. The continued presence of inflection in this area made it necessary for historians of the language to disregard such arguments as those that Jespersen and Richter were to make central. One had to proceed in some other way, and one began by comparing the Germanic sentence with its Indo-European ancestry.

We have seen how **Jacob Wackernagel** introduced a powerful new argument to support John Ries's 1880 basic position, and that his "law" was soon to be adopted and adapted by both Ries and Delbrück. Wackernagel's 1892 law explained how in Old Indic the verb, originally in end-position, was stressed (*betont*) in the dependent clause, unstressed in the independent one; consequently in the Indo-Germanic independent clauses the short (mono- or bisyllabic) verbal forms, being unstressed, tended to become enclitic and, by the law governing all enclitics, to move toward the front and attach themselves to the first words (Wackernagel 1892, p. 428).[27] This would be the rhythmic foundation of the second position for short verbs in declarative clauses. Of course, one might feel that some further reasons must have intervened to strengthen this option until it would become a general rule for all verbs in the face of other possibilities — and such reasons may have derived from the morphologically grounded need to differentiate between subject and object (or topic and comment). But more on this later.

Wackernagel's law meant that only short verbal forms were susceptible of becoming enclitic, hence longer and heavier forms remained in last place in both main and secondary clauses (p. 428). All languages did not, however, behave uniformly in this respect: Greek, for example, developed a particular degree of freedom in the placing of the verb (ibid.).

As far back as 1878, the date of his *Die altindische Wortfolge*, the starting point for **Delbrück** (1842–1922) had been that "Originally the verb must have come at the end of all types of Indo-Germanic clauses, therefore also of dependent clauses."[28] He explained conjecturally the shift to second place in main clauses on the ground of an increasing reliance on stress: The front part of the clause carried stronger stress than the last, and in main clauses it drew the verb toward itself. It was an argument somewhat allied to Wackernagel's theory of intonation. But before arriving at his definitive position, he wavered toward the views of Tomanetz and Erdmann.

Delbrück 1911 contains the most detailed and conclusive statement of his thesis. There he recalls (p. 6) that in *Vergleichende Syntax* III (1900) he had been guided by the conviction that the favored Proto-Germanic construction for both independent and dependent clauses was SVX (he used the symbol SVA = *Subjekt, Verbum, Anderes*), although the aversion to postposing atonic object pronouns introduced the type SXV for some dependent clauses. Now, however, he has changed his mind and still holds the opinion already expounded in his review of John Ries, *Die Wortstellung im Beowulf* (1907), which appeared in the *Anzeiger f. dt. Altertum u. dt. Litt.*, 31 (1907), 65–76, namely, that Wackernagel must have been right in seeking to trace the source for the variations of German verbal position back to Indo-European, and that in both types of clause, the typical original schema was SXV. The stress patterns of the Old Germanic clause also were similar to those of Old Indic. The weak-stressed verb of main clauses was pulled toward the strong-stressed first element, eventually preempting the second place, whereas the strong-stressed verb of the dependent clause remained in final place (p. 6).[29] In short, he now wants to establish a point-by-point correspondence between Germanic types of construction and those of Indo-European (p. 70). As he had shown in 1878 (*Die altindische Wortfolge*), Old Indic prose had four types of main clauses: (1) SXV, the *habituell* or normal construction; (2) the "occasional" construct whereby a stressed element other than the subject steps into first place: This element can be (a) the verb itself, (b) the nominal predicate, or (c) a complement; (3) a conjunctional particle opens the clause without affecting the position of the verb (which can remain last or also first, i.e., after the particle); (4) a *Nachtrag* may follow the verb (he calls it *etwas Ergänzendes*, which produces *relative Endstellung*). Now the first type of Germanic construction corresponds to the normal one of Old Indic SXV, but the verb has gradually moved to second place. Similarly, the verb has taken second place in Germanic in correspondence to the "occasional" Old Indic constructs of the types 2.b and 2.c, an "inversion" that did not occur in Old Indic. As to the dependent clause, the rule of the normal ordering SXV held fast in Germanic (pp. 70–3). In conclusion, in Proto-Germanic the verb stood normally at the end in both main and secondary clauses, yet in the former a leftward movement started toward second position (p. 74).

But further on, in trying to explain the later strengthening of end-position in dependent clauses, Delbrück made what Fleischmann regards as a counterproductive *salto mortale* (p. 68): The verb of dependent clauses was sent back by the fact that syntactic subordination was marked by the development of sufficiently strong subordinating conjunctions, which moved to the dependent clause from the main one, where they had previously been as markers pre-announcing, as it were, the forthcoming of a substantial qualifier in the form of what was to become, precisely, a dependent clause. Indeed, this explanation is as complicated as it is ultimately unconvincing, although C. Biener felt satisfied with it as it stood. The reelaboration of the thesis by **Wunderlich** and **Reis** does nothing more than confirm the nature of the vicious circle implicit in Delbrück's hypotheses (Fleischmann, p. 72).[30]

Nevertheless, these hypotheses of Delbrück's on the genesis of modern conjunctions contain an important nucleus of truth that even Fleischmann is forced to acknowledge, thus invalidating to some extent his critique of Delbrück. The difficulty of describing primordial conditions is due to a predicament common to many languages in the early stages, but particularly acute in the Germanic group, that the distinction between adverbs and conjunctions as grammatical categories is comparatively weak; and one cannot even speak properly of relative clauses.[31] Thus the distinction between main and dependent clause, like the concept itself of subordination, is partly impractical in Old High German.

The case of the particle *thaz* (later *daß*) is typical. It has been conjectured that its function in Old Germanic was that of coming at the end of a clause as a sort of notice for a forthcoming clause. It then, supposedly, stepped beyond this boundary and became the introductory part of the second clause. It was, at any rate, not tied to end-position of the verb. The "neutral" introductory particle *thaz/daz* strengthened itself between the thirteenth and fifteenth centuries, in Middle High German, thus announcing itself as the first purely conjunctional introductory particle.[32] Furthermore, it must be noted that in Middle High German the *Nebensatz* did not yet function as a *Satzglied*, as in New High German, that is, it did not cause inversion of the subject when it preceded a main clause.[33]

In conclusion, it must be noted that Fleischmann's implication that the two schools of thought just surveyed are mutually contradictory and exclusive is unwarranted. Indeed, Fleischmann overlooks Behaghel 1878, an early statement of his belief that SOV was the original rule for the Germanic group. That statement, which was found in an article concerned with other matters, offered an interesting combination (pp. 283–5) of phonetic evolution, morphological evolution, and word order change, which can find some confirmation in more recent research (and which has an important parallel in Saussure's remarks on the shift from adverb through preposition to preverb — *Cours*, 1949, p. 247). Beginning with the observation that inseparable verbal compounds are older than the separable ones, since their particle has lost its original meaning, Behaghel went on to define the stages in the formation of compounds. "Ein Compositum wie *du übertréibst* ist also nur denkbar, wenn es eine Zeit gab, in welcher das Adverb seinem Verbum nicht wie heute nachfolgte, sondenn vorausging. Diese durch unsere Composita verlangte Wortstellung ist aber genau diejenige, die uns noch heute im Nebensatz vorliegt, und wir erhalten somit den wichtigen Satz: DIE URSPRÜNGLICHE DEUTSCHE WORTSTELLUNG IST NICHT DIE DES HEUTIGEN HAUPTSATZES, SONDERN DIE DES HEUTIGEN NEBENSATZES. Die Ausbildung des späteren Wortfolge im Hauptsatz ist also der Zeitpunkt, vor dem die untrennbaren Composita sich gebildet haben." In other words, the original group was Noun + Adverb + Verb, just as in Greek νεὼν ἄπο ἔρχεται → ἀποέρχεται, and in German *er, der die Nacht durch schlief* → *durchschlief*. Earlier, the adverb was not needed because flection was sufficient to express the full complement-sense. (In a postscript, p.

292, Behaghel noted that he had become aware that Bergaigne 1878, p. 140, had expressed the same hypothesis concerning the original Germanic word order system.)

Had Behaghel held forth on such premises, which were those of Wackernagel and Delbrück, his thesis on the impact of Latin — acceptable or not — would have fitted simply as an identification of the impulse needed to bring back in full force the original SOV pattern, at least in the dependent clauses, at a time when the incipient shift toward SVO had become arrested and the uncertain syntactic predicament of the German language was ready to welcome a clear device to distinguish the dependent from the independent clause.

All in all, however, the heritage of these early masters was leading to an impasse. Although research and speculation were vigorously carried on with the same methods in the first four decades of our century, only the lack of a comprehensive "universal" theory prevented the specialists from reaching meaningful conclusions. An excellent early example of this relative impasse is the learned dissertation by **Emil Hammarström**, *Zur Stellung des Verbums in der deutschen Sprache* (Lund: Håkan Ohlsson, 1923). See, especially, pp. 194–202 for a discussion of prior authorities and the author's interpretation of his findings. His statistical analyses of a large body of varied documents authorized Hammarström to conclude with a sort of harmonization of the Behaghel and Delbrück theses. Around 800 A.D., one witnesses a crystallization of the differential treatment between *selbständig* and *abhängig* clauses by virtue of the verb's second position in the former and final position in the latter. In due time, German overcame the uncertainty whereby dependent clauses were occasionally affected by the movement acquired by the main clauses, even while the main clause pattern became the dominant one in other Germanic dialects. Eventually, Latin influence intervened to sanction the feeling for verb final position through the literary language. This Latin influence was already visible in Old German, as translations show, but it became decisive in the seventeenth century after the learned models of the chancery style (*Kanzleistil*). The explanations of the various drifts sound forced and often rather half-hearted in Hammarström, as they did in the masters on which he drew, perhaps because only a general theory of typology, not yet available, could have provided convincing causes.

Nevertheless, without realizing the full meaning of what had been taking place, German grammarians had now reached a point of great maturity thanks to the implicit discovery of the peculiarities of a correct and comprehensive description of German word order as a closed system. It was **Jean Fourquet**'s (1938)[34] merit to focus attention on these features by stating two basic theoretical points concerning German syntax: (1) The central knot or decisive element of the German sentence is the verb (p. 25); (2) the description of positions concerns not just phrases or groups of words or elements, but clauses as wholes (p. 22). With regard to this second point, it must be borne in mind that the predication of position as applying mainly to groups is the case of Latin (*civis romanus* or *romanus civis, bonus est* or *est bonus*), French, or English, where, when one speaks of the order SVO, one disregards the fact that any number of other elements can precede or follow this group without affecting its relative internal order (the order of its discrete parts as limited to one another). But unlike English (*today*) *it rained*, German *es regnete* is transformed into (*heute*) *regnete es*.[35] Therefore a correct method of description for German will speak not of the verb before the subject etc., but of verb first, second, or last (plus *Nichtzweitstellung*, as we have seen).

Fourquet then proposes his own paradigm (pp. 24–32). Considering that coordinating conjunctions (*und, oder, aber* . . . , all those that are nonadverbial, I should add) do not affect order; they are not tied to the verb but bear only on the clause as a whole (hence they do not call for the verb-noun construct like other elements, adverbial or complemental, when these appear in first position); and considering that the verb is the clausal knot (*noeud de phrase* — a term borrowed from L. Tesnière, "Comment construire une syntaxe," *Bulletin de la Faculté des Lettres de Strasbourg*, Mai-Juin 1934), he posits the following nomenclature for the basic elements of the clause: I = "elements" introducing syntactic subordination (conjunctions, relative pronouns); V = personal verb; M = "members" that carry a single syntactic tie (subject, object, adverbial phrase — all can be complex phrases). We will then have the following possible constructions: V MMM . . . ; M V MMM; I MMM . . . V (p. 31). Order alone cannot represent dependence: one cannot say *Man sagt, er krank ist*.[36]

As Fourquet carries on his analysis, the following interests us particularly for the elaborations of terminology and definition in some of his major points:

1. Granted that, as we have seen, the central feature of the German

clause is not the relationship between subject and verb, but the position of the verb in first, second, or last place (pp. 2–3), we must accept the suggestions made by Reis 1901 and Diels 1906. Both conclude that what characterizes the subordinate clause is not the final position of the verb, but that before the verb there appears one element more than in independent clauses (p. 11).[37]

2. The subordinate clause is, therefore, characterized by the rule that the verb does not immediately follow the first element (which links the clause to the preceding statements), but is separated from it by at least one other element, often by several, at times by all (p. 291).

3. Modern usage confuses the true infinitive with the participle without *ge-* of *lassen* and the modal verbs, in the rule of rejecting the finite verb to the last but one place when it is accompanied by a "double infinitive" (. . . *hätte machen sollen*) (p. 29).

4. Fourquet opposes himself to the predominant thesis whereby the "neutral" Germanic clause ended with the verb (neutral here meaning simply declarative, neither interrogative nor imperative) (p. 293). Yet he concludes (p. 294) by admitting that this thesis was founded on two correct observations, which were carried to hasty conclusions: It is true that in the opposition main-subordinate, so well known in German, the latter clause preserves the ancient features of the language, whereas the main clause is the one that innovates. However, the ancient Germanic subordinate clause was in no way characterized by the final position of the verb. Its characteristic is negative: The verb is found at any place beyond the second. The stabilization of the verb in final position is a recent development, and the work of grammarians (sic). It is also exact to say that the second position of the verb in the independent clause is the upshot of a secondary evolution, and that if we go back to early Anglo-Saxon, the differentiation between main and dependent clause tends to fade out; the verb is usually closer to the end and often at the absolute end.

Displaying a welcome aptitude to systematic theoretical statement, Fourquet critically reexamines all previous hypotheses on German word order through a broad, punctual analysis of selected texts from the various branches of the Germanic family, from Anglo-Saxon to Frisian, Scandinavian, High and Low German dialects. The impression that he is skeptical about the possibility of generalizations is, however, dispelled by Fourquet's recent restatement of his position (1974).[38]

In this 1974 paper Fourquet recalls and in part rephrases what he now considers the most relevant historical findings of his 1938 book. After noting the contrast between the neutral or "unmarked" second position of the verb in the independent declarative clause (*unabhängig Aussagesatz*) and the "marked" (i.e., "bearing special meaning") first position in interrogative and imperative clauses (*Fragesatz* and *Aufforderungssatz*), he goes on to his early identification of two "systems" or stages of sentence construction in Old Germanic (but one must be aware that Fourquet was using large sample texts from different dialects, so that deductions applying to Old Germanic could be arrived at only by extrapolation), with an Intermediary Stage, *Zwischenstufe*, represented by the first part of the *Sachsenchronik* before 891 and the *Hêliand*. From the First Stage, best represented by the *Beowulf*, to the second (*Sachsenchronik* 891–925, *altnordisch Edda*, OHG *Isidor*) one witnesses the generalization and regularization of second position of the finite verb (fV) in main declarative clauses, whereas in the Intermediary Stage a pronominal subject or object still took its place between the initial element and the verb, the "inversion" being apparently relegated to the presence of a nominal element: Cf. *se papa hine heht Petrus* 'der Papst ihn hieß Petrus' or *þy ilcan geare he for to Rome* 'that year he traveled to Rome' versus *þy ilcan geare for se cyning* ['went the king'] *to Rome*. Alongside these constructions, all unmarked (*unmarkiert, merkmallos*), we have the marked (*merkmalhaft, markiert*) type with *þa/þær* + verb: *þa for he to Rome*, as well as the unmarked type where second place is taken by the verb by default, as it were, to wit, in the absence of pronominal objects or complements: *He for to Rome*. In all stages the dependent clause is characterized by end- or later-than-second position of the verb. For example, even *qui nascitur in Sion* becomes *dher in Sion ward chiboran* in the OHG *Isidor*.

While noting that the earliest Germanic sources, including Gothic and the Runic inscriptions, are less clear than other dialects, Fourquet concludes that verbal second position, common to all Germanic dialects in independent declarative clauses, was not *urgermanisch* but an innovation that entered all dialects (German, Dutch, and Scandinavian) from approximately the sixth century on, as a signal case of *convergence des langues* in Meillet's sense. This departure from the Indo-European heritage that took place after System I, i.e. the *Zweitstel-*

lung, may have been caused at least in part by the phonetic changes in the nature of accent and rhythm (p. 322).

In any event, to obviate the frequently heard objection that no clear overall pattern, or even such an occurrence as a regular end-position of the fV, is discernible in older stages of the language, one must bear in mind that Fourquet is always speaking not of complete sentences, but of a core segment, "ein zentraler Teil mit festem Bau, innerhalb dessen das Vf am Ende steht." Before and after this core segment are located "peripheral constituents, some of them coming in front of the clause in the role of "topic" in the sense of modern linguistic theory: these might be either a nominal subject (stressed) or a complement of circumstance (place, time); others going after the central segment (beyond the fV), this position being a possible index of heavy semantic content" (p. 316). He recalls a typological similarity between German and Turkish and also Japanese (p. 321) with regard to the modifier → modified and dative + accusative order, which in New High German prevails equally in independent and dependent sentences (Fourquet uses the formula . . . $g_3g_2g_1v$ = verb preceded by complements in progressive order according to their weight, similar, we might recall, to H. Weil's "ascending construction").

For Gothic, Ulfila's Bible shows "that, like in Latin, there were no restrictions binding the position of a constituent to its grammatical class (e.g. noun, pronoun) or its function (subject, object)" (p. 321).

The *absolute Endstellung des Vf* reached a peak in the eighteenth century. The modern loosening of this trend was a consequence of the Romantic taste for archaic "popular" rhythms. The *gv-Folge* of all the Germanic group except Gothic must then be an Indo-Germanic heritage (Gothic exceptionally undergoing an evolution toward free word order, FWO, like Latin: See the Hittite pattern in *URUan zahhijaz katta dahhun 'urbem bello sub misi'* — p. 322).

3. Modern Theory[39]

3a. THE PRAGUE SCHOOL

In contemporary applications of structuralist methods, mention is often made of the Prague School, a label that covers three generations of scholars of different origins and from different fields. Their notion of "structure" is somewhat akin to Platonic and Romantic "organicism" as well as to the German definition of *Gestalt* or *Form*. We will find this approach variously applied to sentence analysis in contemporary attempts to understand statements as contextual wholes, whose parts are meaningful only in an organic relationship to the whole. Linguistic structuralism thus becomes a multiform phenomenon drawing on multiple converging sources, from Saussure to Russian-Czech Formalism and Structuralism.

The broadest horizons became open when aesthetics became the target. It is widely recognized that specific aesthetic structuralism began in Prague in the 1920s, and later semiotic theories were to draw on those early ideas. Under the influence of Russian formalism, the Prague linguists began to theorize on literary structures as systems "based on an inner unification of the whole by the mutual relation of its parts," as Jan Mukařovsky was to put it in *K pojmosloví ceskoslovenské teorie umění*. "In such a system, or structure, each element was held to have meaning only in relation to all other elements within it."[40]

But even before such broader developments took place, the Prague structuralists were focussing on matters of language, and specifically of word order. **Vilém Mathesius** (1882–1945) began with his "Studie k dějinam anglického slovosledu (Studies in the History of English Word Order)," *Věstník České Akademie*, 16–19 (Prague, 1907–10), and continued to work on the subject until his death (two of his main volumes were published posthumously in 1947 and 1962).

Mathesius took as his starting point Henri Weil's pioneering work of "general grammar" *De l'ordre des mots* (1844), which had demonstrated the importance of the principle according to which the order of words is determined by the progression of ideas (*la marche des idées*), the "normal" or most natural order being that which proceeds from what is known to what is not yet known.[41] The reverse order, from the unknown to what is known, usually serves as a vehicle of emotion (see pp. 12, 25, 49, 132 of 1844 ed. — this "oratorical" order was Weil's rewriting of the traditional theories of "inversion"). Weil held this to be a universal principle of general grammar, although he was aware that the structure of a given language will control the manner in which it is applied.

Starting from Weil's principle, Mathesius evolved a theory of "functional or actual sentence analysis" (the investigator's discovery of the inherent "functional sentence perspective" — he used the German term *Satzperspektive*, and "functional" here meant both "relational" and "carrying meaning"). As distinct from formal sentence analysis, which is concerned with "parsing," the new method was concerned with the semantic structure of the sentence and its relation to the verbal and situational context.[42]

Mathesius called "theme" or "communicative basis" the already known element of the sentence, and "rheme" or "communicative nucleus" the "statement" of new information — a distinction analogues to the now widely used binomium of "topic" and "comment." This distinction (reminiscent of Greek *onoma* and *rhema*) was given greater circulation by Jan Firbas, but it was introduced into German usage as *thema/rhema* even before Firbas by H. Ammann (*Die menschliche Rede* II, Lahr/B., 1928, see p. 3) and especially K. Boost (*Neue Untersuchungen*, Berlin, 1955, see p. 31), as Firbas himself recalled.[43] More specifically, the prominence first position gave to an element other than the subject had been regarded as particularly significant in German, and accordingly Georg von der Gabelentz, in a wide-ranging comparative essay of 1869, had started speaking of the psychological subject and psychological predicate as distinct from the grammatical ones — a distinction that has remained rather popular in German.[44] Almost any part of the clause, or even a whole clause, could become the psychological subject — just as Mathesius' "theme."

In carrying out Mathesius' method, **Jan Firbas 1956** found that languages can differ in the spatial distribution of the elements. By comparing 400 English sentences of the most frequent declarative type (the type that opens with a thematic subject, that is, a subject that functions as an actual theme) in D. H. Lawrence's *Sons and Lovers* and in the Czech translation, he found that English tends to place those elements first that, viewed in the light of the actual situation, are less important and weaker in communicative dynamism, i.e. more thematic, than those placed first in Czech.[45] Second, often the weak thematic beginning is followed by weak transitional elements (auxiliaries, verbs with wide semantic application, such as *give*, *take*, *put*, etc.), which indicates the time of the action or state concerning the theme. This whole initial section is weak in communicative dynamism "and as a rule has no counterpart in Czech." This is in connection with the analytic and synthetic characters of English and Czech, respectively. Czech has free word order, hence it can throw statement elements into prominence by shifting them to frontal position.

After praising D. L. Bolinger's study on "Linear Modifications" (*PMLA*, 67, 1952, 1117–44) as a valuable contribution to the theory of functional sentence perspective, though with a different approach from that of Mathesius, Firbas, "Some Thoughts on the Function of Word-Order in Old English and Modern English" (*SPFFBU*, 6, 1957, 72–98: see p. 73), went on to compare seven versions of St. Matthew's Gospel from different periods from Old English to Modern English. The essay is less conclusive than the previous one and ends with more questions than answers. What is wanting is a convincing method of evaluating the individual languages' comparative means (diachronically and synchronically) whereby they give the desired prominence or dynamism to the most communicative (rhematic) elements. The question, once again, had been first posed by H. Weil, who had distinguished the two ways different languages have of establishing the *marche des idées*, either by *reprise de la notion initiale* of the previous sentence or by picking up again its end or 'goal' (*le but*).

In a subsequent long paper (1959) on verbal function in English, German, and Czech, Firbas reached the conclusion that "in all three examined languages the verb ranks below the noun in that it displays a definitely lower frequency as conveyor of the rheme proper. In all three languages this detracts from the communicative value of the verb and promotes the shift towards nominal expression" (see "More Thoughts . . . ," p. 74).[46]

One possible application of the Prague functionalists' focussing on differential communicative contents within the sentence is a new perspective on the traditional notion of inversion. Since the rhythm or basic intonation of the German sentence (somewhat like that of the Latin one) places the greatest weight on frontal and final elements, the sentence has these two positions for selective emphasis or focus (focalization). When the final focalized element is other than the verb in a dependent clause (or other than the nonfinite verb in a main clause containing a complex verb), we have an "afterthought" or *Nachtrag*. The first position, in turn, can be given to an accented fronted element, which thus acquires a rhematic function (for example, an object as part of the rheme-predicate); or an unaccented fronted element that, subject or other, has a thematic function, referential toward antecedent, previously given information. In other words, fronting and topicalization cannot be equated, and neither can, of course, subject and topic. Some further examples are supplied by J. Haiman 1974 (pp. 43f.): In *A woman's voice broke the silence*, if we know there was silence, the predicate phrase is the topic, the subject is then the comment; similarly in *Only Max eats peas* or *Who came?* Here, too, the subjects are the focus or comment.[47]

Despite its wide application, the theme-rheme or topic-comment nomenclature is not without its critics. Aside from the difficulty (and perhaps subjectivity) of deciding which element is which in real sentences, Manfred Bierwisch, for one (*Grammatik des deutschen Verbs*, 1963, 1966³, p. 169 fn. 27), finds with reference to Boost, *Neue Untersuchungen* . . . , that this type of distinction (also adopted by Boost, as we have seen) belongs rather to the psychology of the speech situation, and that in this sense it has nothing to do with internal linguistic structure.

In any event, the Prague "functionalist" or "perspectivist" approach has been carried further, and rather valiantly, by **Eduard Beneš**, who has also contributed several important applications to the analysis of German (1962–64, 1971, 1973).[48] His conclusion is that in this language the articulation of the sentence into thematic and rhematic communicative parts obtains fully in the SVX (independent declarative clause) or VSX type (question, command, condition). It also obtains, but only as a secondary phenomenon, in the SXV type (dependent clause with verb-final position). The verb conserves its full communicative and dynamic value in all types. In type I, in particular, the "inversion" of the subject serves the purpose of compensating (as a *Kompensationsmittel*, that is) for the relatively fixed position of the verb when communicative or expressive needs demand that some element of the statement be placed into relief. The formula for this is: v VF S x x X (PV) and its variants (x – X = "other complements" in order of importance, the most important, X, coming last; VF = *Verbum finitum*; PV = *Paraverbium*, i.e., *Prae-* or *Postverbium*, particle or nonfinite form. The formula is derived from Boost — see below).

As a consequence of the Prague terminology, Functional Sentence Perspective is referred to in recent studies as a level of semiotic processes — but this would shift our discourse to a broader area well beyond our purpose.

Since we have started this review of the Prague school with the name of H. Weil, and are about to consider some contributions of German structuralism, it may be fitting to take a quick look at two French structuralists whose ideas seem to establish a point of contact between the work of H. Weil and the chief concerns of later typological approaches.

Among the professed structuralists outside the Prague school, **Henri Frei**, in *La grammaire des fautes* (Paris: Geuthner, 1929), and then in a book review of 1931,[49] proposed, first, that the order of the basic sentence elements must be viewed as tendentially akin to that of the elements of the nominal group, so that the sequence subject → predicate carries with it the tendency to postpose the adjective to the noun (1929), and, then, that the order of words and that of morphemes inside the word have the same foundations (1931). As a general point, "il existe, entre les divers groupements d'éléments significatifs, un parallélisme certain, quoique souvent caché et souvent contrarié, et telle langue qui, dans la phrase indépendante, présente un type de séquence donnée, par example l'ordre sujet-prédicat, ne s'en écarte pas, dans les autres groupements, sans de bonnes raisons" (1931, pp. 135–6). It is well to remember that the first systematic statement of such a principle was, once again, due to H. Weil, with his classification of languages according to an ascending or descending order of construction (modifier → modified or modified → modifier).

This division of basic possibilities was carried further by another eminent French structuralist, **Lucien Tesnière**, who divided all languages according to whether they normally place the modifier before or after the modified; indeed, in an unwitting echo of Weil, he labeled the former possibility as *construction montante* or *ordre centripète*, the latter as *construction descendante* or *ordre centrifuge* (French being, of course, of the latter type, so that in that language a pre-posed adjective must respond to an expressive option).[50]

But before we go any further, and because of the ideal connection of some of his ideas with the specific developments we are about to consider, it is appropriate to enter at this point a brief reference to Ferdinand de Saussure. Even though his *Cours de linguistique générale* (Lausanne-Paris, 1916; I cite from the Paris edition: Payot, 1949, checked against Engler's critical edition) contained only a few scattered remarks on word order, they are of momentous import within our context. Starting from the axiom of the "blind character of sound evolution" (p. 209), which carries the consequence that phonetics cannot distinguish between morphemes and grammatical forms — since in such a case we would have a confusion between sound and meaning, diachrony (phonetics) and synchrony (grammar), an *a priori* impossibility (ibid.) — he indirectly established the implied principle that word order, as a fact of syntax, makes adjustments for the disorder caused by phonetic change. Thus (p. 247), from the absence of prepositions in Indo-European, since the flectional cases took care of the functions occupied by prepositions in other language systems, one went to a state wherein cases are replaced by the analytic nexus of preposition + noun. Saussure did not say this much, but we can interpolate that the transitions from (Proto-)Latin *ire mortem ob 'to go to death before' to *ire ob mortem* and *obire mortem* 'to go before death, to die,' or Greek *óreos baínō káta* 'I come from the mountain down' to *katà óreos baínō* and then *katabaínō óreos* 'I descend from the mountain' (where *ob* and *káta* were originally adverbs, not prepositions or preverbs) are as much cases of grammatical evolution from adverbs to prepositions and preverbs, as Saussure maintained, as they are grammatical corrections of the vacuum being left by the phonetic weakening of case-endings. Thus *katá* assumes the meaning once carried autonomously and synthetically by the desinence *-os*, which will in time disappear altogether. (Engler ed., p. 410.)

Elsewhere Saussure made more explicit the relationship of cause and effect that ties together the weakening of the case system to the drift from free to fixed word order, since the latter necessarily takes over the functions of the former as the only alternative. He pointed out this movement as being characteristic of the whole family of Indo-European languages, with Slavic and English being at the extreme ends of the greatest and least resistance (maximum retention of flection in the former, almost nil in the latter — p. 314). Similarly, he underlined the relationship between "a word order tied to strict rules" and "an underdeveloped flection" in the Semitic group — an unusually constant characteristic of this group throughout its history, although it too does show a slight evolution oriented in the same direction as Indo-European (p. 315).

3b. THE STRUCTURALISTS

Leo **Weisgerber** is one of those much-quoted masters whose intellectual and verbal gait will strike many readers as both provocatively lucid and frustratingly elusive. He is the foremost representative of an idealistic school of thought often labeled Neo-Humboldtian. Philosophically, Weisgerber represents an extension of the Condillac-Michaëlis-Herder-Humboldt tradition that places thought and speech on an equal plane of mutual conditioning (the theory of the *Weltbild der Sprache*, akin to the Sapir-Whorf theory — see my *CTC*). Linguistically, he represents a reaction against the uses of structuralism in a merely phonological and morphological direction. His advocacy of an *inhaltbezogene Grammatik* is to be understood according to an equation *Formbezogenes: Inhaltbezogenes* = structural syntax: semantic syntax. The most concise phrasing of the leading idea within this long tradition is probably that of Hjelmslev, "Du rôle structural de l'ordre des mots" (1950), p. 55: "puisque le signe fournit la forme à la pensée même, la pensée se subordonne non seulement au système des signes, mais aussi à leur agencement dans la chaine. L'ordre des signes est l'ordre de la pensée."

From the large number of Weisgerber's writings, not much can be derived that constitutes a concrete, specific contribution to a technical analysis along the lines we have pursued. Quite understandably from his vantage point, his occasional references to technical literature usually aim at showing its inconclusiveness or inadequacy. With regard to *Satzlehre* and *Wortstellung* he cites and discusses most approvingly — especially in his 4-volume treatise *Von den Kräften der deutschen Sprache* 1962^3 — [51] Erich Drach, *Grundgedanken der deutschen Satzlehre*, 1937, a landmark in the formation of the German Structuralist School that will make a good start for an observation of this productive group of grammarians. But for an adequate understanding of the work of what is usually referred to as German structuralism, it will be helpful to bear in mind that, as opposed to the generally positivistic-behavioristic orientation of their American counterparts, most of these structuralists show a marked idealistic frame of mind of broadly Kantian imprint.

Drach's little work, which was destined to a durable success, presented itself chiefly as a pedagogical manual for Germans as well as foreigners learning German. The author's originality lay both in his

134 ☐ MODERN THEORY AND NINETEENTH-CENTURY BACKGROUND

ideological framework — the semantic stress on "die Denkfunktion des Wortinhaltes" rather than "die grammatische Funktion des Wortkörpers" as the decisive factor, the one that "entscheidet über die Stellungsbeziehungen" (p. 17) — and in his aptitude to propose such clear formal diagrams of *Vorfeld*, *Mitte(lfeld)*, and *Nachfeld*, which, with much of the attendant nomenclature, became standard in scholastic and scientific presentations of the subject — even including the use of the three-box rectangle ⊔⎯⎯|⎯⎯|⎯⎯⊔ (see below, section 4). The former argument was probably the one that endeared Drach to Weisgerber in his *inhaltbezogene Grammatik*. The neat format of his well-organized presentation commended itself to future generations for its cogency and adaptability.

In Drach's system, between *Vorfeld* and *Nachfeld* the sentence moves from known antecedent to yet unknown consequent or goal (*Ziel*, *Ergebnis*, p. 17), while the *Mitte* contains the statement of the action (*Geschehen* = *Vf*). In inverted constructs, the *Vorfeld* is then either the *Ausdruckstelle*, expressive locus of something we want to stress, or the *reprise* of antecedents (p. 18). The pivotal formal rule is, therefore, that the *Mittelfeld* is occupied by the finite verb, whereas the subject, object, or complements shift according to the variations just described.

The conclusive formula for the declarative independent clause is pregnant with future developments: The *Geschehen*, 'event,' invariably takes second place; all other *Satzglieder*, 'elements,' occupy either the *Vorfeld* — which is the *Ausdrucksstelle* or 'expressive place' of the 'meaningful term' carrying either emotion or will, *gefühls- oder willensgeladenes Sinnwort* — or the *Nachfeld* — which is the *Eindrucksstelle*, 'impressive place" of the information or thought-content, the *gedankliches oder lehrhaftes Sinnwort* (p. 19). We are clearly on the way toward the theme-rheme or topic-comment distinction that will play an important role later on. The same schema also applies, with the appropriate shift of the verb, to question and desire.

Drach gives the name of *Satzplan* to this articulation of the sentence. He does not yet use the key term of *Rahmen*, 'frame,' but he does speak of *Satzklammer* — or, more precisely, *Klammersatz* (p. 39) — which he ideally likens to the much-maligned *Schachtelsatz* (see chs. 9–11, "Die Umklammerung," "Pole und Spannung," "Der Schachtelsatz," pp. 38–50). Indeed, he aligns himself with the defenders of the encapsulated periodic sentence, which, if correctly and elegantly conceived and handled, is, together with the *Umklammerung*, the supreme trademark of the German way to think and speak; it is a synthetic striving toward unity, rather than division and separation, so that a thinking process is appreciated only when it is ready to be presented as an orderly, hierarchically organized whole with a beginning and an end. He even cites, without strictures (p. 39), Burdach's characterization of the extreme traditional ideal that found its expression on German soil (p. 39):

In der lateinischen Kanzleisprache herrscht die Regel: der einem anderen Nebensatz übergeordnete Nebensatz muß jenem, der ihm untergeordnet ist, ganz oder mit einem Teil voranstehen. Die Nebensätze ersten, zweiten, dritten Grades müssen in dieser ihrer logischen Anordnung aufeinanderfolgen. Hierzu wurde reichlich Gebrauch gemacht von der Teilung der Sätze, und es entstand die allbekannte Einschachtelung.

Hans Glinz, *Die innere Form des Deutschen* (1952, 1961^2),[52] contrasts his method, as first and foremost "syntactical and semantic" ("syntaktisch und inhaltlich orientiert"), with the American structuralists' and Bloomfieldians' inclination to fragment grammar into phonology, morphology, and syntax, entailing the separation of discrete "minimal units": phonemes, morphemes, and tagmemes (pp. 3–5). Yet, he characterizes his own method as *strukturalistisch-empiristisch* (p. 8). Aside from the general method, his influence rests in particular on the full nomenclature he proposed, some of the terms of which already were gaining currency, e.g. *Kernsatz* (Satz mit finitem Verb an der zweiten Stelle); *Stirnsatz* (. . . an der Spitze); *Spannsatz* (. . . am Schluß). His partly successful and enduring terminological experimentation covered every detail: For example, he proposed the key term *Spannfügteil*, defined as follows: "unterordnende (d.h. die Personalform ans Satzende verweisende) Konjunktion" (see the "Beilage zur 2. Auflage," p. 14, and, in general, the Glossary on pp. 484–91).

His aptness at definition was equally impressive. See, for example, his effort to comprise in one compact and articulated formula all the essential variations in position for a key constituent (pp. 136–42). He defines thus the arrangement of the nonfinite verbal form: "Das feste vorletzte Glied im Spannsatz (letztes im Stirnsatz, letztes-erstes im

Kernsatz)." Examples: *daß da nur zwei Türpfosten* sein *sollten; weil sie keine Freude an dem Spaße* haben *konnte* or gehabt *hatte* or *zu haben schien* (I am making up a multiple-choice example to show all the possibilities discussed by Glinz); *konnte (hatte, schien) sie keine Freude an dem Spaße (zu)* haben (or gehabt)?; *sie konnte (hatte, schien) keine Freude an dem Spaße (zu)* haben (or gehabt).

For an idea of the (rather taxing) terminological richness Glinz achieved it will suffice for the reader to glance through the "schematic exposition" (*schematische Darstellung*) at the end of the volume (pp. 455–74). It contains a series of "results" (*Ergebnisse*) and an eight-page center-fold (after p. 472) that in a continuous diagram analyzes on all linguistic levels a prose-paragraph by Goethe. This last piece displays Glinz's supreme effort at total organization from the minutest analytical divisions to final synthesis.

Karl Boost, *Neue Untersuchungen zum Wesen und zur Struktur des deutschen Satzes* (Berlin, 1955), is generally credited with the introduction of the theme-rheme perspective as a central problem of German *Wortfolge*.[53] Beneš 1962–64, p. 10, has derived from Boost's analysis of the basic types of German sentences with *Rahmen* or Full Frame a set of schematic representations that bears repeating:

Type I. $\underline{S}\ VF\frac{x}{S}\ x\ x\ X\ (PV)$ } independent clause

II. $VF\quad S\ x\ x\ x\ X\ (PV)$ } question, imperative, conditional

III. $\begin{matrix}\text{Konjunktion}\\ \text{Relativum}\end{matrix}\ S\ x\ x\ x\ X\ (PV)\ VF$ } dependent clause

The *Satzklammer* is indicated with a dotted line when it is made apparent only by a sufficient number of elements; x – X = complements by degree of importance; PV = *Paraverbium*, i.e., *Prae-* or *Postverbium*, particle or nonfinite form; VF = *Verbum finitum*.

Boost opens his discourse (p. 7) with a request to look beyond a description of the German sentence, which is clear and detailed enough as transmitted by the tradition, for an explanation of its unitary form, that inner structure that will make the general principle manifest through the individual variations. The sentence is to be defined phonetically, morphologically, and semantically as a unity in all three senses. This applies to all languages, but the unitary principle to be sought must fit the German sentence specifically.

Language, he states, is communication on the basis of an interchange between speaker and hearer, in which the *thema* is a question and the *rhema* an answer, each step or element of a statement being governed by a tension, to be resolved in the interchange between two elements or parts of an element all the way to the end of the sentence as a whole (pp. 85f.).

He praises Drach for the articulation (*Gliederung*) of the sentence into *Vorfeld-Mitte-Nachfeld*: This division overcame the type of syntactic analysis that was destined to failure because it was based on isolated grammatical elements, and placed the sentence squarely on the semantic plane (*auf der Sinn-Ebene*), where it belongs (p. 30). Our construction or word order is "free" on the grammatical level, not so on the semantic one. The basic principle is that a tension is created by the setting of a "given" as theme at the beginning of the sentence, and the expectation thus aroused is then resolved at the end. The remainder of the volume studies the articulation of this *Spannungsprinzip* that governs all sentences.

In conclusion, we hear that "the sequence of the constituents is determined by their communicative value; the highest value comes as close to the end as the particular sentence form will allow. Hence a certain hierarchy whereby the undetermined noun has a natural priority over the determined one, etc." (p. 86).

Boost's Humboldtian drift is disclosed by an approving quotation from **Walter Porzig** 1928:[54] "Forms (*Gestalten*) are always totalities. . . . The whole is circumscribed; it has an inside and an outside that are qualitatively distinct. . . : Its elements are mutually related. . . . It is greater than its parts. [The word is more than the sum of its phonemes, and the sentence dominates and determines its words.] . . . The expression 'interiority' means that the parts can neither be augmented nor diminished nor exchanged between one another without affecting the whole qualitatively. . . . [Hence there are no isolated mood- or case-forms; they stand inextricably inside the sentence they qualify.] . . . The second type of determinant for the

Forms is their ordering . . . whereby the order of the parts is essential to the whole. [Consequently word order and intonation must be reciprocally coordinated in an unambiguous manner.] . . ." (pp. 7f.).

All this commentary on the true value of *Gestalt* will be seen in proper perspective if one keeps in mind that this brand of "structuralism" has been essentially a translation of German *Gestalt* through its Slavic (Czech and Russian) equivalents, first *Forma* and then *Struktura*.

In the wake of these structuralist masters (including Drach 1937, Glinz 1951, Boost 1955, and later Admoni 1967 and Guchmann 1969 — see below), the description and analysis of the German sentence has become increasingly formalized, the main terminological effort going to the definition of the typical frame, bracketing or bracing system — *Satzrahmen*; the identification of its principal constituents — *syntaktische Glieder*, i.e., the *Verbalglied*, traditionally *Prädikat*; and the *Ergänzungen* or complements, often subdivided into *Objekte* or *Objektergänzungen*, etc. Both the system and its possible variations or exceptions, including Incomplete (or Partial) Frame or No Frame as distinct from the Full Frame — *vollständiger* or *unvollständiger Rahmen* (generally *Ausklammerung*, including the *Nachtrag*), *Sätze ohne Rahmen* — also have been studied in their historical development, for example, by M. M. Guchmann 1964–69 and Ulrich Engel 1970.[55]

3c. TRANSFORMATIONAL GRAMMAR

The convergent schemes gradually evolving from the work of these grammarians become the basis for later linguistic schools, first and foremost that of the transformationalists. The same paradigms are coopted by literary critics and "contextualist" philologists whose interests go beyond technical analysis. We shall pause briefly to consider an example of this latter possibility in a much discussed book of a brilliant linguist and philologist, both for the theoretical thesis it contains and the documentary material it summarizes.

Harald Weinrich 1964 restates, in a quick historical survey, the notion that the basic feature of German word order is the position of the verb, which can have first place (in questions, imperative constructions, and in the style of popular ballads or even prose romances — *Volkslieder*: Cf. Goethe's *Sah ein Knab ein Röslein stehn*; *Spricht zu ihm das schöne Weib*; to which we must add the inversion in hypothetic or concessive constructs with ellipsis of conjunction), second place (normal in independent clauses), or last place (normal in dependent clauses).[56] Weinrich proposes a shrewdly comprehensive formula for dependent clauses: The verb can take any place in the clause except the second — which neatly takes care both of the first place as just seen above, i.e., in hypothetic or concessive constructs such as *Trittst du im Garten hervor, / So bist du die Rose der Rosen*, and of cases with *Nachtrag*, whereby the verb is sent back from the end but not as far as second place (p. 218).

He criticizes both the partisans of the Behaghel thesis and those of the Delbrück thesis because in each case there remains to explain the departure from the norm either in the secondary or in the main clause. In the case of the latter thesis, it may appear absurd to derive the explanation of order in the main clause starting from the secondary one (p. 219). As we shall see farther on, the absurdity disappears if one assumes that, SOV being the original order in all clauses, the change started in the most important part of the sentence, the main clause, and has so far remained limited to that part.

Likewise, Weinrich attacks the thesis of rhythmic reasons, principally represented by Behaghel, because there is conflict between Latin *cursus*, by which a sentence or clause must end with a polysyllable (*amāre vidētur*), and Germanic cadence, since German has no objection to ending with a monosyllable.[57]

On the stylistic-rhetorical level, Weinrich makes an appropriate remark that amounts to applying to German the classical rules of ancient rhetoric. He maintains that the distribution of second and end-positions in a sentence is also subject to a criterion of equilibrium (roughly corresponding to a balance of main and secondary clauses according to the classic principles of periodic variation): "The classic ideal for German prose wants a fairly balanced distribution of clauses with second verb position and clauses with final verb position. It holds the middle point between excess in end-positions (*Schachtelsätze*) and excess in second positions (*lakonischer Stil*)" (p. 227). It is interesting to see here a reference to the separation, which started in the Baroque age, between periodic or Ciceronian and coupé or Senecan styles.

Coming to his own theory of *Relief*, Weinrich explains the position of the German finite verb through its function for purposes of articulation and emphasis within the clause (*gliedern, Relief geben*): Second place indicates *Vordergrund*, last place *Hintergrund*. Since German is morphologically poor both in verbal tense and mood forms and in conjunctions with a clearly and unambiguously subordinating function, it became necessary to mark subordination through differentiated verbal placement. Consequently, one can say that forms apparently identical really belong to different *Tempora* according to position in the clause.[58]

Essential to this theory is the principle whereby the clause must be seen not as isolated or self-enclosed, but in its connection with other clauses and therefore with the greater unity that is the text (p. 211). An outcome of the theoretical premises is the observation that "One can thrust a clause into the background in two ways: first, by sending the verb to the end (*Er glaubt, daß er singen kann*), second, through a subjunctive in second position (*Er glaubt, er könne singen*). Each type perfectly fulfills the principle of syntactic emphasis, or, rather, de-emphasization. On the other hand, we have hypercharacterization with *Er glaubt, daß er singen könne*, hypocharacterization with *Er glaubt, er kann singen*. Therefore there is competition, as it were, between the use of the subjunctive mood and the position of the verb in the play of syntactic emphasis. Today the subjunctive plays the weaker role."[59]

But then Weinrich appears to defeat his critique of the traditional notion of hypotaxis (which he proposes to replace with *Hintergrund*) when he concludes with the acknowledgment that in German, "when the speaker wants to assign a content to the background, he must arrange the sentence in such a way that the syntax entails end-position for the verb. He must then start the clause with a conjunction or a pronoun" (p. 227) — which is precisely the definition of secondary clause within the framework of hypotaxis. We may be left with the impression that we are back where we started. Weinrich's explanation of the origin of final position in German secondary clauses may lack a compelling force of conviction also because in analyzing other languages he does not recognize that their formal tenses (e.g., in English and in the Romance languages) as they are used on different syntactic levels are also semantically different, whereas in German the difference in position cannot be regarded as a way to make up for the paucity of German verbal forms, in so far as it does not amount to a semantic difference. And in criticizing the $X + V$ theory (which, however, he mentions only in the indefensible form of the Wunderlich-Reis theory), he does not take into account the best proof of its truth: the presence in German of the operator → operand pattern, which we discuss below (pp. 154–5). Nor does he sufficiently recognize the formal character of grammar; hence he constantly tends to merge logic with grammar. Likewise, he produces a paradox when he concludes his critique of the traditional nomenclature of subordination and hypotaxis by saying that the elimination of conjunctions (as in Voltaire) results in a stylistic variation, not a logical one (since the meaning does not change) nor a grammatical one (pp. 165, 212–3). Indeed, the transformation is not logical, but grammatical it undoubtedly is, since grammar is a formal matter and conjunctions are morphological facts.

Since the transformational-generative approach, which we are now ready to consider, is intertwined with typological universals, we must first turn our attention to Greenberg's seminal paper. The most decisive step toward establishing a firm basis for typological description and evaluation of word order patterns came with **Joseph H. Greenberg**'s 1961 (published 1963) paper on "Some Universals of Grammar with Particular Reference to the Order of Meaningful Elements." Greenberg held the following criteria as basic for the typology of order: The discrimination of preposition from post-positive case elements; the order of S, V, and O in declarative clauses; and the place of adjective vis-à-vis the noun (NA or AN), with the additional position, in some cases, of the genitive with respect to the governing noun (GN or NG). He found that OV is "harmonic" with post-positions, whereas "prepositions, NG, VS, VO, and NA are 'harmonic' with each other. Thus, there is a 'tendency' in certain languages to put the modified before the modifier" (p. 78). He noted the "general tendency for comment to follow topic," hence to accompany SV order with NA, and attributed the harmonic correspondence between orders of single groups to the psychological principle of "generalizing" (p. 79). To anticipate later criticism, it seems fair to state that Greenberg *was* interested in finding "reasons" for his statistical observations, even though his statement of such reasons was brief and apparently marginal.[60] Greenberg's schema immediately became the necessary point of departure for all later speculation.

Transformational grammar is sometimes praised, sometimes criticized for opposing reasons: Some maintain that it postulates a deep linear order, others that it fails to do any such thing. Haiman 1974, for example, finds that "the base component of a transformational grammar of German is totally indeterminate," so that "specifically, given the surface structure orders that appear in German sentences of various types, it is possible to construct equally plausible derivations for these sentences which proceed from any of three given bases: SOV (as in subordinate clauses), SVO (as in declarative sentences), and VSO (as in questions)" (Haiman, p. 37).

Let us, then, look at the proposals recently advanced by three transformationalists that illustrate the contrasting possibilities in the order just given. A fourth one, more recent still (P. Ramat 1976), concludes by denying the validity of each of the three possibilities. We shall begin with **Emmon Bach** 1962 (German version in H. Steger 1970).

Starting with Zellig S. Harris's threefold distinction in the relative ordering of morphemes into restricted, contrasting, and descriptively equivalent order, Bach submits a rule that, though complex, will be simpler than others offered so far (e.g., by R. B. Lees) and will achieve this degree of simplicity precisely by proceeding from the SOV order of dependent clauses rather than from the SVO order of main clauses. Such a rule will, as one must, "set up the verb phrase in one order and derive the other orders from this one by shifts of the finite verb" (p. 266). This SOV order is, as opposed to Lees's, not a "fictitious intermediate sequence," but a (real) "basic order in which the verb phrase is a continuous sequence, namely, the order of explicitly dependent clauses." In other words, "rules of constituent structure given here take the order of dependent clauses as a 'base order.'" Bach claims that his rule covers all permutations, including first place for finite verb in yes-no questions, second place in declarative sentences and suppletive questions (or w- questions), the giving of first position to any "element" or *Satzglied* (which thereby, often by *reprise* of an antecedent, becomes the topic rather than the grammatical subject), and the end-placing of *nicht* and other negatives (before final verbals). Essentially, German order is "exactly the reverse" of English order. "By including the finite verb as a possible topic we are preparing the way for yes-no questions" (p. 268). In particular, the rule also accounts for the difference between (1) *Lange wurde getanzt* and (2) *Lange wurde es gesungen*: (2) is legitimate only if *es* replaces a neuter NP (e.g. *das Lied*), whereas in (1) we have deletion of the "disappearing

MODERN THEORY AND NINETEENTH-CENTURY BACKGROUND □ 143

es" of *es wurde lange getanzt*, demonstrating "the existence of a situation which entails the use of transformational rules" (p. 265).

Bach does not address here the question as to how to relate this model to the simultaneous base of deep structure expressed elsewhere by some transformationalists, nor to deeper implications in the diachronic sense. We may be entitled to draw hopeful conclusions as to the eventual mutual adaptability of the two levels of speculation.

Particularly, Bach proposes that a dummy node Ø should be generated by the phrase structure rules, so that the underlying order of constituents would be somewhat like S O Ø V (verb then originating in clause-final position). Verb frontal position would be explained by the obligatory rule of question formation, triggered by the presence of a clause-initial Q (or Question) morpheme, which places a w- morpheme at the head (w- becoming a w- adverb, pronoun, or the verb itself when it is the element being questioned). Insofar as Bach's rule depends on the presence of the Ø node, it appears doubly questionable (cf. Haiman's 1974 apt strictures, pp. 39–40).

The SOV thesis Bach proposed was also expounded at the same time by the leading East German generative grammarian **Manfred Bierwisch**, *Grammatik des deutschen Verbs* (Berlin, 1963, 1973[8]), pp. 30 ff., and both were followed by **Elizabeth Closs Traugott** 1965 and 1969.[61] Traugott 1969, p. 5, also quoted Bacquet 1962 as supporting evidence, along with Bach, that "the subordinate order is the basic one" (meaning the one operative on a deep level, hence to be used for derivation of all surface orders). This 1969 paper by Mrs. Traugott is particularly interesting as a rather early attempt to map out a theoretical approach to the typology of syntactic change from a transformational viewpoint, at a time when the subject of syntactic change was still largely unexplored, and before typological hypotheses began to gain some ground (see below). The results of these earlier papers were incorporated into Traugott's 1972 book.

In his much-quoted paper on Gapping, **John R. Ross** 1970 rejected SOV for German and proposed SVO, with a complex argument drawing on conditions for identical-verb deletion in such cases as: (a) *Bill kicked Sam, and Max kicked Harry* → (b) *Bill kicked Sam, and Max, Harry* [(c) *Bill, Sam, and Max kicked Harry* is not allowed in SVO English as a derivation of (a) because, though grammatical, it would not be synonymous with (a)]. Now if German were an SOV language it would, conversely, have to produce only the (c) type, but it allows both (c) *and* (b). Cf. (a) . . . *weil Max ein Narr ist, und Moritz ein Edsel ist* → both (b) . . . *weil Max ein Narr ist, und Moritz ein Edsel* and (c) *weil Max ein Narr, und Moritz ein Edsel ist* 'because Max is a fool, and Moritz an ass.' The kind of forward gapping implied in (b) would never, under any circumstances, be permitted by a true verb-final language, Ross contended. Yet one must conclude that, even if his argument were found to be convincing, it would not lead to SVO for German, as Ross claimed it did, but either to SVO *or* VSO. Indeed, in a 1971 paper Bach returned to the question and changed his mind, claiming that not SOV but only SVO or VSO were conceivable for German, and he now opted precisely for VSO.

This last possibility had been just advanced by **James McCawley** 1970, who through a purely abstract argument, specifically predicated about English but potentially investing all superficial SVO languages, proposed VSO as the general base, hence allegedly applicable to German also. The subject would normally precede the verb by the operation of a fronting rule that sends the topic to the left — and the subject is the most common topic.

In an elegant paper in which the conciseness of the presentation does not hide the breadth of information, **Paolo Ramat** 1976 begins by going over the three discrete and divergent proposals by Bach (I), Ross, and McCawley, and then submits a "new" approach: The question, he says, must be taken beyond the surface order into the deep structure, in search of universal principles that will have to be of a logical nature (predicates and arguments). But the deep level cannot be conceived as linearly arranged. Ramat's answer to Bach, Ross, and McCawley's multiple question seems to be, then: None of the above. Of course, as far as it goes this last answer must be considered correct; nevertheless, we might comment that, whatever the results of this investigation below the "surface," such results will no longer interest German or any other positive language, since they will be purely and abstractly universal.

Ramat's suggested solution with regard to the surface ordering is made intriguing by a clever combination of Wackernagel, Mathesius, and modern typology: The original order SOV, potentially akin to its mirror image VOS (turning to VSO by the law that the theme tends to precede the rheme, and by Greenberg's Universal 1, hence S + O), became SVO both by Wackernagel's law and by the need for topicalization (topic, or S, first) and focalization (O taking last, emphatic place as the most informative part of the predicate) (p. 32). This formula is presumed to define a unitary principle (*ein einheitliches Prinzip*) for all diachronic manifestations of the language — Ramat's contribution to that ongoing effort toward synthetic representation that we have seen expressed even in the handling of surface empirical rules in all quarters. The reader may recall, for example, Glinz's structuralist definitions of verbal position.

In any event, we are also entitled to wonder: Is not something wrong when "scientific" methods of investigation end up by producing *all* the possible answers to a given question? Could this mean that the problem was put in the wrong terms; that perhaps the only productive approach, for the time being, is the historical one: surface diachrony? More important, could it not be that, in Ramat's own words (p. 26), "transformational grammar is, above all, not in a position to clarify the problem of ordering, because it starts from the wrong premise that the deep structure contains a linear, time-bound arrangement," whereas it contains only hierarchic relations of semantic elements within a logical configuration?[62]

In short, perhaps it has been a mistake to seek deep-structure solutions to such complex problems before much more surface clarification has been attained. Above all, it was a mistake to assume, or even imply, that the ordering types discussed by Greenberg could refer to or exist in the deep structure (that so much is sometimes understood to be the implication of Greenberg's typology is visible in R. Jakobson 1963 and Ross 1970, "Gapping . . . ," pp. 249–50, besides, of course, Greenberg himself).

We need not dwell on the provocative perspectives introduced into the understanding of syntactic processes by Charles J. Fillmore's Case Grammar, a radically modified version of transformational grammar. We need not do so because, despite Fillmore's own direct interest in questions of word order, at least for English, the possible specific applications of such an approach to the peculiarities of the Germanic area remain unfulfilled to date.[63] Suggestions from this quarter of which Germanists should remain aware are those that concern the spatial divergence between languages in ordering those cases that they are all supposed to host in the deep structure. The "agentive" *John* in both *John opened the door with the key* and *John's key opened the door* etc. comes first in English but last in, say, Welsh, although it is the same "case" in both languages as a form of universal — assuming it exists at all. Thus, whereas most transformationalists look for some kind of deep ordering of elements, Fillmore sees no correspondence between the order of elements in surface structure and the system of the cases. Furthermore, since syntax and, emphatically, German constituent ordering cannot be divorced from meaning, it must be borne in mind that Fillmore's model reverses Chomsky's relative location of semantic fields within the broad sphere of linguistic analysis. Instead of moving from the Base Component to Meanings through Deep Structures and Semantic Interpretation Rules (on a parallel track to the movement that takes syntax from the Transformational Component to sounds through Phonological Interpretation Rules), with Fillmore we should get a progress from Initial Element → Semantic Component (which includes the set of Cases) → Transformational Component → Surface Structures.[64]

East German linguists have been particularly active in transformational grammar and **Manfred Bierwisch** deserves a high degree of attention as a leading member of this group. His work is of particular interest in indicating what a transformational grammar should include at this juncture in the evolution of the method. His *Grammatik des deutschen Verbs* 1963, 1973[8] begins with a general section on theory and then articulates the syntactic treatment of the verb into subsequent chapters on constituent structure (*Konstituentenstruktur*), simple transformations and position (*einfache Transformationen, Verbumstellung*, etc.), embedding (*Einbettungstransformationen*), and finally tenses and moods.

The most pertinent aspect of the study for our purpose begins with the observation that the facts concerning the ordering of the principal constituents have been clearly and surely described by traditional grammar, but that little has been done so far on the grammatical regularities that pertain to the ordering of nonverbal constituents. Bierwisch excludes both Boost's theme-rheme distinction (as we have already seen) and Drach's *Vorfeld-Nachfeld* division from the grammatical domain as merely psychological (p. 31 and fn. 27 p. 169). Their concern is the speech situation or point of view, not the formal structure of the sentence. They address questions of expressive or stylistic choice, not the sort of regularities that, however limited, remain to be discovered.

Coming to the main problem of verbal position, to be tackled in terms of transformations and explanation beyond empirical description, Bierwisch believes, in agreement with Bach 1962 and Fourquet 1959,[65] that the most efficient way to reconstruct the German sentence is by starting from the chain that characterizes the dependent clause, that is, SOV (p. 34). He regards Bach's thesis as a confirmation of his more detailed analysis, which he has evolved independently by following the same (transformational) method. (It is somewhat ironic that, without any change in method, Bach was soon to change his mind and produce opposite conclusions, as we have seen.)

His first and most compelling argument for this thesis is that synchronically speaking the last place of the sentence naturally belongs to the verb because, when the finite verb is permuted into a verb phrase with a modal or auxiliary, the nonfinite form of the original main verb goes to the end, thus making a *Satzklammer* (p. 35). Likewise for the verb of an infinitive clause: For example, *der Versuch, im Haus einen neuen Leiter zu finden*; we also naturally say *jemandem etwas geben*, not *geben jemandem etwas*.

For word order Bierwisch also uses the term *Topologie* (remember Herling's and Bauer's *Topik*). Now, since the topology of the fV starts from the typology of dependent clauses, these latter are excluded from verb-topological permutations (p. 108). In other words, final position is practically fixed in dependent clauses — with one exception, the case of the *Verbalkomplex*: *Wen er hat treffen wollen* (traditionally dubbed as double infinitive). We should add here the apparent exceptions defined as *Nachtrag, Nichtzweitstellung*, or *Distanzstellung*.

Turning then to *Einbettung* (p. 121), he traces transformations that produce such sentences with embedded relative clauses as: *Ich habe von dem Vorfall, den du erwähnt hast, auch gehört*; or embedded infinitive clauses, as: *Ich habe . . . seine Frau ein Brot kaufen sehen* (p. 122), or: *Man fand ihn im Sessel sitzen* (p. 129), or *Infinitivkomplexe mit zu*: *Der Wunsch, das alles abzulegen, kam zu spät* (p. 145).

Bierwisch considers the syntax of infinitive constructions one of the few areas of German grammar that have been systematically, coherently, and exactly described, thanks to **Gunnar Bech**'s work, *Studien über* *das deutsche Verbum infinitum* (Copenhagen: Munksgaard, 2 Bde., 1955–57). The glossematic framework of Bech's method is said to have brought his results into harmony with the soon-to-be-formulated theories of Harris and Chomsky (pp. 176f., fn. 61).

For **John Haiman**, *Targets and Syntactic Change* (The Hague: Mouton, 1974), German word order is a good field for testing surface syntactic targets, that is, "conspiracies" of several independently motivated and formally unrelated rules of deep transformations working together to produce a surface feature (or, vice versa, of several surface features having a common target in the base, pp. 25f.). Verbal position, in particular, lends itself to exploitation in this manner, because it is also a formal constraint existing in almost total isolation from meaning and style if we take the chief feature of second position in independent clauses (*V/2 Constraint* — pp. 9–11). He proposes to demonstrate that the surface structure constraint that requires the presence of subject pronouns in clauses of Perlmutter's 1968 Type-A languages is a consequence of the *V/2* Constraint and that the latter is a diachronic precondition to the former: Only *V/2* languages can become in due time Type-A languages. Since the process turns out to be essentially the same in all Type-A languages, its one basic principle can be seen as a mechanism of linguistic change. Furthermore, the study will show that even in a strictly formal domain syntax and semantics reveal themselves as ultimately inseparable (p. 12).

Haiman concentrates on the special type of *V/2* represented by the *es*-construct because this construct is made particularly fruitful to the analyst by its being, differently from the other types, heavily constrained. "Dummy *es*" constructs are taken as proof of the *V/2* Constraint. The rule is so phrased by Beneš 1962:8: "This particle (even though it may be more or less semantically colored) functions only as an introductory element or 'filler'; it occurs as a place-holder, in order to allow the finite verb to occur as the first communicative element, without thereby destroying its grammatical second position." Confirmation: When the (first) place of *es* is taken by another element it must disappear from the sentence altogether; hence dummy *es* is never found in questions (where the verb *can* have first position); similarly, dummy *es* is never found in subordinate clauses (pp. 19–20). In other words, its only function is to satisfy the *V/2* Constraint. Since these same constraints apply, for example, to *es*-insertion in impersonal passives (*es wird gefoltert* [*in Brasilien*] 'torture is practiced in Brasil' but only *in Brasilien wird gefoltert*, not *in Brasilien wird* [**es*] *gefoltert*), one can conclude that the transformational rule of *es*-insertion is constrained in at least two ways: It can apply only in those clauses where the V/2 Constraint holds, and it must be ordered *after* rules that front or pre-pose constituents in the sentence (p. 23).

Fronting (pp. 39f.) is essentially of two kinds, the first one carrying emphasis or prominence (*Ihm werde ich kein Geld pumpen* 'to him I will [surely] lend no money'), while the second is *resumptive,* since topicalization is a way of referring back to a relevant antecedent (*Da öffnete sich ein zweites Tor* 'Then a second door opened').

Haiman concludes (p. 49) that German is a VSO language because the hypothesis of a VSO underlying structure provides the most efficient or simplest base from which to derive *ZV* . . . and *esV* . . . sentences, while holding firm that the V/2 Constraint is a target ($Z = $ a constituent other than the subject). The passage from base VSO to surface SVO would be dominated by the Fronting Rule (p. 43) — Haiman's version of McCawley's hypothesis — in consequence of which the canonical order will be SVO simply because in most cases, that is in unmarked constructs, the subject as the most common topic will be the element to be fronted. *Es*-sentences will then be those in which fronting has simply failed to occur (ibid., but see the difficulties p. 113).

In I.3 (pp. 63ff.) Haiman attempts to demonstrate that the V/2 Constraint, now shared by all Germanic languages, also was once (though not rigidly) common to Old English too, whereas Modern English is now the only exception. Nor is it limited to the Germanic group: It extended once to medieval French and still controls modern Romansh. Yet Haiman strives to make a case for the Germanic origin of this feature in Old French and Romansh through direct influence (pp. 69f.). One further qualification is, however, in order: Within the Germanic group two more languages appear to have been exempted from the V/2 Constraint, namely Gothic and Old Icelandic (pp. 92f.).

The remainder of this penetrating study is a complex discussion of the target-nature of the V/2 Constraint conducted on the basis of the final theoretical outcome of the ambiguous situation whereby *es*-insertion in Old German was required only of impersonal verbal predicates, not of impersonal adjectival and nominal predicates (pp.

102–104): Cf. *es donnert* 'it thunders' but Old High German *iz abandet* versus New High German *es wird Abend*, both translating Latin *vesperascit* 'evening is coming.' Old High German has no (dummy) subject here; nor did it need one in *Ube tag ist, licht ist* 'When it is day, it is light' or *So heiz wird zi sumere* 'It gets so hot in the summers,' where an element other than the subject happens to be fronted and, once again, the impersonal is a nonverbal predicate. Now Modern German can behave likewise in such cases, or more precisely it offers an optional *es*-insertion (when the dummy pronoun is not required by the V/2 target): Cf. *Es wird bald Sommer* but *Bald wird (es) Sommer*; *Es ist Essenszeit* but *Nun ist (es) Essenszeit*.

3d. TYPOLOGICAL SYNTAX

A relevant segment of the most recent work on German word order has appeared under the heading of the typological approach, especially at the hand of two Germanists, **Winfred P. Lehmann** and **Theo Vennemann**. Although criticism has been directed from several quarters both at their specific assumptions and at the general implications of their method, they deserve our detailed attention because they offer the most articulate and systematic study of word order, especially German, to this date.

A central feature of this typological work is the close relationship it posits between morphology and syntax, specifically between inflection and ordering. We have seen the earliest hypotheses on such possible relationships in scholars of the eighteenth and nineteenth centuries, and we have noted O. Jespersen's and E. Richter's position on the matter. We must now enter another early authority before proceeding any further.

In the seventh chapter of **Edward Sapir**'s *Language* (1921), while speculating on the meaning of the gradual replacement of Modern English *whom* by *who*, the great pioneer of modern linguistics postulated a theory of language "drifts," which he found to be essentially threefold: (1) The trend toward elimination of case markings, and specifically of the distinction between the subjective and the objective (subject and object cases); (2) the tendency toward fixed position in sentence parts; and (3) the drift toward invariable words. In praising Sapir for having correctly identified these fundamental phenomena and postulated a causal relationship between them, Theo Vennemann 1975 feels compelled to underline the weakness whereby Sapir was unable to carry his discovery to its logical consequences.[66] First of all, even while Sapir attributed the loss of case markings to their being "nibbled away by phonetic processes . . . ," these being manifestations of "the old drift toward reducing final syllables, a rhythmic consequence of the strong Germanic stress on the first syllable" (*Language*, pp. 164, 175, 181), he failed to see how this phonetic "reduction" occurs in all languages, not just the Germanic ones; and furthermore, he remained skeptical as to the true impact of phonetic change on syntax, so that he failed to establish a relationship of cause and effect between his two first "drifts," loss of cases and stabilization of word order. Finally, precisely as he could not see the universal import of his observations (these drifts being of a general nature, and not simply language-specific to English), he also neglected to pinpoint the exact nature of that fixed order, to wit, an order of SVO, so that we get one last drift to be formulated, namely the shift from SOV to SVO, from Indo-European through Old English to Modern English.

Charles C. Fries 1940 and Robin Lakoff 1972 have attempted to carry out Sapir's intuitions in ways that, in Vennemann's opinion, mark more a regression than true progress.[67] In particular, R. Lakoff completely ignores Jespersen's and especially Richter's hypotheses, with the result that she declares insoluble and unanalyzable the crucial points (signally, the causal relationship of case loss to fixation of order) that both Richter and, although with excessive caution, Sapir had clearly posited.

At the date of this paper (1975), Vennemann, a German-born, American-trained linguist now at Munich, had already formulated, although only in a cluster of still scattered papers, his own paradigm for our subject. He claimed that his system was both descriptive and "philosophical," in the sense that it explains what it describes, assigning reasons and causes. The thinking of Vennemann and his collaborator Renate Bartsch (formerly of Berlin, now at Amsterdam) is to be understood against the background of their critique and revision of Chomskian transformational grammar, toward what they designate as "natural generative grammar." The critique is based on the charge that the transformationalists have misunderstood deep structure as being linearly ordered, hence they have neglected the basic semantic value of word order in the surface structure.[68] Vennemann begins by pointing

152 ☐ MODERN THEORY AND NINETEENTH-CENTURY BACKGROUND

out that "phonetic representations . . . must model the linear unidirectional flow of speech in time. It follows from this that each grammar needs at least these two kinds of rules: lexicalization rules which introduce elements that can be converted into physical signals, and serialization rules which arrange these elements in linear order interpretable as temporal order." "The problem of grammar is that it relates structures which are hierarchical (semantic structures) to structures which are non-hierarchical (phonetic representations)."[69]

Vennemann addresses himself next to the question: "Why do some languages have grammatically functional word order while others do not?" (p. 24) — which is complemented by the other: "Why do languages with grammatically functional word order have the kinds of word order that they do?" (p. 47).[70] And he notes that "grammatical relations can be expressed either by morphology with no reliance on word order (as in Latin and Sanskrit) or by word order (as in Chinese) or by both (as in German and English, German relying more on morphology than English, which relies almost entirely on word order)" (p. 24). To exemplify, "*Roderich seduced Erdmuthe* means what it means only with the linear order in which the words occur in it," whereas "*Rodericus Erdmutham seduxit* means what it means with any one of the six word orders" (ibid.). (We could then conclude, I should say, that Latin is "naturally" an SOV language, stylistically *de facto* a FWO [free word order] language.) A subtle example is the distinction between de-adjectival manner adverbs (referring specifically to the verb) and de-adjectival sentence adverbs (investing the whole clause), which German tends to achieve by marking the latter with -*er* + *weise*, whereas English can achieve this distinction simply by word order: See *Mary sang "America the Beautiful" strangely* versus *Strangely Mary sang "America the Beautiful"*; compare with *Seltsam sang Maria "America the Beautiful"* versus *Seltsamerweise sang Maria "America the Beautiful"* (ibid.).[71]

The failure of transformational grammar to appreciate and accommodate this traditional and simple insight that morphology and word order are alternative devices for expressing semantic relations on the surface is aptly criticized in Bever and Langendoen 1972. Transformational grammar had to ignore it because one basic assumption of this model of grammar is incompatible with it: the assumption that deep structures (both of Chomsky's model and of generative semantics) are linearly ordered. Assume that deep structures are ordered. An earlier stage of

MODERN THEORY AND NINETEENTH-CENTURY BACKGROUND □ 153

English (Proto-Indo-European and, to a lesser extent, Old English) marked grammatical relations morphologically rather than by word order. (Word order was "free," i.e., not used to express basic grammatical functions, but to express stylistic or discourse functions such as topicalization.) Old English thus had a rich set of morphological rules, plus a set of "scrambling rules"[72] to undo the linear order of the deep structures. Modern English has a very rigid word order and very little morphology. Historically speaking, it has lost most of its morphological rules and almost all of its scrambling rules. . . . A transformational grammarian must conclude that English has become simpler, because fewer rules (hence, fewer symbols) are needed to describe it (viz. no rules to express the basic grammatical functions where Old English had the morphological rules . . .). The conclusion that English has become simpler cannot, of course, be accepted. Languages, if anything, are evolving toward greater rather than lesser complexity. . . . Languages develop cyclically from "morphology with few grammatically functional word order rules" to "word order with few morphological rules" and back again, with sound change being the causal factor throughout (p. 25).

In this manner we enter the area of Vennemann's comparative theory of linguistic evolution and genetic linguistics, whereby he will arrive at a universal scheme showing the genetic relationship between different but related languages. He bases the shifts from one type to another on the impact of phonetic change. "First sound change grinds off the morphology and thus forces the grammar to respond by substituting word order rules in order to counter the threat of ambiguity. Next sound change degrades the positionally fixed independent function words of the language into a new morphology, which makes the word order rules redundant and leads to their loss. And so on indefinitely" (ibid.). This latter sound change would reproduce in a new way the once lost morphological markers, presumably by processes similar to the combination of preposition and noun. I should add here that an aspect of this phenomenon might be seen, for example, in the formation of Latin *illico* from *in loco*, or *tecum* for *cum te*, Spanish *con tigo*, Italian *teco*, and Medieval Latin metrically limited *vereórte* or *melíorme*.[73]

Vennemann had offered (p. 40 in Kimball) a diagram of language change that he later felt compelled to replace with one that, besides eliminating the still little understood phase of FWO, also inserts an intermediary phase (TVX before SVX, where T = topic) and replaces

O with the more general X (= "everything else," to wit, all complements of the verb including and starting with the object).[74] Whereas the older diagram was clearly unworkable, since it did not allow a number of drifts that are definitely documented, particularly in the evolution from Latin to Romance, the new one remains highly conjectural, and leaves completely aside the very natural patterns SOV → FWO and FWO → SVO.[75] It does, nevertheless, deserve attention as a start toward further exploration:

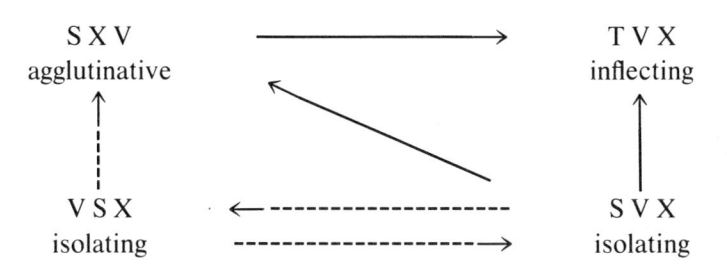

```
    S X V         ───────────→        T V X
 agglutinative   ←───                inflecting
     ↑                  ╲               ↑
     ┊                    ╲             │
     ┊                      ╲           │
    V S X        ←----------------     S V X
   isolating     ---------------→     isolating
```

For an answer to the question, How and why does the evolution occur?, we must turn to the fundamental syntactic principles that govern the linear surface ordering, out of the deep simultaneity of the elements, spacially and temporally. We start with the Principle of Ambiguity Avoidance or Disambiguation Principle, which contains two special series of cases to be subsumed under the headings of Principle of Natural Serialization and Principle of Natural Constituent Structure (p. 26). The former holds that "the natural way of serializing the operator-operand relationship of all complex expressions is from right to left in OV languages, and from left to right in VO languages."[76] One must, of course, keep in mind that the argument or topic, i.e., the subject, normally precedes the rheme or predicate in all languages (except VSO), and that the model or basic pattern of a given language hinges on the position of the object vis-à-vis the verb. Serialization thus means unidirectionality in arrangement of elements that must go together by the Principle of Natural Constituent Structure: The basic relationship between an operator and an operand, namely, a qualifier, modifier, determinant, or governor and their targets, must be arranged consistently either as operator → operand or operand → operator (pp. 40–41).

For further elucidation we may turn to Greenberg's Universal 7: "If in a language with dominant SOV order there is no alternative basic order, or only OSV as an alternative, then all adverbial modifiers of the verb likewise precede the verb. (This is the 'rigid' sub-type of SOV.)" But since German is not in this class (OVS is the alternative), it consequently mixes the operator ↔ operand patterns. Conversely, "The left-to-right order tends to be employed by SVO and VSO languages, including English" (Vennemann in Kimball, p. 42).

Winfred P. Lehmann recently has recapped his and other linguists' researches on the matter by showing how in "consistent" OV languages descriptive adjectives and genitives precede their head nouns; complements and relative clauses precede their governing (main) verbs; in the comparative nexus, the standard precedes the pivot, which in turn is followed by the adjective; and the cases are marked by suffixes or postpositional particles rather than prepositions or prefixes. Consistent VO languages (both SVO and VSO) tend to do exactly the opposite. Variants may be due to affective (emphatic) pressures, as in French *une étroite amitié* — or, we could add, Latin *Romanus sum civis*, including the particular sense of national pride underlined by Marouzeau.[77] This ordering pattern also extends somehow to dependent clauses vis-à-vis main clauses, as in Muršilis's (Hittite, an OV language): "That a scape-bull should be given, that it should be burned with fire, that birds were to be offered, was determined." Lehmann offers the basic explanation whereby at a very early stage of language learning the child acquires the transformational habit of always placing the governor before its target (VO) or after (OV).[78]

We are now ready for Vennemann's explanation of the reason that only the first three of Greenberg's orders (SVO, SOV, VSO, VOS, OSV, and OVS) obtain in fact. "In unaffected speech, the subject represents the topic of a sentence, and the object is part of the comment (or what is predicated of the subject). The topic is what the speaker is going to make a predication about; he will naturally introduce it first" (pp. 27–8).

This corresponds, we might want to add, to the general point of view affirmed by the Prague structuralists and most recently by Roman Jakobson, who speaks of order being "iconic" in the sense that it represents the hierarchy of grammatical concepts: "Si le seul ordre — ou du moins l'ordre fondamental prédominant — dans les phrases énonciatives comportant un sujet et un objet nominaux — est un ordre

156 ☐ MODERN THEORY AND NINETEENTH-CENTURY BACKGROUND

dans lequel celui-là précède celui-ci, il est évident que ce procédé grammatical reflète la hiérarchie des concepts grammaticaux. . . . C'est le sujet, seul terme indépendant de la proposition, qui met en évidence ce à quoi s'applique le message."[79] Hierarchy then means: More important first. This, we can interject, was the most commonly identified principle of word order in classical grammar: Cf. Quintilian's examples of *naturalis ordo*, whereby the chronologically prior usually precedes, as does the more important: "*viros ac feminas, diem ac noctem . . . dicas potius*"; "*quia interim plus valent ante gesta, ideoque levioribus superponenda sunt.*"[80] Again, Jakobson: "L'ordre temporel des procès d'énonciation tend à refléter l'ordre des procès d'énoncé, qu'il s'agisse d'un ordre dans la durée ou d'un ordre selon le rang."[81] See also his earlier phrasing of the matter: "The nearly universal precedence of the subject with regard to the object, at least in unmarked constructions, points to a hierarchy in focusing."[82]

Universal 41 states that "If in a language the verb follows both the nominal subject and the nominal object as the dominant order, the language almost always has a case system." Vennemann then proposes, "as a tentative conclusion, that in SVO languages it is the placement of the verb between S and O which is the syntactic device separating S and O" (p. 29) — in the absence, of course, of a case system.

If this conclusion is correct, then it is correct to say that SOV represents the sentence pattern with the natural verb position because in this type the verb has only the semantic function of specifying the relation of the comment O to the topic S, while in SVO languages the verb has the additional syntactic function of separating S and O (pp. 29–30). There is, fortunately, further support for this conclusion. In Old English, the sentence pattern is, roughly, SOV for dependent clauses and SVO for independent clauses. Proto-Indo-European had SOV, with many free word order possibilities because of its rich inflections,[83] and contemporary English has SVO in both clause types. English thus changed SOV to SVO first in main clauses, and only subsequently in dependent clauses. Contemporary German represents the same syntactic type as Old English. Let us boldly conclude that when languages change from SOV to SVO, they do this first in independent clauses and only subsequently in dependent clauses. Why should this be so? The topic-comment relationship plays an important role only in main clauses, not in dependent clauses (p. 30).

Rather typically, although somewhat peculiarly in the case of German, "English preposes *concerning* and German postposes the semantically equivalent *betreffend*, because both adpositions derive from present participles, i.e., from verbs" (p. 31). This is a consequence of the verb following the head noun in German dependent clauses, since the adverbial phrase with *betreffend* is a derivative of a dependent clause.

"SOV languages have the finite verb at the end. If there are modals or auxiliaries, they will be finite and thus follow the nominalized main verb (i.e., infinitive or participle). In an SVO language, it is the other way around" (p. 34). Cf. *(daß) Hans Maria gebracht hat* but *(that) John has brought Mary.* Universal 16 tells us, furthermore, that "In languages with dominant order VSO, an inflected auxiliary always precedes the main verb. In languages with dominant order SOV, an inflected auxiliary always follows the main verb." Vennemann concludes that "VSO languages are 'old' SVO languages because they have invariably completed the V-Aux inversion" (ibid.). Examples of the rule for SOV German: *(daß) Hans es gebracht haben muß* versus *(that) John must have brought it* (p. 43).[84]

Lehmann has added a number of particulars that confirm Vennemann's analysis. In a 1971 paper topically concerned with the rise (or perhaps, more generally, regularization) of some SOV features in New High German, he points out that, since genitives and adjectives derive from relative constructions, like these they tend to follow their head noun in VO languages, to precede it in OV languages.[85] Furthermore, VO languages have prepositions, OV languages postpositions. This is because, like verbs, prepositions and postpositions govern objects. "Both verbs and noun-governing particles may therefore be expected to occupy the same position with regard to their object" (p. 20). Turkish or Japanese, consistently SOV, have only postpositions, while Arabic, consistently VSO, or Spanish, consistently SVO, have only prepositions. Latin (ambiguous) had prepositions in general, but they were late as a syntactic class. *A porta abiit* came from *portā ab iit*. Cf. *anno post* . . . (ibid.). Now "from the beginning of the early NHG period, a number of particles have developed which are used as postpositions: *entgegen, entlang, gegenüber, gemäß, halber, nach, wegen, zufolge, zuwider.* . . . " We could add *voraus: seinem Jahrhundert voraus* "in advance of his century." And I also want to add that even nominal phrases can be constructed postpositionally in relation to their governed terms: See *aller revolutionären Emphase zum Troz* 'in spite of all revolutionary emphasis.'

German is inconsistently SVO, for its attributive adjective precedes the noun, *ein reicher Mann*, and AN patterns are characteristically SOV (p. 22). "AN has become more prominent in contemporary German than it was in MHG." See Middle High German *der künec guot*, Goethe's *Röslein rot* (poetic), *Karl der Grosse*. "By the medieval period, German was comparable to the Romance languages of the time in exhibiting SVO characteristics. But subsequently, with the fixing of subordinating word order in which verbs are final, German has introduced a remarkable number of SOV characteristics" (p. 23).

Proto-Indo-European had no prefixes, yet all derived languages have them; they also have prepositions, comparative constructions reversing the order *te maior*, and postposed relative clauses (contrary to Hittite "Whoever is a son of second rank, he shall become king" — p. 23).

The classification of such a complex and contradictory case as that of German is an important test. If we are correct in considering Latin a basically SOV language, like its parent Proto-Indo-European, shall we also place German alongside Latin as still essentially close to its origin? Concomitantly, how must we project the trend of its future development? Vennemann, as he has more specifically pointed out in 1971,[86] claims that "transformational grammar makes the wrong prediction when it assumes for German the deep structure order of an SOV language, plus a transformation moving the finite verb to the second position in main clauses. This is the simplest analysis, but it characterizes German as a syntactically simple language, which it is not. And it makes the incorrect prediction that German may revert to a pure SOV language by losing that one movement transformation. Natural generative grammar assumes German to be an SVO language with very many complicated rules arranging all constituents in an unnatural order. The theory predicts that German will develop into a pure SVO language by replacing its unnatural serialization rules with natural ones" (pp. 46–77) (natural in the sense of corresponding to its basic language type). The problem with German (and foreign learners, we can interject, are therefore correct in finding it difficult) is that it "has a very bad syntactic system due to its incomplete shift from SOV to SVO. The finite verb has shifted in main clauses, but not in dependent clauses" (pp. 30 and 46). "The order of all other constituents is still that of an SOV language: adverbials are serialized from right to left (in English, from left to right)" — cf. *die für die Milchversorgung verantwortliche Behörde* versus *the personnel responsible for the delivery of milk*; "verbs serialized from right to left (in English, from left to right); direct and indirect objects are serialized from right to left (in English, from left to right in *John gave the book to Mary*, with *John gave Mary the book* still available from old SOV days).[87] All these concomitants of the SOV pattern are perfect for dependent clauses, but for the main clauses they are all 'bad.' Since the verb position of the main clause pattern is basic (it is 'unmarked': most frequent, learned earliest by children, etc.), Bartsch's principles predict that . . . , in short, German must undergo similar syntactic development in the future as English has in the last 1500 years" (p. 46).

All this well explains the peculiar "difficulties" of German. Germans themselves began to be acutely conscious of such "irregularities" in the late seventeenth century, mainly in the wake of the French grammarians' criticisms of German literary style as awkwardly complicated, unnecessarily involved, and ultimately irrational. Yet there was little that the Germans could do about it beyond trying to bring into their habits at least some regularity and consistency — which is the story of the stylistic literary process going on in eighteenth-century German writing.

On the basis of their conviction that the principles of natural constituent structure and natural serialization "have predictive power for language change," and that "they explain many of the word order changes that follow the basic verb shift which is at the heart of all syntactic type changes," Bartsch and Vennemann offer the example of what is going on in Contemporary German as a "very transparent" test of the above observations.[88]

To return to the general diagram, Proto-Indo-European, as an SOV language, produced a number of SVO languages, which then could evolve only into FWO or, eventually, VSO languages. Now "Proto-Indo-European is a 'very old' SOV language coming ultimately from an 'old' VSO language, because it has S-V agreement after the verb root and inflectional case marking after the noun root" (p. 37). Furthermore, "VSO languages always develop from SVO languages." "Adjectives, as modifiers on nouns, tend to precede the head noun in

SOV languages but to follow in SVO languages. Let us assume that a 'consistent' SOV language . . . has AN (adjective-noun) as the only pattern. As an SOV language changes to SVO [as Latin changed to Romance], the tendency will be to change AN to NA. This tendency does not seem particularly strong because English still has the adjective before the noun even though its change to SVO began more than 1200 years ago'' (p. 32).

Elsewhere Vennemann raises, though rather summarily, a point that in the light of the preceding historical survey deserves further stressing. The customary way for a language to strengthen its hypotactic aptitudes is to develop its conjunction system. Germany, under the influence of humanistic "Ciceronian" Latin (and Italian) and the particular keenness of its administrative classes to develop a hypotactic *Beamtensprache*, went further than any other country in evolving a taste for the periodic style, even in the over-structured and complicated *Kanzleistil*. Oddly enough, however, it was unable to create a clear enough system of subordinating particles. Under these circumstances, word order was called upon to fill an additional role, that of marking subordination by applying an effective double standard, that is, by introducing a clear separation in word order structure between main and dependent clauses.

Thus it is typical of German that so many particles are at the same time coordinating and subordinating conjunctions, prepositions, and sometimes also adverbs, often not without some degree of confusion. Think of *weil* (now weakening in colloquial speech, always weak in dialects), *obwohl-obgleich* now disappearing, *da, denn, während, trotzdem* (for example, *Maria nahm die Pille, trotzdem sie schwanger war* — where *trotzdem* is a subordinating conjunction meaning 'even though' and carrying XV construction — versus *Maria nahm die Pille, trotzdem war sie schwanger*, where *trotzdem* is adverbial-coordinating, meaning 'nevertheless' and carrying VX construction [examples supplied verbally by Vennemann]). And one should add that the plurivalence of *der, die, das* — articles, adjectives, and relative pronouns — points up the weak morphological distinctions in a syntactical direction, as also did the ancient use of *so* as a relative pronoun.

I was referring above to some of the difficulties of German. Here is another one to which Vennemann has not jet addressed himself explicitly. Why has the inversion Verb-Subject become necessary when the Object (Complement, Adverb) is placed first? (We have seen how this compulsory inversion has been judged, e.g. by Albert Dauzat, as an index of the "impressive" nature of German.)[89] After all, other languages, notably Italian or Spanish, even in the complete absence of case markings, can antepose complements without prejudice of the normal order in the remainder of the clause, or at least without entailing compulsory inversion. This impulse to invert is present in Contemporary English, but weak. The answer could be that the evolution of German toward SVO status has overcome the lingering presence of cases, however reduced and weakened, by inculcating an unusually strong need of the verb as a syntactic marker of separation between S and O in the main clauses. This explanation would appear acceptable if one regards the inversion brought about by anteposition of O (*Das glaube ich nicht* — a pattern equally strong in the dialects: Cf. Viennese *des glaub i net*) as the model for all other antepositions. More important, however, we must see here a peculiarity of the Germanic group, most clearly felt in German itself, whereby the truly central feature of the clause is not the interrelationship and order of S, O, V, but the position of the verb alone. We have seen how realization of this feature evolved in modern linguistic research.

To conclude with a quick summary of most relevant points: In the absence of a case system, in SVO languages a nonmorphological device is needed to mark the distinction between S and O; this device, which can only be syntactic, is the separation of S from O by the placement of V in between.[90] The shift from SOV to SVO thus represents "an emergency measure to separate S and O" — a separation that is made semantically necessary once their sequence has become morphologically unclear, hence ambiguous, in consequence of phonetic grinding off of the case endings. German has the most complicated word order rule system because, of all the Indo-European languages, it is the typologically most mixed.

Word order is essentially a feature of style in free order languages, whereas in SVO languages it is essentially and firstly syntactic, hence semantic. By underlining the stylistic nature of word order in FWO languages we revert to the classical vantage point, at least insofar as Greek and Latin can be still regarded as FWO, and we confirm the validity of that classical system which had precisely placed the matter of word order, as part of *synthesis* or *compositio*, not within grammar or linguistics but within rhetoric or stylistics.[91]

Indeed, a new perspective has been opened up for the study of poetic discourse, if we only keep in mind the observation that inversion has traditionally been a basic feature of poetic language at all times and places — a principle first systematically, and drastically, stated in 1717 by Jean-Antoine Du Cerceau, for whom rhyme, rhythm, and verse are nothing but the "mechanical form" of poetic style, whereas the arrangement of words, in which inversion plays the most typical role, is its "internal form" and "objective criterion."[92]

In taking up Sapir's notions on "drift," and in the context of her generative-semantic approach, Robin Lakoff 1972 had expressed skepticism as to a causal relationship between phonological change and loss of case endings — hence between the latter and the development of the "segmented" or analytic order, or between the suffixional and the prepositional order (pp. 280, 284). We have seen how Jespersen could envisage the opposite causal movement and how then Elise Richter started the approach that is paralleled by the Vennemann hypothesis. Somewhat similarly to Lakoff, Larry M. Hyman 1975[93] objects to Vennemann's proposed explanation of syntactic change through disambiguation and topicalization, on the ground that: "First, there are SOV languages which have no trace of case markings on nouns — and which have never had any. The Niger-Congo family, which in its proto days was SOV, is a case in point, with present day Ịjọ having retained the SOV order of the proto language. Second, there are many languages which have already imposed fairly rigid word orders, but which have not lost their case markings, e.g., Russian. In particular, there seems to be evidence that the rigidification [i.e., fixation] of an SVO word order in many languages temporally precedes at least the major case levellings. This should not be surprising, since case markings do not drop overnight — they weaken gradually through time" (p. 117). Hyman mentions W. P. Lehman for the suggestion that word order change also comes through contact with a neighboring language (pp. 115–6).[94]

Vennemann 1975 agrees with the criticism that his 1973 papers (Kimball, Prague, Edinburgh)[95] lacked one essential step in the explanation of the shift from XV to VX, namely, as to how speakers go about organizing their sentences in the course of that transition (p. 289). He accepts Larry Hyman's suggestion (in Li) that the mechanism consists in the grammaticalization of afterthought patterns. Since, however, some consistent XV languages use afterthought syntax very sparingly (*vide* Japanese, where it is common only in oral usage), how does "afterthought" become so important in changing some other languages from XV to VX? He had tried to answer this in 1974 (in an unpublished paper, "Exbraciation as a Mechanism of Word Order Change"). Essentially (Vennemann 1975, p. 289), take the case of *weil Hans Maria Peter Paul vorzustellen bat*, 'because John asked Mary to introduce Peter to Paul.' The XV principle of complements preceding their head nouns produces here an extreme case of ambiguity, since recognition of relationships has become too difficult (pp. 289–90). In other words, *Peter* must be the direct object (A or accusative) and *Paul* the indirect object (D or dative), yet the XV pattern of this dependent clause would call for DA order, not AD: Cf. *to give Mary the book*, where XV (for English, archaic) produces DA or iO → dO.

Vennemann, "Topics, Subject, and Word Order," in Anderson and Jones, especially pp. 362–5, has further developed the *Satzklammer* notion (sentence brace construction) and pointed out that the *Nachtrag* effect, also studied by others, indicates ongoing drift toward consistent VX order. He exemplifies the mirror image relation between XV and VX patterns thus:

Hans | muß | gestern | auf dem Balkon | seinen neuen Freunden |
0   1   7   6   5
das Buch | gegeben | haben;
4   3   2
John | must | have | given | the book | to his new friends |
0   1   2   3   4   5
on the balcony | yesterday.
6   7

During the transitional phase between SXV and SVX, word order has not yet taken over the function of case-endings and these latter have already begun to lose their effectiveness through phonetic grinding. In German the drift could begin to take place, not surprisingly, even while the case system remained relatively strong (as in Old High German and Middle High German), yet it had lost much of its operative quality through the weakening of stress in the final syllables and the change in intonation patterns.

Susumu Kuno 1974[96] shows that "because of perceptual difficulties inherent in center-embedding, a consistent verb-final language tends to place subordinate clauses, and noun phrases with subordinate clauses, at the beginning of the sentence." There result some patterns that seem to contravene the basic unidirectional flow of constituents, so that at times, to avoid ambiguity, subordinate clauses and especially relatives will follow their head nouns and verbs rather than preceding them.

Vennemann 1975 (p. 297) further states that "The change from XV to VX is universally accompanied by a change from agglutination to flexion to isolation. The explanation follows from (1) and (7): In a consistent XV language, prefixes are operators on their stems, and stems are operators on their suffixes." By the principle of natural serialization these patterns will be reversed in the VX stage. "The period of isolation is merely one of transition: The stage is set for a new system of agglutination, prepositive if it develops in the VX stage, postpositive after a change to XV." And (p. 298) "The basic order of Verb, Direct Object, and Indirect Object in consistent languages is IDV or VDI, according to the principle of natural serialization. Shifting to VX order changes IDV to the inconsistent VID.[97] A new prepositional pI develops, serialized as VDpI, in conformity with the principle. ID order lingers for awhile, most commonly used for topical I, in accordance with Behaghel's Second Law." In other words, English *I gave Jane the book* is "unnatural," archaic as compared with the "consistent" *I gave the book to Jane*, the more modern or later phase. And, again (pp. 300–1): "The development of adverbs with postpositive *-mente* is, together with the postpositive future and conditional morphology from forms of *habere* 'have,' the last creation of XV character of a language well on its way to VX."[98]

Pattern formulas can be streamlined by omitting the subject (S) and subsuming all complements under X (= "everything else"), which includes O. Indeed, Lehmann 1973[99] had begun to offer a simplification of Greenberg's classification by reducing it to a typology of VO versus OV (with implied primacy of verb phrase over noun phrase), a rubric roughly involving a Modifier/Modified parameter. Arthur Schwartz 1975[100] attributes to this reduction the collapse of SVO and VSO types, "a conflation which seems desirable in view of the number of characteristics shared by these systems (e.g., prepositions, WH-fronting, auxiliary before the main verb, etc.) and the current depreciation of the notion 'grammatical subject.'" He then adds a reminder that data have now become available on the relatively infrequent but still, despite

MODERN THEORY AND NINETEENTH-CENTURY BACKGROUND □ 165

Greenberg, extant, VOS system ("Subject-Final"), and goes on to show that Spanish, for example, not only could be regarded as ambiguously bordering between SVO and VSO, but also offers numerous cases of VOS possibilities.[101]

This last remark raises the important question of the extent to which the Romance languages, specifically Spanish and Italian, can be regarded as fitting a specific pattern "consistently." Italian, for one, does display a dominant SVX type, but Old Italian showed clear traces of SXV origins. Cf. the patterns Nominal Verb + Auxiliary and the further evolved Aux . . . X . . . Participle, successively, in *rispose che cenato aveva* and *m'aveva di paura il cor compunto* (Dante); likewise, XV in the proverb *Cosa fatta capo ha*; often with free exbraciation and hyperbaton, as in *refutar lu* volio *presente* but alongside voliote *pregare* (*Ritmo di S. Alessio*, vv. 233 and 168; *avereme non* puoi *in tua podesta* (Cielo d'Alcamo, *Contrasto*, 149).[102] In Contemporary Italian XV is still documented, even though it may be literary-flavored: *Brevi fantasie come quelle da Francesco Lanza raccolte e ricreate* (Leonardo Sciascia, *Il mare colore del vino*, 1973, p. 10).

Furthermore, see the pattern VS, [SOnVAux], nV in *non pensando gli Amidei di ciò che loro offeso avea curarsi* (Bandello I, 1).[103] End-position for the verb (but with all sorts of possible variations, including separation of the auxiliary and afterthoughts) is so common in literary Italian, at least from Boccaccio until the eighteenth century, that at times it becomes almost a conspicuous (and notorious) rule: *Conchiusero . . . che così vituperosa macchia non si poteva che non con l'istesso sangue del nemico . . . lavare* (ibid.); *che dodici botte erano quel giorno a li giostranti per guadagnar il premio ordinate, e chi prima le faceva senza impedimento alcuno il premio ne portava.*

In Old Italian XV is felt as a relatively more grave and dignified rhythm than VX, hence as an element of high style. Boccaccio uses it in the graver sections of his *Decameron* (see, for example, the Introduction), while he uses ostensibly more often the VX order in "comic" direct speech (see the Calandrino stories). Although there is no steadfast rule — because the main point is the desire to imitate the free-order aspect of Latin through hyperbata (such as Dante's *io non avea la mia donna veduta*) — main clauses, as in German, carry VX more often than secondary ones, where XV tends to be the rule. Hyperbata may disrupt the more conspicuous rhythm of one or the other pattern by inserting other elements between the various parts of a verb (*non avea l'amico tentato* — a case of imbedding that produces a limited *Satzklammer*), but as opposed to German, the modal and auxiliary tend to precede the infinitive or participle at all times.

As to modern Italian, take the following examples from Pirandello:[104] "La macchina è fatta . . . , ha bisogno d'ingoiarsi la nostra *anima*, di divorar la nostra *vita*. E come volete che *ce le ridiano, l'anima e la vita*, in produzione centuplicata e continua, le macchine?" (p. 1050); "Ma l'anima, a me, non mi serve. Mi serve la mano; cioè serve alla macchina. L'anima in pasto, in pasto la vita, dovete dargliela voi signori, alla macchinetta ch'io giro" (p. 1051). (Note the stylistic, nongrammatical chiasm.) An explanation is available through Condillac-Weil's 'train of thought' as *liaison des idées*, since the inversion is called for by the throwback to the previously mentioned topics *anima* and *vita*, which become the psychological subject even though they remain the grammatical object.

All in all, one must conclude that, through the centuries, Italian has behaved in many respects as a very free language with regard to word order, at least in its literary usage. And, of course, Italian shares with all other Romance languages and many others from other groups the need to throw weak atonic pronouns (proclitic) to the left of the verb (German tends to throw the reflexive *sich* to the left of everything else): Cf. French *je le vois*; Italian *lo vedo*; Portuguese *não me procura, quem me procura?* 'he is not looking for me,' 'who is looking for me?'; Rhetian *l'vez* 'I see it'; Rumanian *îl văd* 'I see it.'[105]

The bracing pattern of German is important to understand even from a general vantage point because, although it is typical of German in its uniquely elaborate and systematic form, it is to some extent characteristic of all languages that, like the Romance and Germanic groups, including English, have moved from SXV to SVX through the intermediate phase of TVX (T = topic). French shows bracing in the *ne* + V + *pas* pattern, Italian in such constructions as *Il Milanese rispose che cenato aveva*.[106] For English, see the *Look it up* and dat. + acc. construction, etc. Characteristic of the TVX phase is the different behavior of dependent clauses from main ones, extreme in German but also witnessed in Old English and Old Romance.[107]

To sum up: Indo-Germanic and Indo-European, like Sanskrit, Greek, and Latin, being sufficiently inflected, showed a strong tendency to place the predicate last and the object after the subject, although the strong autonomy afforded by a fully or almost fully functional flection allowed a high degree of FWO. Phonetic grinding voided the Latin flectional system, thus promoting the drift to SVO in Romance. The same phonetic grinding, aided and strengthened by the development of strong initial accent in the Germanic group, reduced and in part eliminated the case endings or rendered them unfunctional in that group also, thus encouraging the separation of S from O through the interposition of the verb. It could be added here that the flectional system of Old German was comparatively weak, so that a minimum degree of further weakening brought it close to being inoperative, hence to cause the shift to SVO. But in performing this shift, German did not manage to reverse the original basic movement from operators to operands, with a resulting coexistence of contradictory movements, each of them especially but not exclusively obtaining in the main or in the secondary clauses respectively. On the other hand, the persistence of the two orders, though contradictory, was made possible and indeed strengthened in the course of time by the need for formal markers of subordination, even while the need for periodic structures was increased by the prestigious examples of humanistic Latin. End-position of the verb thus became the syntactic marker of subordination, in a language that was singularly weak in clearly identifiable subordinating conjunctions, the only possible morphological markers.[108]

Should one object that Sanskrit as well as Latin and Old High German were essentially free in word order, not SOV, we can answer that this is only relatively true and only a relative distinction. Analysts generally have admitted that the strongest and clearest preference with regard to position in these languages was for verbal end position. In short, Vennemann has restated Delbrück's thesis with new arguments but also in a manner that raises new problems. For a problematic difference remains within this line of thinking with regard to the main cause of the drift, insofar as Vennemann's postulation of a change conditioned by loss of inflection cannot diachronically harmonize with Wackernagel's attribution of the same drift to questions of accent or intonation. Wackernagel (the chief source of Delbrück's arguments) was referring to essentially phonetic events that occurred many centuries before the morphological changes referred to by Vennemann — and the latter does not take account of the former. Supposing they are both right, we shall have to assume that the later morphologically based drift reinforced and generalized the earlier phonetically based one — and that the original end-position of the verb remaining in the dependent clause was then, in turn, reinforced by syntactic needs in conspiracy with Latin influence, if we also accept the seemingly valid part of Behaghel's thesis.

We might want to interject here that, if the criterion of natural serialization is acceptable as a basic principle of ordering, only two orders might appear to be natural and theoretically intelligible, as exemplified by *Paul gave a present to Mary* and **To Mary a present gave Paul*, to wit, SVX or XVS. Unfortunately, this latter is not documented as an existing common type by Greenberg. When Du Marsais postulated the former order as the only natural universal, he explained thereby not only the order of succession of nominal modifiers vis-à-vis their referents, but also that of subject and predicate. When Adelung tried to explain the principle of German serialization by reversing Du Marsais' order with his formula *unbestimmt → bestimmt*, he ran up against the difficulty of the SP sequence, which contradicts the order of other constituents in German, both in main and secondary clauses. Indeed, this aspect of the question of order still constitutes a major difficulty, since no linguistic system has yet satisfactorily explained the relationship between SP serialization and that of all other constituents. It is not to be hoped, at this stage, that some evidence can be found whereby XVS can be posited as the transformational point of departure of a number of positive languages.

Starting with Greenberg (who had moved with the aid and support of Roman Jakobson's advocacy of what he called "implicational universals")[109] and then on through Lehmann and Vennemann, we have followed the growth of a typological approach to syntax that seems to imply or explicitly to advocate the placing of word order patterns in the form of "ordering of meaningful elements," namely, some selected elements: S, O, V, and some special pairs: NA, NG, NC, relative pronouns + NP or VP, at the center of syntax. As we have noticed through this part of our survey, this school of thought, though widely cited, discussed, and sometimes accepted, has not been without its critics. I wish to consider here, because of their exemplary character, four direct attacks. They deserve some attention, if only as antidotes to possibly excessive expectations.

The first, **Wolfgang Klein**, "Eine Theorie der Wotstellungsveränderung" 1975,[110] is specifically a review article of some of Vennemann's earlier work. Klein focusses on some weaker aspects of Vennemann's exposition (e.g., diachronic documentation, topicalization and, especially, the "predictive" claims concerning allegedly undemonstrable drifts).

The second, **Calvert Watkins**, "Towards Proto-European Syntax: Problems and Pseudo-Problems" 1976, also voices strong, general demurrers against typology and language classification through basic word order. Without ever mentioning Vennemann, he directs his barbs at Lehmann for the manner in which he proceeds to claim OV order for Indo-European and, even more sharply, at Paul Friedrich, *Proto-Indo-European Syntax: The Order of Meaningful Elements*, 1975,[111] who, instead, argues for VO. For Watkins, Lehmann's problem is not that of siding with Delbrück and relying too heavily on him, as Friedrich claims, but, on the contrary, not heeding Delbrück's data closely enough — these data and the consequent claim of OV as the unmarked order of constituents in Proto-Indo-European being eminently correct, in Watkins's view (p. 308). One may agree with the specific strictures as to use of sources and methods of inference, and even with our not yet being ready for certain kinds of generalizations, but the central charge that typologists attempt to make phonology or "syntax coextensive or coterminous with word order" (pp. 306f.) seems to overshoot the mark. Vennemann, for one, clearly underscores that word order is one specific device of semantics or syntax, acting historically as a substitute for morphological markings when these disappear or become inoperative.

Another objection (by **P. Ramat**) against Vennemann relates to the historical circumstances of the shift to second position and to its function as a discriminating device between S and O (or S and X). As I have already stressed, this twofold assumption runs into the difficulty that Wackernagel's law shows this shift as dating from very early times within Indo-European, and when inflection could not be assumed to be weakening, hence to be a determining factor. Furthermore, the same law establishes rhythmic causes as sufficient ground for the shift (accent and enclisis), without any reference to morphology.[112] Another difficulty Ramat points out concerns the apparent contradiction between the SOV-type operator → operand movement evidenced by the "natural serialization" of Genitive + Noun and Adjective + Noun (*determinans* or *regens* + *determinatum* or *rectum*) and, on the other hand, the contrasting operand → operator sequence of Object + Predicate, since this latter is conceived as an operator on the former. It would seem that Vennemann leads to an impasse somewhat reminiscent of Fulda's and Adelung's predicament.[113]

Similarly, K.-P. Lange takes to task both Lehmann and Vennemann, focussing on the principle of natural serialization, which, he claims, was invented by Lehmann and then named by Vennemann (p. 14).[114] Both linguists assumed that for the purposes of typology it is more expedient to postulate, rather than Greenberg's three basic types (VSO, SOV, and SVO), two basic ones: OV and VO, because it is these two possibilities that correlate with the opposite choices of either operator → operand or operand → operator. However, notes Lange, neither linguist provides reasons for the verb's leading role in this latter choice.

Lange then goes on to propose a new principle of serializing operators, which would be based on a semiotic syntactic system of a kind unlike that of Chomsky's *Aspects* 1965 (= autonomous syntax, postulating an undefined mental capacity that organizes word order without regard to meaning), and more like Chomsky's original (1957) proposal of a semiotic set of meaning-creating transformations that control word order. The remainder of the paper is concerned with a tentatively formulated rule that "suffixed operator indicators require preposing of operators with respect to their operands, whereas prefixed operator indicators require postposing," as in *die heut-ig-e Jugend, die Jugend von heute, die Jugend heute*, etc. (pp. 19–22: -*e*, *von*, etc. are called operator indicators).

Nevertheless the typological approach continues to make headway, producing new affiliations. I shall mention a recent paper that provides information on attitudes prevailing in some far-away circles, **László Dezsö**, "Towards a Typology of Theme and Rheme: SOV Languages," 1978.[115] He begins by informing us about the work of the "Leningrad Group of Typology" and the "Cologne Project on Language Universals." His compact paper brings together the typological dimensions of a transformational search for relations between base and morphological structures, with rules of order being viewed from the angle of functional sentence perspective, conceived as a common term for both diathesis and theme-rheme rules. Invariant structures are said to be needed to derive the basic diatheses of active, passive, and impersonal as well as to form the various types of sentences. Such invariants "consist of a predicate, of obligatory arguments or *actants*, of free arguments or *circumstants*." Further on he exemplifies the processes as they apply to SOV languages and their changes.

Another typological study (in the wake of Lehmann) is that of **Paul J. Hopper** 1975, which one can regard as a partial confirmation of Fourquet's findings.[116] The author also places *Germanisch* at an intermediary stage between Indo-Germanic prevalent SOV and the SVO status of individual Germanic languages. Germanic would have inherited from Indo-Germanic a marked *Anfangsstellung* of the *Vf* and an unmarked *Endstellung* for dependent clauses as well as an unmarked *Zweitstellung* for one- or two-syllable enclitic verb in independent sentences, in line with Wackernagel's law. This last option became generalized among other Germanic languages. Hopper submits (p. 94) that "the most important conclusion from the point of view of comparative Indo-European syntax is that the Germanic languages in their earliest recorded stages contained syntactic patterns similar to those of the most archaic, peripheral Indo-European dialects. Just as the Proto-Germanic phonological system can be compared in conservatism only to that of Greek and Armenian, so do its basic syntactic configurations stand beside those of Hittite, Vedic Sanskrit, and Old Irish."

But this work is also of particular interest in that it explicitly attempts to combine the traditional analysis with the postulates of modern linguistics, yet only to conclude that such traditional concerns as word order, or more properly "surface constituent order," "the position of the verb, the placing of enclitics, and so on, which characterized the work of the first decades of the twentieth century in this area, is in fact relatively trivial, since the rules which govern these aspects of syntax are late-level adjustment rules, and hence might be more susceptible of dialectal and individual variation. Furthermore, the diachronic changes in syntactic patterns are more satisfactorily accounted for by an investigation of the deeper constant structures from which the point of divergence between later stages of the language can be stated" (p. 13). (After the results we have considered above, we may feel, nevertheless, still entitled to wonder whether we are in fact ready to account for the phenomena of surface constituent order through deeper constant structures.)

I should like to close with a few observations on additional desiderata.[117] First, in the light of all the above, a central issue appears to deserve more attention than it has received in this context. I mean the uneven development and contradictory character of available choices that correspond to different language types. Think of the fundamental and, for English and German, unlimitedly productive pattern of serialization by mere succession, i.e., juxtaposition without prepositions, hierarchically arranged as operator → operand, as in *gooseberry wine* versus French *vin de groseille* (operand → operator + preposition), and the simultaneous availability in English of the opposite construct as in *he is a know-it-all* (like French *un mêle-tout*), a pattern full of possibilities in a number of typologically heterogeneous languages, as in the interesting French (cf. Molière) and Italian (cf. Rossini) pseudo-Latin formation *factotum*. This openness of contrasting options will extend to prolonged phrases too, as in English *flanked by police carrying machine-guns* versus *by machine-gun carrying police*.[118]

Another question not often raised, and which we have not encountered in the literature surveyed here, is that of the order of phrases within the dependent clause. One first rule is that complements will be anteposed that would take first place in the clause if it were independent. An example from Bertolt Brecht:

Wir waren fest entschlossen, nach der Ergreifung der Macht im Interesse der Besitzenden den Kommunismus so zu treffen, daß er sich von diesem Schlag in Deutschland nie wieder erholen sollte.[119]

(This is Brecht's rewriting of Göring's "Wir waren fest entschlossen, nach der Ergreifung der Macht den Kommunismus so zu treffen, daß. . . .") In a main-clause construct it would read: "Nach der Ergreifung der Macht und im Interesse der Besitzenden werden wir den Kommunismus so treffen, daß. . . . " The object *den Kommunismus* is therefore postposed to the complements *nach . . .* and *im. . . .*

But position also may be determined by phonological causes, as with a particle that cannot easily bear an accent: In "Ueber die Frage, ob es Hitler ehrlich meint" (Brecht, ibid., p. 199), the weak pronoun object

MODERN THEORY AND NINETEENTH-CENTURY BACKGROUND □ 173

es precedes the subject. This is somewhat similar to the case of the reflexive *sich*, which is normally anteposed to everything else (when it is not, it strikes immediately as an idiosyncratic stylistic twist, as in Theodor Adorno).

In one of the most authoritative and detailed treatments of modern German, **George O. Curme**, *A Grammar of the German Language* (New York: Macmillan, 1922[2]), pp. 597–8, observes that when the subject of the dependent clause is a noun or pronoun (other than an introductory subordinating pronoun as the *einleitendes Element*), it is quite commonly preceded by an unaccented pronominal object, including a reflexive form: *Ich liebte ihn auch, weil ihn álle lieben.* But the reflexive goes immediately before the verb when it is itself emphatic: *Sie wußte instinktiv, daß solch ein Herr Sohn und Österreicher oft lieber sích sélbst gehört als einem Berufe* (R. H. Bartsch, *Die Haindlkinder*, p. 23). An adverb and some complements can also precede the subject without changing the order of the remainder: *Wie heutzutage in unserer und durch unsere Weltliteratur die Gegensätze der zivilisierten Nationen aufgehoben sind, so . . .* (Mommsen, *Römische Geschichte*, I, xv). Curme makes these remarks while discussing the "transposed order" of subordinate clauses introduced by subordinating conjunctions or relative pronouns/adverbs (transposed order meaning, as very commonly used, verbal end-position, as distinct form the "normal order" of verbal second position in declarative main clauses and the "inverted order" of subject-after-verb). This transposed order is declared to have been the original Germanic or Proto-Germanic order (cf. p. 586, § 284.I.3.a), and to be based on the rule that the more important follows the less important, hence that modifiers must precede the word they modify. (Complements of the verb would then be understood as its modifiers.)[120]

The attentive reader cannot have failed to observe that one important category has been historically underrepresented, namely, the peculiarity whereby "adverbial" coordinating conjunctions, like true adverbs, cause the inversion of the subject when they come at the head of the clause, but do not if, thanks to the relative positional freedom of adverbs, they come in later places: *Er ist reich, daher braucht er* (or *er braucht daher*) *solche Ausgaben nicht zu scheuen.* Furthermore, some such conjunctions offer all three possible constructions: purely coordinating (no inversion), adverbial-coordinating (inversion), postposed adverb (no inversion): e.g., *Es regnet, also ich gehe nicht aus*; . . . *also gehe ich nicht aus*; *ich gehe also nicht aus.*[121] Traditionally, it appeared normal to treat such conjunctions either as regular adverbs or as conjunctions without special qualifications.

Another peculiarity of the German clause that has been understood relatively late is that its intonation places particularly heavy stress both at the beginning and at the end. The consequence is that simple topicalization of a secondary element can achieve what in other languages requires special periphrases (French *c'est lui qui* . . . ; English *did he not* . . . ; *it is he who* . . . , etc.): Cf. *Herr, ér hatte es leicht! Ér ging von hinnen, aber dír ließ er als Erbe das halb zerstörte Reich* (*Lord, did he have it easy!*).[122]

The main conclusion of our survey must be that German word order has been gradually recognized as presenting one central feature that suffices by itself to characterize that language within the whole Indo-European group, namely: The principal rule of order in the main clause is determined not by the SVO pattern but by the pivotal function of the Verb in Second Position.[123] As to the secondary clause, it is not characterized by Final Position of the Verb but, more exactly, its Later-Than-Second Position (*Nichtzweitstellung*), with a possible *Nachtrag* if anything follows it:
MC = | . . . | V² | . . . ; SC = | . . . | . . . | V²⁺ | (. . .) might be one way of representation. Another conclusion might be that German has proved so challenging a subject for analysis for the very reason that makes it, like all real languages, mysteriously elusive to definitive explanation. For not only are the rules of German, which seemed so unusually systematic, open to an endless effort at definition, but their "exceptions," synchronically and diachronically, can be manifold and meaningful, especially when they have something to do with rhythm of intonation — in other words, accent or weight, the living realities of delivery. A compact illustration is provided in some of the examples supplied by E. Drach to summarize the foreign learner's dismay when confronted with such disorienting facts, and also cited, not without irony, by L. Weisgerber in order to introduce his desire to transcend the formality of grammar in the mechanical sense:[124]

The inverted subject should follow the verb immediately, but it can also wait until later: *Hundert Jahre hindurch wuchs um Dornröschens*

Schloss eine dichte Hecke [focalization — AS]. The predicate of the *uneingeleiteter Nebensatz* goes after the subject, but it can also precede it: *Er sagte, in dieser Gefahr müsse die Wache vorsichtig sein.* Complements of time precede those of place, but: *Er kam zum Ziel in weniger als drei Stunden* [a clear case of Behaghel's *Gesetz der wachsenden Glieder* — AS]. The separable particle goes to the end, unless it does not: *Er trat auf mit den Ansprüchen eines Herrschers.*

The verdict is, obviously, not one of ruling disorder, but, simply, that an exhaustive explanation requires more than one level for our analysis.

4. The Practical Paradigms

It may be convenient at this point to supply a summary of current standard presentations. This will help the reader to locate single issues within a systematic framework, after he has been offered an opportunity to trace them back through their historical evolution. I have therefore chosen two different though convergent presentations, each of them interesting for discrete and opposite reasons: One is by a specialist theoretical student, the other belongs to one of the most popular and authoritative manuals.

In the study already cited, *Verbstellung und Relieftheorie* (1973), **Klaus Fleischmann** conclusively identifies three possibilities for verbal position in dependent clauses: (1) End-position in *Gliedsätze* introduced by conjunctive particles of the "subordinating" kind; (2) initial position in (a) *Konditionalsätze* (with subjunctive mood): *Hättest du Peter das Bild gegeben, so müßte er nicht kommen* — p. 28 and Part C, ch. 3; b) *Konzessivsätze* (with indicative): *Hat Peter das Bild auch bekommen, so verlangt er es doch ein zweites Mal* — p. 29; (c) *Nachgestellte Kausalsätze: Er fiel beinahe um vor Müdigkeit, hatte er doch zwei Nächte nicht geschlafen* — p. 29 (the latter two are an interesting addition to traditional grammar, which had hardly noticed them explicitly; note that the causality in (c) is determined by the *doch*, which in fact would fall off if the clause were "transformed" into an end-verbal *Gliedsatz* introduced by *da* or *weil*); (3) second-position with some "non-subordinating" conjunctions (pp. 29–30); we find here the (archaic) type of the *Exzeptivsatz: Er ist verloren, es hülfe ihm denn Gott*, transformable by addition of *wenn . . . nicht* or *falls . . . nicht*, with consequent dropping of the second-position of the verb, of the subjunctive mood, and of the *exzipierende denn*; likewise, we have here also the type of optional second place when final position would be more normal, typically in the indirect question (*Ich weiß nicht, wo ist er*) and some relatives (*Es war einmal ein Mann, der ging in den Wald*, Romantic fable style, where, we must add, *der* is felt by most speakers as a demonstrative, not a relative, pronoun); the dependent clause is somehow perceived as independent — therefore, we could add, we have a case similar to declarative dependent clauses after *verba dicendi, credendi, sapiendi: er glaubt, er kann (könne) dies tun;* (4) special cases (pp. 31–2): *Distanzstellung* with *Nachtrag: daß der Reiche nicht lebendig fühlt seinen Reichtum* — Goethe. Fleischmann defines this as a *relative Endstellung*, since the verb appears later than in second position but not quite in final place. The elements that follow the verb as an afterthought are normally adverbial phrases, but they can also be objects or even subjects, as fill-ins or nonobligatory complements (*Ergänzungen*). They can be so placed either optionally or necessarily. Likewise, "double infinitives" and compound verbal phrases (*Doppelinfinitiv* and *mehrgliedriges Verbum*) also fall in a sense into this category: *Weil ich ihn habe kommen lassen; weil er sonst von der Überzahl der Feinde wäre getötet worden.*

One will note that these rules explicitly cover finite verbs only. Grammarians have seldom addressed themselves to the question of dependent clauses lacking a finite mood, notwithstanding the important and influential antecedents of Latin with its subjective and objective clauses as well as clauses with verb in participial, gerundive, or supine forms. In German this concerns chiefly the case of (end-positioned) infinitives introduced by (*um* . . .) *zu*, but is not limited to this most common possibility.

For an analysis of German in all periods it is good to keep in mind the three basic variants identified by W. Admoni, "Der Umfang und die Gestaltungsmittel . . . " 1967, and M. M. Guchmann, *Der Weg zur deutschen Nationalsprache*, Bd. 2, Berlin: Akademie Verlag, 1969, pp. 79 ff., namely, with specific reference to independent sentences: (1) Sentences with No Frame (*ohne Rahmen*), as *Reussen ist ein groß mächtigs landt und ist gelegen under dem vorgenanten Stern Tramontana*; (2) full Frame (*vollständiger Rahmen*), as *Ich hab dich meinem frewnd Johanni empfohlen*; (3) incomplete Frame (*unvollständiger*

Rahmen) or *Ausklammerung* of some elements, as *darin ward Maria Gottes müter begraben mit großer reinigkeyt.* (Guchmann's examples, p. 79. Cf. R. P. Ebert 1978, pp. 39 f. In forthcoming studies Ebert applies this schema to extensive statistical analyses of texts from several centuries — see his "Social and Stylistic Variation in Early New High German Word Order: The Sentence Frame (*Satzrahmen*)," to appear in *Beiträge zur Geschichte der deutschen Sprache u. Literatur*, Tübingen.) The options *daz er ez hat getân* vs. *daz er ez getân hat* are disregarded and both included in the fully bracketed construct.

The most current description of the *Satzrahmen* or *Satzklammer* focusses on the independent declarative sentence and defines the *Klammer* proper as the two parts of the verb phrase (VP), that is, finite verb (fV) + nonfinite form, separable particle, or nominal predicate (NP); the *Mittelfeld* will be occupied by the object(s) or other *Ergänzungen*, while the *Vorfeld* and *Nachfeld*, both outside the *Klammer*, will house the first element (subject, topic, or adverb) and the *Nachtrag*, respectively (this last term now no longer in great favor). In the dependent clause the Frame typically begins with the *einleitende Partikel* and ends with the final verb (whereas in the independent clause it includes only the various parts of the verbal group).

For a thoroughly informed and methodologically up-to-date presentation, see Ulrich Engel, *Syntax der deutschen Gegenwartssprache* (Berlin: Schmidt, 1977), pp. 190–225, with graphs on p. 192. This manual is also of great value to the student for its rich bibliographies and glossary (*Fachausdrücke*).

Der Grosse Duden, vol. 4: *Grammatik* (1973 ed., pp. 620 ff.) organizes the matter of sentence construction (*WORTSTELLUNG: SATZSCHEMATA*) as follows:[125]

I. Die PRÄDIKATSTEILE
1. Die Stellung der Personalform (einteiliges Prädikat)
   a. Personalform an zweiter Satzgliedstelle: KERNSÄTZE
   b. Personalform am Anfang des Satzes: STIRNSÄTZE: questions, etc., also In Konditional- und Konzessivsätzen ohne Einleitewort: *Ist es auch dunkel, wir . . .*
   c. Personalform am Ende des Satzes: SPANNSÄTZE. In eingebetteten Sätzen mit Einleitewort steht die Personalform am Ende des Satzes oder — bei Ausklammerung — zum Ende des Satzes hin: *Weil Peter schneller gelaufen ist als Frank*

Exception: Im irrealen Vergleichssatz mit *als* steht die Personalform unmittelbar hinter der Konjunktion:
Er tat so, als hätte er von all dem nichts gewußt.
Endstellung der Personalform (in main clauses) in Analogie zu Parallelsätzen mit Endstellung ist selten:
Wes Brot ich ess', des Lied ich sing (obviously archaic with proverbial ring)
2. Stellung der Prädikatsteile bei mehrteiligen Prädikaten
   a. In Kern- und Stirnsätzen   (here are given the rules on separation
   b. In Spannsätzen   of the finite form from the participles and infinitives)
II. Die SATZKLAMMER und die Stellungsfelder: Die Satzglieder

[———————————————]
Peter   ist   schneller   gelaufen   als Frank

| Vorfeld | 1. Klammerteil | Mittelfeld | 2. Klammerteil | Nachfeld |

(fester, unfester Verbzusatz — trennbare Praposition; a separable particle can be used *isoliert*, meaning with ellipsis of the verb: *Wir haben frei (bekommen); Das Licht ist aus (geschaltet).*)
Präpositionen: *entgegen, entlang, gegenüber, gemäß, unbeschadet, ungeachtet, wegen, zufolge, zugunsten, zunächst, zuungunsten* go before or after the noun. *Nach* nur bei modaler Verwendung nachgestellt. Nur nachgestellt *halber* und *zuwider*.

One might add to *Duden* that the *Nachfeld* (elsewhere called *Nachtrag*) will mostly occur for reasons of: Logical connection with the following (*liaison des idées*): *Sie tauschten ihre Erfahrungen aus über die beste Art, die Zigarre aufzubewahren*; emphasis on a complement: *Tonio versuchte ihre Stimme zu unterscheiden, in welcher es klang von warmem Leben*; or just to break up the overlong complement sequence: *Zuweilen hatte ihm geträumt, daß er wieder daheim sei in dem alten, hallenden Haus an der schrägen Gasse* (all the examples from Th. Mann). The *Nachtrag* is an exception to the *Satzklammer* insofar as it breaks through the sentence "braces."

There is no well established terminology to refer to the different types of clause structure. Some refer to the normal construction of the independent clause with verbal *Zweitstellung* as *direkte Wortfolge* or *gerade Gliedfolge*; conversely, the dependent clause with *Spätstellung* or *Nichtzweitstellung* will be said to show *ungerade Gliedfolge*. But this last formula also can designate the "inverted" order in a *Hauptsatz*.

Within the *Satzlehre* we must take note of the interesting phenomenon that reverses, as it were, the *Satzklammer* from a "braced" to a chiastic pattern, when the *Nachsatz* is anteposed to the *Vordersatz*, thus calling for inversion of the subject in the latter. The result is a striking encounter of the two main verbs: The dramatic tension is often marked by a heightening of the tonic accents: *Warum er das gethan hat, begreiffe ich nicht* (Adelung),[126] *Wenn der uralte heilige Vater mit gelassener Hand aus rollenden Wolken segnende Blitze über die Erde sät, / / küß' ich den letzten Saum seines Kleides* (Goethe).[127] If a speaker may feel that the *Satzklammer* and indirect construction produce a satisfying, centripetal circularity (the closest that a modern language can come to ancient periodicity), the reverse phenomenon just seen is effective for opposite, centrifugal reasons. The sentence now moves, almost explodes from the center "out," rather than from the extremes "in."

This is, in its essential lines, the present situation. If we look to the historical picture that has emerged from all the preceding, it should have become clear that popular manuals, even by informed experts, tend to give a simplified and at times distorted view of the complex factors involved. To take one example, Peter von Polenz, *Geschichte der deutschen Sprache*,[128] states that "die Endstellung des 2. Prädikatsteils (Infinitiv, Partizip, Adverb) im Hauptsatz und die Endstellung des finiten Verbs im Nebensatz" began to be prescribed as the sole term as early as the sixteenth century. We have found no trace of such a clear situation in any of the texts. Incidentally, Polenz's useful term of "Second Part of the Predicate" presents the advantage of subsuming under one concept the infinitive or participle, the nominal predicate, and, presumably (Polenz does not specify), the separable particle.

According to Polenz (p. 95), in harmony with the new situation that was reflected in grammatical theory, in the second half of the sixteenth century a transformation took place in the word order of administrative German that extended to further linguistic areas in the seventeenth century. The result was that German became, in a highly systematic manner, a language of *zentripetale Wortfolge* as contrasted with the *zentrifugale Wortfolge* that is characteristic of, say, French — this on the basis of *das syntaktisch untergeordnete Wort* preceding the *übergeordnete.*[129] Yet the words whose syntactic function applies to the whole group are excluded from the centripetal rule (p. 96). The overall picture of the clause is, then, characterized by the *Satzklammer*, the bracing of the dependent element or clause within the conjunction and the finite verb, of the main clause within the finite verb and the second part of the predicate (or the separable particle, we should add), and, furthermore, of the extended attribute between the article and the noun (p. 97). This term of "extended attribute" (*erweiterte Attributgruppe*), another useful terminological addition, refers to a key aspect of natural constituent serialization in the direction operator → operand (remember the example *die für die Milchversorgung verantwortliche Behörde*).[130] Polenz assumes that the extended attribute began to be all preposed in the late sixteenth century, whereas earlier the elements beyond the second tended to be postposed (pp. 95–6). The length and complication of this extended attribute, practically unlimited, are characteristic of the *Kanzleistil*. But, once again, Polenz is incorrect in dating the "resistance" to the *Schachtelsatz* from the nineteenth century (p. 97). We have seen how much earlier and consistent it had been among grammarians and rhetoricians.[131]

NOTES

NOTES

Notes: Introduction

1. *Either/Or*, trans. D. F. and L. M. Swenson (Princeton: Univ. Press, 1944), I, p. 246 (I, pp. 295–96 in 1959 ed.).

2. So that, in a limited sense, it can be said that Old Italian and Modern French exhibit aspects of that famous *Klammercharakter* commonly regarded as a unique feature of G. In Chapter Three we will further expatiate on some of these correspondences. At this point it may suffice to exemplify with some simple cases, e.g., the inversion of subject after the verb when a "strong word," adverb or adverbial phrase, starts the clause: French *à peine se fut-il assis que le train partit* 'hardly had he sat down, than the train started'; Italian *invano si faticherebbero molti* 'in vain would many labor'; Ru. *asa ere frate-mieu* 'thus was my brother'; Spanish *entonces se comenzó el juego* 'then began the game.' Or the inversion of subject after the verb for emotive or stylistic emphasis: French *vint la guerre* 'then came the war'; Italian *gran destino è il mio* 'mine is a great destiny'; Spanish *no quiero yo el caballo* 'I don't want the horse.' Examples from Rebecca Posner, *The Romance Languages: A Linguistic Introduction* (Garden City, N.Y.: Doubleday and Co., 1966), p. 173.

3. Interview recorded September 23, 1966 by the staff of *Der Spiegel* and, according to the philosopher's wishes, published only after his death: See *Der Spiegel*, 30, 23 (May 31, 1976), pp. 193–219. Cf. p. 217: "Ich denke an die besondere innere Verwandtschaft der deutschen Sprache mit der Sprache der Griechen und deren Denken. Das bestätigen mir heute immer wieder die Franzosen. Wenn sie zu denken anfangen, sprechen sie Deutsch; sie versichern, sie kämen mit ihrer Sprache nicht durch. . . . Weil sie sehen, daß sie mit ihrer ganzen großen Rationalität nicht mehr durchkommen in der heutigen Welt, wenn es sich darum handelt, diese in der Herkunft ihres Wesens zu verstehen."

4. "Lettre sur les sourds et muets" (1751) in Diderot, *Oeuvres complètes*, ed. J. Assézat, I (Paris: Garnier, 1875), pp. 371–2.

184 □ NOTES

5. *U.N.C. Studies in Comparative Literature*, 53 (Chapel Hill: U.N.C. Press).

6. See especially Hans Aarsleff, "Thoughts on Scaglione's *CTC*: The Survival of Eighteenth-Century French Philosophy Before Saussure," *Romance Philology*, XXIX, 4 (1976), 522–38.

Chapter 1: The Theory of Sentence Structure

1. B. Delbrück, "Einleitung" to Ch. 48, "Das Satzgefüge," of his *Vergleichende Syntax der indogermanischen Sprachen*, 3. Theil, in Karl Brugmann, ed., *Grundriß der vergleichenden Grammatik der indogermanischen Sprachen* (Strassburg: K. J. Trübner, 1900), pp. 406–15: see p. 413.

2. For an analysis of these hypothese, see Manfred Sandmann, "Beiordnung," esp. pp. 174–188. (See title in fn. 9 below.) Since this sign can be defined differently in standard linguistic usage, I must clarify that here and hereafter I use the arrow → to mean "linear movement from preceding to following element."

3. For a shrewd close analysis, see, e.g., Ladislao Mittner, *Grammatica della lingua tedesca* (Milano: Mondadori, 1933, 1941[5]), pp. 198–202.

4. *Cicero numerosus: Studien zum antiken Prosarhythmus*. Oesterreichische Akademie der Wissenschaften, Philosophisch-hist. Klasse, Sitzungsberichte, 257. Bd. (Wien, 1968).

5. B. L. Hijmans, Jr., *Inlaboratus et facilis: Aspects of Structure in Some Letters of Seneca* (Leiden: Brill, 1976), leans on Primmer for definitions of compositional styles (see pp. 99 ff.), but this study is somewhat pedestrian and unacquainted with the better background literature.

6. Cf. Hijmans, pp. 102–3.

7. Peter von Polenz, *Geschichte der deutschen Sprache* (Berlin: W. de Gruyter, 1972[8]), pp. 98–9 for the following examples.

8. See the sharp stylistic appreciations in Eric A. Blackall, *The Emergence of German as a Literary Language, 1700–1775* (Cambridge: U. Press, 1959), pp. 53–4.

9. Sandmann, "Zur Frühgeschichte des Terminus der syntaktischen Beiordnung," *Archiv für das Studium der neueren Sprachen und Literaturen*, 206 (1969–70), 161–88. Also, Id., *Subject and Predicate. A Contribution to the Theory of Syntax* (Edinburgh: Edinburgh University Press, 1954).

10. (Paris: J. Delalain, 1862). Cf. Gérald Antoine, *La coordination en français*. Diss. Paris, 1954 (Paris: D'Artrey, 1959–63, 2 vols.), pp. 195–216.

11. Kjell-Åke Forsgren, "Zur Theorie und Terminologie der Satzlehre. Ein Beitrag zur Geschichte der deutschen Grammatik von J. C. Adelung bis K. F. Becker, 1780–1830," Diss. Göteborg, 1973, 217p.

12. Max Hermann Jellinek, *Geschichte der neuhochdeutschen Grammatik von den Anfängen bis auf Adelung* (Heidelberg: Karl Winter, 1913–14, 2 vols.). See also, for the non-Germanic areas, A. Scaglione, *The Classical Theory of Composition, from Its Origin to the Present* (Chapel Hill: U.N.C. Press, 1972).

13. Cf. Charles Thurot, "Notices et extraits de divers manuscrits latins pour servir à l'histoire des doctrines grammaticales au Moyen Âge," in *Notices et extraits des manuscrits de la Bibliothèque Impériale et autres bibliothèques*, XXII, 2 (Paris, 1868).

14. III, *Art d'écrire*, Book I, chs. vii–ix: cf. *Oeuvres philosophiques*, ed. Georges Le Roy (Paris: Presses Universitaires de France, 1947–51, 3 vols.), I, pp. 529–39.

15. Cf. Forsgren, pp. 56, 192–3.

16. Jellinek, II, p. 473 and Klaus Fleischmann, *Verbstellung und Relieftheorie*. Münchener Germanistische Beiträge, 6 (München: W. Fink, 1973), pp. 342–3.

17. The edition quoted bears only the printer's mark on the title page. The *Initia rhetorica* saw a second edition (Leipzig: C. Fritsch, 1784), whereas the major work, *Initia doctrinae solidioris*, has many editions (Leipzig, 1734–5, 1745, 1776, 1783, and 1796). Cf. Jellinek, II, p. 471. Jellinek's bibliographic titles in fn. pp. 471–2, all rhetorical like Ernesti's, show the German sources of period description and sentence structure (six titles between 1706 and 1735).

18. Jellinek, I, p. 257 and II, p. 475; Fleischmann, p. 351.

19. Bodmer's work, independent from that of Gottsched, appeared anonymously in 1768, according to Jacob Baechtold, *Geschichte der deutschen Literatur in der Schweiz* (Frauenfeld: T. Huber, 1892, reprt. 1919), p. 677.

20. Forsgren, p. 178.

21. Fleischmann has painstakingly reconstructed the story of this question as crucial for the understanding of subordination and verbal position. See his pp. 359f. on Hemmer.

22. Jellinek, II, 484 on Aichinger and Meiner. See, now, Meiner's *Versuch* in the Faksimile-Neudruck der Ausgabe Leipzig 1781, ed. H. E. Brekle (Stuttgart-Bad Cannstatt: Frommann-Holzboog, 1971).

23. Cf. Forsgren, p. 179.

24. Forsgren, pp. 31 and 187f.

25. Forsgren, p. 193.

26. German translation, *Die Entwicklung des Deutschen zur Literatursprache, 1700–1775*, with appendix (Stuttgart, 1966). In the following section I shall refer the reader often to this basic work for further elaboration on several of the points I summarily raise. The most authoritative histories of German, particularly, for English-speaking readers, John T. Waterman, *A History of the German Language* (Seattle and London: Univ. of Washington P., 1966, 1976^2), are also valuable whenever they specifically turn to major changes in sentence arrangement. See, e.g., Waterman, pp. 140ff. on "The Grammarians" of New High German, not well represented in Blackall.

27. Quoted by Waterman, p. 121, from George O. Curme, *A Grammar of the German Language* (New York: Macmillan, 1905, 1922^2, 1952^2, F. Ungar, 1960^2), pp. 263, 267.

28. Cf. Waterman, p. 151. See Weise, *Curiöse Gedancken*, 1692, pp. 124–213, esp. 141.

29. See it now in the edition by Paul Pietsch in *Wissenschaftliche Beihefte zur Zeitschrift des Allgemeinen Deutschen Sprachvereins*, R. 4, Heft 30 (Berlin, 1908), pp. 327–56, and in Leibniz, *Philosophische Werke*, eds. A. Buchenau and Ernst Cassirer. II: *Hauptschriften zur Grundlegung der Philosophie* (Leipzig: Felix Meiner, 1924^2), pp. 519–55: See, esp., Nos. 57, 80, 110, 113, pp. 538, 546, 554, 555 for the use of the terms *Reichtum* etc.

30. See it in Leibniz's *Philosophische Schriften*, ed. C. J. Gerhardt (Berlin: Weidmann, 1875–90, 7 vols.), vol. IV (1880). Cf. Blackall, pp. 8–9.

31. Blackall, p. 4. Quoted from Leibniz's *Ermahnung an die Teutsche, ihren Verstand und Sprache besser zu üben* . . . (1682–3 ?).

32. P. 76 of "Akademische Rede, zum Abschiede aus der vertrauten Rednergesellschaft zu Leipzig, 20. August 1728" in Gottsched, *Gesammelte Reden*, ed. Eugen Reichel, Bd. 6 of J. Ch. G., *Gesammelte Schriften* (Berlin: Gottsched-Verlag, n.d. [1904?]), or in his *Ausgewählte Werke*, IX, 2, ed. R. Scholl (Berlin: W. de Gruyter, 1976), p. 524.

33. Cf. *Saggio sulla filosofia delle lingue* (1800, a revision of the *Saggio sopra la*

lingua italiana of 1785), Part IV, ch. xvi, p. 140–7 in Cesarotti, *Opere scelte*, ed. Giuseppe Ortolani, I (Firenze, 1945). See my *CTC*, pp. 309–16. On Leibniz's ideas on language considered from a modern linguistic viewpoint see Marcelo Dascal, *La sémiologie de Leibniz* (Paris: Aubier-Montaigne, 1978), and his article, "About the Idea of a Generative Grammar in Leibniz," *Studia Leibnitiana*, 3 (1971), 272-90; also Sigrid von der Schulenburg, *Leibniz als Sprachforscher*, ed. Kurt Müller (Frankfurt: Klostermann, 1973).

34. Cf. Blackall, pp. 30–3, who used, for Wolff's text, the 1725, 4th ed. copy in the British Museum. Several of the texts referred to hereafter are relatively rare, even among German libraries. Blackall used mostly copies in London or Zürich. The date of completion of Wolff's manuscript is 1712 (the "Vorrede" is dated October 18, 1712); the Logic was first published in 1713. It is now available in Wolff's *Gesammelte Werke*, eds. J. École, J. E. Hoffmann, M. Thomann, H. W. Arndt, 1. Abt., Bd. 1, ed. Hans Werner Arndt (Hildesheim: Georg Olms, 1965, 1973). In fairness to Thomasius it must be noted, however, that he was not personally the translator of the *Einleitung*.

35. Cf. Blackall, p. 33.

36. Cf. Daniel J. Cook, "Leibniz and Hegel on the Language of Philosophy," *Studia Leibnitiana — Supplementa XV* (Wiesbaden: F. Steiner, 1975), pp. 229–238, esp. 233.

37. Blackall, p. 16.

38. Blackall, pp. 75–76.

39. Jellinek, I, p. 361, quoting Adelung, *Umständliches Lehrgebäude*, 1782.

40. Gottsched, *Ausgewählte Werke*, ed. P. M. Mitchell (Berlin — New York: W. de Gruyter, 1975), VII, 1, ed. Rosemary Scholl, pp. 334–5.

41. *Der Patriot* is most easily quoted from the 2d ed. (Hamburg, 3 vols., 1737–8). But see it now in the edition by Wolfgang Martens (reprt. Berlin: W. de Gruyter, 3 vols. + 1 vol. of commentary, 1969–70).

42. *Der Patriot*, reprt., vol. I, p. 7 (1969): first issue, Mittwochens, den 5ten Jenner, 1724.

43. This 5th ed. of 1759 is the one reprinted in the *Ausgewählte Werke*, ed. P. M. Mitchell, op. cit., 7. Bd., 1. Teil and 2. Teil (1975), ed. R. Scholl. The 2d tome contains the Specific Part.

44. Ulrich Wendland, *Die Theoretiker und Theorien der sogenannten galanten Stilepoche* (Leipzig, 1930), relates Gottsched to the stylistic manuals of 1670-1730. See also Blackall's schematic notes pp. 154, 163–177. For a recent survey and discussion of the development of Senecan or Neo-Stoic stylistic theories, see Scaglione, *CTC*, chs. 3 and 4.

45. On general French contempt for German, see Paul Lévy, *La langue allemande en France*, I, (Paris, [1951]), pp. 117ff.

46. Blackall, p. 164.

47. This is the passage cited by Dornblüth; see below in my Chapter 2 on Word Order. *Redekunst* 1739, p. 292.

48. This concession appeared in the 5th ed. of the *Sprachkunst*, which will be more specifically analyzed in Chapter 2, on Word Order. See Blackall, pp. 176–7, without reference to Senecanism in the matter of these participles.

49. See Lessing, *Sämtliche Schriften*, ed. Karl Lachmann — Franz Muncker, VIII (Stuttgart: Göschen, 1892[3]), p. 50.

50. Blackall, pp. 266, 283–4.

51. Blackall, p. 266.

52. Cf. Georg Steinhausen, *Geschichte des deutschen Briefs: Zur Kulturgeschichte des deutschen Volkes* (Berlin: R. Gartner, 1889–91, 2 vols.). Blackall, p. 178.

53. See E. Blackall, "The Observations of Father Dornblüth," *MLR*, L (1955), 450–63.

54. *Consuetum* in the title is meant as 'advisable': *ratsam* replaces it at head of text in chapter.

55. For a detailed analysis of the principles and literary impact of what one could regard as a late stage of the medieval *ars dictaminis*, cf. Reinhard M. G. Nickisch, *Die Stilprinzipien in den deutschen Briefstellern des 17. und 18. Jahrhunderts* (Göttingen: Vandenhoeck & Ruprecht, 1969).

56. Cf. Blackall, *MLR*, L (1955), p. 450. By the middle of the century the intellectual leaders had unequivocally turned against the pseudoperiodicity of "officialese" both in the manner of the bureaucrats and that of the traditional pulpit preachers, which could be lumped together in growing ridicule, as exemplified in Lessing's satirical self-defense (against Basedow) for having offended the preacher Cramer in his attack on "Kanzelstil": See his 105th *Literaturbrief* in the 6th Theil (of 1760) of the *Briefe, die neueste Litteratur betreffend*, 1759–65, in Lessing, *Sämtliche Schriften*, ed. Karl Lachmann-Franz Muncker, vol. VIII, pp. 236–7.

See p. 463 of Blackall's 1955 article, and especially Blackall, "The *Parnassus Boicus* and the German Language," *German Life and Letters*, n.s., VII (1954), 98–108, for further details on the 1723–24 article in the *Parnassus Boicus*. The three unsigned installments, due to the pen of Gelasius Hieber (1671–1731), a celebrated Augustinian preacher in Munich and one of the three editors of the periodical, were entitled "Von der Kunst und Wissenschaft der sogenannten Grammatica oder Sprach-Lehr und ihren Eigenschafften." The concepts that had been introduced with such terms as *Mannhafftigkeit (Männlichkeit)* and *Helden-mässig* were carried on in a later article, "Einige Anmerckungen über die Teutsche Sprach," by another of the three editors of the *Parnassus Boicus*, Agnellus Kandler (1692–1745), that appeared in the fifth issue of the continuation of the *Parnassus Boicus* (after an interruption between 1727 and 1735) under the title *Neu-fortgesetzter Parnassus Boicus*, after Hieber's death. Kandler also spoke of *"Helden-Sprach"* (Blackall 1959, p. 106).

Chapter 2: Theory of Word Order from the Renaissance to Adelung

1. "Symbebēkós" is Dionysius's term for accident.

2. Jellinek, II, pp. 430–1. In Vol. II of Jellinek's work, "Wortstellung" is Section IV of Ch. 16 (Syntax), and covers pp. 425–64, followed by Section V, "Satzlehre."

3. Let us note, incidentally, that however the matter may stand, in Dionysius's discarded doctrine the verb came practically last, namely, after both subject and object — or at least after the object if there was no expressed subject, as in the example.

4. Keil III, 89, 14ff. Cf. Jellinek, II, p. 429 fn. Note that Alexander de Villadei's *Doctrinale* of 1199 placed the adverb after the verb, in true SVO pattern.

5. Jellinek, II, p. 439.

6. Piper, ed., *Die Schriften Notkers und seiner Schule* (Freiburg/B. and Leipzig: J. C. B. Mohr, 1895), I, p. xxx, 26ff. Following quote on p. xxiv, 17ff.

7. J. Müller, ed., *Quellenschriften und Geschichte des deutschsprachigen Unterrichtes bis zur Mitte des 16. Jahrhunderts* (Gotha: E. F. Thienemann's Hofbuchhandlung, 1882).

8. For precise references to these early treatises see Fleischmann, pp. 326–8.

9. Jellinek used of this important work the reelaboration by Caspar Fink (1578–1631), *Grammatica latina ex praecipuis veterum et recentiorum grammaticorum redacta: nunc*

188 □ NOTES

denuo recognita . . . opera C. Finckii et C. Helvici (Giessae, 1615^2; Lipsiae, 1621), referring to it as Finck-Helwig. See Jellinek, II, p. 3. Cf. H. E. Brekle, "The Seventeenth Century," in Th. A. Sebeok, ed., *Current Trends in Linguistics*, 13/1: *Historiography of Linguistics* (The Hague-Paris: Mouton, 1975), pp. 277–382; see pp. 312–317.

10. *Teutsch Grammatick oder Sprach-Kunst . . . per Laurentium Albertum Ostrofrancum* (Augustae Vindelicorum: Michaël Manger, 1573). Reprt. *Die Deutsche Grammatik des Laurentius Albertus*, ed. Carl Müller-Fraureuth. Ältere deutsche Grammatiken in Neudrucken, III (Strassburg: Karl J. Trübner, 1895), with an Introduction.

Laurentius Albertus or Albrecht de Malleis (perhaps von Schlägel according to Jellinek, rather than von Hammer according to Schellhass), born in Thuringia as a subject of the Saxon kings, appears as matriculated in 1557 at the University of Wittenberg under the name of Laurentius Albrecht Neapolitanus Francus. Neapolitanus could stand for an inhabitant of Neustadt an der Saale or Neustadt an der Aisch. In 1565 he went to Würzburg and met the Domherr Johann Egolf von Knöringen, to whom he later dedicated his grammar, and through him the Bishop Friedrich v. Würzburg.

11. I must refer the reader to my *CTC* for explanations concerning the terminology used here and elsewhere.

12. Fleischmann, pp. 328–9, in his succinct observations on Albertus, also underlines his being the only sixteenth-century grammarian who, to his knowledge, attempted to grasp the concept of *Nebensatz*.

13. Reprt. in *Die deutsche Grammatik des Albert Ölinger*, ed. Willy Scheel. Ältere deutsche Grammatiken in Neudrucken, IV (Halle/S.: M. Niemeyer, 1897).

14. See, on Ölinger, Fleischmann, pp. 329–31.

15. *Grammatica germanicae linguae M. Johannis Claii Hirtzbergensis, ex Bibliis Lutheri germanicis et aliis eius libris collecta*, 1578, reprt. *Die deutsche Grammatik des Johannes Clajus . . .* , ed. Friedrich Weidling. Ältere deutsche Grammatiken in Neudrucken, II (Strassburg: Karl J. Trübner, 1894).

16. Fleischmann, pp. 331–3 on Claius.

17. (Marburg: Rudolf Hutwelcker.)

18. Cf. A. Scaglione, *Ars grammatica* (1970), passim.

19. Fleischmann, pp. 333–4.

20. (Cöthen im Fürstenthume Anhalt.)

21. (Braunschweig: Balthasar Gruber.)

22. (Ibid.: Christoff Friedrich Zilliger.) Cf. Fleischmann, pp. 335–7.

23. Brekle in Sebeok 1975, cited, pp. 314–7, and G. Fricke, "Die Sprachauffassung in der grammatischen Theorie des 16. und 17. Jahrhundert," *Zeitschrift für deutsche Bildung*, 9 (1933), 113–23; see pp. 120f.

24. Cf. *Sprachkunst* 1641, pp. 414, 417ff., 653; *Ausführliche Arbeit* 1663, pp. 549, 551ff., 788.

25. *Ausführliche Arbeit*, p. 755. Fleischmann, pp. 336–7, also takes Schottel to task for his purely semantic orientation in disregard of the formal syntactic structures.

26. See now the reprint of this work, ed. Wolfgang Hecht (Tübingen: Max Niemeyer, 1967, 2 vols.).

27. Pp. 740–61. See esp. §§ 1–5, 11, 23.

28. Jellinek, II, p. 443 on Schottel.

29. (Mühlhausen/Thüringen: Johann Hüter.)

30. Fleischmann, pp. 337–8, points out the problem, but without offering a comprehensive solution.

31. Jellinek, II, pp. 433–5 through Condillac.

32. See, now, reprt. of Morhof, 1700 ed., ed. Henning Boetius (Bad Homburg: Gehlen, 1969), pp. 98 (§§ 164–5), 254–5 (§§ 471–2), 274 (§ 511).
33. See p. 66, 1737 ed. of The Hague.
34. Note the XV order (indeed, XVS, since when the subject was expressed it followed the verb: *fruit vouloir Pierre*), and compare with Dionysius of Halicarnassus's "first" theory. Cf. Condillac, *Essai sur l'origine des connoissances humaines*, II, I, ix in *Oeuvres philosophiques*, ed. G. Le Roy (Paris: Presses Universitaires de France, 1947), I, pp. 83–4.
35. Condillac, *Essai* II, I, xi, pp. 92–3 of *Oeuvres philosophiques*, II. Cf. Jellinek II, pp. 435–7. But Jellinek appears to misunderstand the main thrust of Diderot's argument on the matter of simultaneity or chronological succession (see my discussion below, pp. 58–60, with extensive quotations).
36. Jellinek, II, p. 438.
37. Jellinek, II, p. 439.
38. Cf. Jellinek, II, p. 442, also referring back to pp. 372–4.
39. This rule is reminiscent of Alexander de Villadei's *Doctrinale* of 1199.
40. I.e., absolute.
41. On Christoph Helwig (Helvicus), 1619, and Caspar Finck's reelaboration of his Grammar, 1621, see above.
42. Cölln an der Spree, 1690, 1701, 1709; revised by J. L. Frisch, Berlin: Ch. Gottlieb Nicolai, 1723, 1729; new ed. revised by J. J. Wippel, ibid., 1746.
43. Jellinek, II, pp. 443–4.
44. Jellinek, II, pp. 444–5. The spelling of *Hülf(s)wort* appears to be unstable.
45. Fleischmann, pp. 338–40. The difficulties we have noted were often caused by the application of schemes to unrelated languages, e.g., from Latin to German. But it is around this time that the first systematic attempts were made to study languages comparatively, so as to discover real typological and genetic relationships. According to Hans Aarsleff, "The Eighteenth Century, including Leibniz," in Th. A. Sebeok, ed., *Current Trends in Linguistics, 13: Historiography of Linguistics* (The Hague-Paris: Mouton, 1975), Part 1, pp. 383–479: See p. 413, a lively positive interest in history and broad geographical scopes mark the encyclopedic work of Johann Georg von Eckhart (1674–1730 — name also spelled ECCARD), *Historia studii etymologici linguae germanicae hactenus impensi; ubi scriptores plerique recensentur et dilucidantur, qui in origines et antiquitates linguae teutonicae, saxonicae, belgicae, danicae, suecicae, norwegicae et islandicae, veteris item celticae, goticae, francicae atque anglo-saxonicae inquisiverunt* (Hannover: Foerster, 1711). See Hermann Leskien, *Johann Georg von Eckhart (1674–1730). Das Werk eines Vorläufers der Germanistik*. Diss. Würzburg (München, 1965).
46. Cf. Fleischmann, p. 343; Jellinek, II, p. 473.
47. Jellinek, II, p. 446. These lists are in keeping with the ancient, and especially medieval tradition (see *Doctrinale*) of the *naturalis ordo* (as in Finck-Helwig).
48. Jellinek, II, p. 447.
49. . . . *oder ordentliche Grund-Legung der Teutschen Sprach-Lehre* (Hamburg: in Verlegung des Autoris, gedruckt bey Ph. L. Stromer). Cf. Jellinek, II, pp. 447–8.
50. Pp. 125, 164: "Das Hülffs-Wort hinter sein Haubt-*Verbum*." Cf. Fleischmann, p. 344.
51. . . . *vel succincta et perfecta grammatica linguae germanicae nova methodo tradita* (Rostochii et Parchimi: G. L. Fritsch).
52. Jellinek, II, p. 448.

53. Vol. II of the *Beyträge* (1733) contains a longish essay "Von der Natur der Sprachen, als eine natürliche Sprachkunst," pp. 463–529, as usual unsigned, a section of which on *Wortfügung*, pp. 512–4, rests on a general definition of syntax or construction and simply hints at the choice of modes of expression on the grounds of affections, emotions, embellishment of sound, and emphasis, as a later passage, p. 527, also does. In this latter, reference is made to vol. I, pp. 175ff., where, it is stated, the doctrine is expounded in orderly detail. It is the essay we are examining.

54. 2d ed. 1737, now in Johann Christoph Gottsched, *Ausgewählte Werke*, eds. Joachim and Brigitte Birke, 6. Bd., Teil 1 & 2 (Berlin-New York: W. De Gruyter, 1973). See Teil 1, 9. Kapitel "Von poetischen Perioden und ihren Zierrathen," pp. 351–79. Blackall used the first, 1730 ed.

55. See esp. § 9, pp. 358–9.

56. §§ 7 and 8, pp. 357–8.

57. See below on Bodmer.

58. This translation appeared, as usual in this periodical, unsigned, and is part of the 31st Stück of vol. VIII of the *Beyträge*, which appeared in 1743. Pages 452–4 deal most specifically with word order. Jellinek mentions the *Beyträge* only once, not concerning word order. On the authorship of the translation to Frau Gottsched (Luise Adelgunde Victorie Gottschedin Kulmus) and her further contributions to the *Beyträge* see, e.g., Gustav Waniek, *Gottsched und die deutsche Litteratur seiner Zeit* (Leipzig: Breitkopf & Härtel, 1897), p. 219. As examples of the learning of the translator and commentator, cf. p. 434 fn. on the cultural and linguistic situation in early medieval France (after P. Bayle), and similarly p. 436 fn. In the recent monograph by Veronica C. Richel, *Luise Gottsched. A Reconsideration* (Bern: Herbert Lang, and Frankfurt/M.: Peter Lang, 1973), the translation of Buffier is not mentioned. Cf. the list of translations pp. 55–7, from the appendices to Frau Gottsched's *Sämmtliche kleinere Gedichte* (Leipzig: Breitkopf, 1763). The *Beyträge* have been reprinted Hildesheim-New York: Georg Olms, vol. VIII 1970.

59. The essay appeared in Claude Buffier's *Cours des sciences* (Paris: Cavelier et Giffard, 1732; Geneva: Slatkine Reprints, 1971), cc. 993–1014. It was reprinted in the 1843 ed. of the *Oeuvres philosophiques du P. Buffier*, avec notes et introduction par Francisque Bouillier (Paris: Charpentier), pp. 381–407.

60. Richard A. Ogle, "Natural Order and Dislocated Syntax: An Essay in the History of Linguistic Ideas," Diss. U.C.L.A., 1974, pp. 143–4, refers to J. F. Staal, *Word Order in Sanskrit and Universal Grammar* (Dordrecht: D. Reidel, 1967), as "one of the first major endeavors to reconsider the issue of linear deep structure." After reviewing the opinions of both Indian and Western grammarians, Staal comes to the conclusion that "word order in Sanskrit is 'free'" in the sense that "Sanskrit expressed by means of inflexion what English expresses by means of word order as well as (e.g., in the case of pronouns) inflexion (cf., e.g., Bloomfield 1933, 197 and Hirt 1925, 66 . . .)." (Staal, p. 64.)

61. *Beyträge* VIII, p. 452. The original, here rather freely yet faithfully rendered, had it thus (p. 399 of 1843 ed.): "Au regard de l'arrangement qui se fait de nos idées dans notre esprit, si cette prérogative a quelque chose de spécieux, elle a peu de réalité; car les idées doivent se présenter toutes ensemble à l'esprit pour faire une proposition, sans quoi elles n'ont aucun sens déterminé, et c'est par cette raison que les Latins, pour mettre un verbe à la fin d'une phrase, n'en conçoivent pas moins promptement ni moins nettement tout ce qu'ils disent; il n'y a dans tout cela que l'habitude et un tour d'imagination. L'expérience le montre même dans notre langue," etc.

62. See, likewise, fn. p. 459.
63. See the *Traité* in the 1732 ed. of the *Cours des sciences*, reprt. Slatkine 1971, already cited, col. 433. Du Cerceau is simply referred to as "un homme d'esprit."
64. See the two chapters on cc. 431–5.
65. Aarsleff, "The Tradition of Condillac: The Problem of the Origin of Language in the Eighteenth Century and the Debate in the Berlin Academy before Herder," *Studies in the History of Linguistics: Traditions and Paradigms*, ed. Dell Hymes (Bloomington-London: Indiana U. P., 1974), pp. 93–156, esp. 103f. with references; Id., "Thoughts on Scaglione's *Classical Theory of Composition*: The Survival of 18th-c. French Philosophy before Saussure," *Romance Philology*, XXIX, 4 (1976), 522–38, esp. 533–4, 537.
66. Condillac, *Grammaire* I, iii, part of his *Cours d'études* . . . in *Oeuvres philosophiques*, ed. G. Le Roy (Paris: Presses Universitaires, 3 vols., 1947–51), I, 436b. Aarsleff, "The Tradition," 146 fn. 38, also indicates I, 430a (*Grammaire* I, i), I, 212–4 (*Traité des systèmes*, 1749), and more fully II, 374–8 (*Logique*, 1780, I, chs. ii–iii). Condillac had hinted at this idea in his seminal *Essai sur l'origine des connoissances humaines* (1746), where he had shown "how the inescapable linearity of speech had forced man to decompose the initial unitary signs of the language of action into discrete, arbitrary signs of human language, thus making analysis and ordered reflection possible." (Aarsleff, "The Tradition," 103.) It was, however, I must add, only an indirect implication.
67. Cf. Aarsleff, "The Tradition," 123–31 on Maupertuis, esp. 125. As Aarsleff points out, Georges Mounin, *Saussure* (Paris: Séghers, 1968), p. 54, misses Condillac on linearity, and says that this second feature of the sign, after arbitrariness, was "toujours inaperçu des linguistes avant lui" (i.e., Saussure). Yet Mounin recalls Lessing, *Laokoon*, 1766, ch. 16, with his proposal of an "analyse typiquement saussurienne, où il opposait le fonctionnement de la peinture, où les objets 'coexistent,' à celui de la poésie, domaine de la 'succession.'" For that idea, claims Aarsleff, "Thoughts," 534 fn. 21, "it is surely more relevant to refer to Diderot's *Lettre sur les sourds et muets* (1751), which opened with acknowledgment to Condillac." Diderot made a similar point in a section "de la pantomime" of his *Discours sur la poésie dramatique* (1758), of which Lessing published a German translation in 1760. Lessing's debt to Diderot is generally admitted, also to the 1751 *Lettre*. Richard A. Ogle 1974, pp. 63–4, takes up again the whole question, but whereas Aarsleff fails to trace the doctrine of simultaneity beyond Condillac, Ogle goes no further back than Diderot. As to the first Saussurian feature of the sign, i.e., arbitrariness, Eugenio Coseriu also takes issue with Mounin, showing how it was the heritage of a solid, continuous tradition ever since Aristotle (and, indeed, earlier): cf. Coseriu, "L'arbitraire du signe: Zur Spätgeschichte eines aristotelischen Begriffes," *Archiv für das Studium der neueren Sprachen und Literaturen*, 204, 2 (1967–8), 81–112.
68. See the text in O. Fellows, ed., *Diderot Studies*, VII (Geneva, 1965), p. 64, and in Diderot, *Oeuvres complètes*, ed. J. Assézat, I (Paris: Garnier, 1875), p. 369.
69. Ogle, p. 64, with reference to Chomsky, *Cartesian Linguistics*, 1966, p. 30, and to the nineteenth-century apprehension of language as a "constitutive" rather than a "reflective" medium.
70. "Autre chose est de concevoir clairement sa pensée, et autre chose de la rendre avec la même clarté. Dans un cas, toutes les idées se présentent à-la-fois à l'esprit, dans l'autre, elles doivent se montrer successivement. Pour bien écrire, ce n'est donc pas assez de bien concevoir: il faut encore apprendre l'ordre dans lequel vous devez communiquer l'une après l'autre des idées que vous apercevez ensemble, il faut savoir

analyser votre pensée. Accoutumez-vous de bonne heure à concevoir avec netteté, et familiarisez-vous en même temps avec le principe de la plus grande liaison." Ed. G. Le Roy, I, p. 539.

71. Ogle, pp. 66–7.

72. See the balanced assessment of all this theoretical background in Ogle, esp. pp. 80–90.

73. I use the spelling of the most recent edition by H. Penzl in tomes VIII. 1–2 of Gottsched's *Ausgewählte Werke* (Berlin-New York: W. de Gruyter, 1978), which is based on the 1762[5] ed., while I give the pagination of the original 1762 ed. For a recent, comprehensive assessment of Gottsched's work, see Werner Rieck, *Johann Christoph Gottsched: Eine kritische Würdigung seines Werkes* (Berlin: Akademie-Verlag, 1972).

74. *Frieden* is changed to *Friede* in subsequent editions, and the words in parentheses are also later changes.

75. See *Le Maître de la langue allemande* (Strasbourg: König, 1782[9]), p. 338; (ibid., 1787[10]), p. 391. This way of revising the passage in successive editions shows that it obviously bothered the compiler.

76. Blackall, pp. 180–1, from p. 400 of the Gottsched Gesellschaft edition, ed. Reichel. Within the context of a then fashionable critique of periodicity, Grimarest 1712 had warned writers not to make one wait until the last word of the sentence "pour conoître le noeud de plusieurs propositions jointes ensemble" (*Eclaircissement sur la langue françoise*, 1712, p. 185 — Blackall, p. 169). This was exactly what the German language so often did, but something could be done there too.

77. Cf. Scaglione, *Ars Grammatica* (1970), passim, e.g., pp. 55–7, 59–62, 88–90.

78. See Fleischmann, p. 351.

79. Fleischmann, p. 353.

80. *Le maître . . . ou Nouvelle grammaire allemande méthodique et raisonnée composée sur le modèle des meilleurs auteurs de nos jours et principalement sur celui de M. le Prof. Gottsched* (Strasbourg: Amand König, 1782[9]). First ed. 1754, then 1758[2], 1760[3], 1763[4], 1766[5], 1769[6], 1774[7], 1778[8], 1782[9], 1787[10]. I use the 9th ed. throughout.

81. This rule 2 is Rule 4 in the 5th German ed., pp. 493–4.

82. The phrase in parentheses is not in the original.

83. Cf. Blackall, p. 185.

84. On H.-G. Koll's hypothesis, see Scaglione, *CTC*, pp. 365–9.

85. Jellinek, II, pp. 451–2.

86. (Frankfurt and Leipzig: J. G. Garben.)

87. (München: J. Friedrich Ott, 1765; Johann Nepomuk Fritz, 1775[3].)

88. Cf. Blackall, p. 231, who, however, does not use Du Cerceau.

89. Biackall, p. 215.

90. *Daniel Georg Morhofens Unterricht von der Teutschen Sprache und Poesie* (Lübeck and Frankfurt: J. Wiedermeyer, 1700), pp. 468–71.

91. Blackall, p. 215.

92. Blackall, p. 214.

93. Blackall, pp. 288–9. The full title was *Critische Dichtkunst. Worinnen die poetische Mahlerey in Absicht auf die Erfindung im Grunde untersuchet und mit Beyspielen aus den berühmtesten Alten und Neuern erläutert wird* (Zürich: C. Orell, & Leipzig: J. F. Gleditsch, 1740, 2 tomes). Faksimiledruck nach der Ausgabe v. 1740 mit einem Nachwort v. Wolfgang Bender, Deutsche Neudrucke, Reihe "Texte des 18. Jh." (Stuttgart: J. B. Metzler, 1966, 2 Bde.).

94. Blackall, p. 294.

95. Blackall, pp. 295–313. To Blackall's sources I have added the important 1740 title, which deserves full mention: *Critische Abhandlung von den Wunderbaren in der Poesie und dessen Verbindung mit dem Wahrscheinlichen, in einer Vertheidigung des Gedichtes Joh. Miltons von dem verlohrnen Paradiese; der beygefüget ist Joseph Addisons Abhandlung von den Schönheiten in demselben Gedichte* (Zürich: C. Orell); reprt. Stuttgart: J. B. Metzlersche Verlagsbuchhandlung, 1966. Cf. Johannes Crüger, *J. Ch. Gottsched und die Schweitzer J. J. Bodmer und J. J. Breitinger*, in J. Kürschner, ed., *Deutsche National-Litteratur*, 42. Bd. (Berlin and Stuttgart: W. Spemann, 1883); Enrico Pizzo, *Miltons Verlornes Paradies im deutschen Urteile des 18. Jahrhunderts* (Berlin: Felber, 1914); Herbert Schöffler, *Das literarische Zürich 1700–1750* (Frauenfeld: Huber, 1925); Ernst Busch, "Klopstocks Messias und die poetische Theorie von Bodmer und Breitinger," *Germanisch-romanische Monatsschrift* (NF), 29 (1941), 92–106; Alessandro Pellegrini, *Gottsched, Bodmer, Breitinger e la poetica dell'Aufklärung* (Catania: Università di Catania — Biblioteca della Facoltà di Lettere e Filosofia, 1952); Karl Ludwig Schneider, *Klopstock und die Erneuerung der deutschen Dichtersprache im 18. Jahrhundert* (Heidelberg: C. Winter, 1960); and the important Wolfgang Bender, "Johann Jacob Bodmer und Johann Miltons *Verlohrnes Paradies*," *Jahrbuch der deutschen Schiller-Gesellschaft*, XI (1967), 225–67 and Id., *Johann Jacob Bodmer und Johann Jacob Breitinger* (Stuttgart: J. B. Metzler, 1973).
96. Blackall, pp. 310–1.
97. Blackall, pp. 314 ff., ch. "The Grand Manner."
98. See it in A. L. Back and A. R. C. Spindler's edition of Klopstock's *Sämmtliche Werke* (Leipzig, 1823–30), vol. IV of 6 vols. on linguistic matters, i.e., vols. XIII–XVIII, all published in 1830: See IV, pp. 13–32, especially p. 24 for quote.
99. "Von der Darstellung," Back-Spindler, IV, pp. 1–12 (from *Fragmente über Sprache und Dichtkunst*, Hamburg: Heroldsche Buchhandlung, 1779).
100. IV, p. 6.
101. Blackall, p. 323.
102. Back-Spindler, II (XIV), pp. 271–82. This essay also came from the *Fragmente über Sprache und Dichtkunst*.
103. Blackall, p. 324. See pp. 346–50 for examples.
104. Hamann, *Sämtliche Werke*, ed. Joseph Nadler (Wien: Verlag Herder, 1949–57, 6 vols.), vol. II (1950), pp. 127–36: See pp. 130–1: *Vermischte Anmerkungen über die Wortfügung in der französischen Sprache*. Also in H., *Schriften*, ed. Friedrich Roth (Berlin: G. Reimer, 1821–43, 8 vols.), II, 133 ff., and, now, in a selection of his linguistic writings, still relying on Nadler's text and apparatus; H., *Schriften zur Sprache*, ed. Joseph Simon (Frankfurt/M.: Suhrkamp, 1967). See, also, Hamann's two *Rezensionen* on "Herders Abhandlung über den Ursprung der Sprache" and "des Ritters von Rosencreuz letzte Willensmeynung über den göttlichen und menschlichen Ursprung der Sprache," as well as the "Philologische Einfälle und Zweifel über eine akademische Preisschrift" (all three pieces of 1772), in J. Simon's ed., pp. 129–36, 137–45, and 147–65.
105. Cf. Scaglione, *CTC*, pp. 240–1. Also Jellinek, II, p. 440, and Blackall, pp. 444–5.
106. See, now, Algarotti's *Saggio sopra la lingua francese* (1750), first published 1757 in his *Opere varie* (Venezia: Pasquali), in F. Algarotti, *Saggi*, ed. Giovanni da Pozzo (Bari: Laterza, 1963), pp. 245–61. As to Hamann's quotation from Algarotti, here and on p. 182, it must refer to the French translation of 1772: *Oeuvres du Comte Algarotti*, trans. Belletier (Berlin: G. J. Decker, 8 tomes), and is therefore part of Hamann's later handwritten revision of his printed text (i.e., text B in Nadler's apparatus). See Nadler's fn. p. 401, where he identifies Algarotti's *Oeuvres*, VII, 299 with a "Lettre à M. l'Abbé Gré-

goire Bressani à Padoue, de Berlin ce 17 juin 1752," about some letters by Father Cattaneo written from Paraguay. The exact meaning of notes and apparatus remains uncertain because Nadler relied on G. A. Wiener's critical apparatus (*Hamanns Schriften*, VIII, 1, *Nachträge* etc., Berlin, 1842), where it is not clearly indicated what comes from Hamann's handwritten revision and what from Wiener's research. The only previous edition of Algarotti with a 7th tome was that of 1764 (*Opere*, Livorno: Coltellini, 9 tomes: *Saggio sopra la lingua francese* in t. III, pp. 27–63), and Hamann was apparently writing in 1761–2. Furthermore, it is in the Essay on the French language that Algarotti expressed ideas such as those reported in Hamann's text, whereas the passage referred to in the footnote, though dealing with inversion, has no bearing on the matter. The letter to Bressani, contained in t. VII, pp. 299–305 of the 1772 *Oeuvres*, deals, in fact, with Cattani's letters from Paraguay, which Algarotti had lost by lending them to a friend. Algarotti states that from such letters he had learned that the language of one of the tribes of Paraguay appears to be "si fort rempli d'inversions et, pour ainsi dire, si disloqué," that the Greeks' and Latins' boldest hyperbata would sound easy by comparison. The French, he adds, could find confirmation there that inversions are a mark of a language in a barbarous stage, like English, he says, in which a preposition may be sent to the very end of the sentence. (The translation says simply *article*, but the original exemplifies with *del*, *al*, hence he means prepositions or preposition-article compounds.) See the original in *Opere*, Venezia: Palese, IX (1794), pp. 220–5.

107. On the literary import of Hamann's work, see the recent study by Volker Hoffmann, *J. G. Hamanns Philologie; Hamanns Philologie zwischen enzyklopädischer Mikrologie und Hermeneutik* (Stuttgart: W. Kohlhammer, 1972); on the lively present state of research on Hamann, see Sven-Aage Jørgensen, *J. G. Hamann* (Stuttgart: Sammlung Metzler, 1976).

108. See the *Fragmente* in Herder, *Sämtliche Werke*, eds. Bernhard Suphan *et al.* (Berlin: Weidmannsche Buchhandlung, 1877–1913, 33 vols.), I (1877), pp. 151–158 and 182–197, and in Herder, *Werke*, ed. Wilhelm Dobbek (Berlin-Weimar: Aufbau-Verlag, 1964, 5 vols.), II, pp. 7–76. Only the first Series is included in the Dobbek edition.

109. Suphan ed., p. 157; Dobbek ed., p. 14.

110. See Suphan ed., pp. 191–2, with the example *Die Schlange, fleuch!*, vs. *Fleuch die Schlange*, from Diderot's *Lettre*. Blackall, p. 454.

111. It is worth noting that the Germans defend inversion and free order, siding in this with the *mécaniciens*, but adopt, wisely, the *métaphysiciens*' taste for loose, unperiodic structures with curtailed use of conjunctions (*style coupé*). Their verbs at the end remind them of Cicero, yet they reject this model as *Kanzleistil*, while the official *Amtsstil* continued to cultivate periodicity.

112. Blackall, pp. 455–6.

113. Blackall, p. 456.

114. Blackall, ibid.

115. Hans Aarsleff, "The Tradition of Condillac . . . " (1974), pp. 93–156, has eloquently argued the case for Condillac's *Essai sur l'origine des connoissances humaines* (1746) as the main single source of inspiration, directly or indirectly, for Herder's 1771 *Über den Ursprung der Sprache*, chiefly for the thesis on the origin of language.

For other recent interpretations of Herder's philosophy of language, see the Introduction to Herder, *Sprachphilosophische Schriften*, ed. Erich Heintel (Hamburg: Meiner, 1960), and Joe K. Fugate, *The Psychological Basis of Herder's Aesthetics* (The Hague and Paris: Mouton, 1966). On the background to Herder's prize-winning essay as well as its impact, see the commentary in *J. G. Hamanns Hauptschriften erklärt*, ed. by Fritz

Blanke and L. Schreiner (Gütersloh: Bertelsmann, 7 vols., 1956–78): vol. IV, ed. by Elfriede Büchsel (1963), and Brigitte Schnebli-Schwegler, *J. G. Herders Abhandlung über den Ursprung der Sprache und die Goethe-Zeit* (Winterthur: Keller, 1965).

116. "der Schriftsteller, . . . der durch die Einbildungskraft Aufmerksamkeit, Empfindung, ja öfters Leidenschaft erregen will — der braucht sie nothwendiger." ". . . die Ordnung der Phantasie ist doch gewiß nicht die Ordnung der kalten Vernunft" — ed. Suphan, pp. 195–6.

117. Cf. Lessing, *Sämtliche Schriften*, ed. Karl Lachmann — Franz Muncker (Stuttgart: Göschen, 1892), vol. VIII. *Literaturbrièfe* is the short title for the *Briefe, die neueste Literatur betreffend*, which appeared in periodical form (Berlin: Fr. Nicolai, 24 vols.) first under the editorship of Lessing in 1759, and then with other editors until 1765. Only the articles of Lessing and which appeared in the first series of 1759–60, are included in the editions of his works, but the letter in question at this point in Herder's text was not by Lessing. In some of his own "letters," however, Lessing did raise several of the points on which Herder's *Fragmente* happen to dwell, e.g., in the *13. Brief* of the *Erster Theil*, dated Febr. 1, 1759, where he discussed the aptitude of such orators as Wieland, Mosheim, Demosthenes, and Cicero to vary their style according to audience and purpose or circumstance. Similarly, in the 3rd Theil, 51st Brief, pp. 143–4, Lessing praises the 26th article of the *Nordischer Aufseher* for its worthwhile observations on the means to raise a nation's poetic style above the prosaic. The second means is word order or rather hyperbaton or inversion, following the rule that one must show first that which is most emotionally charged in an idea — "die Gegenstände, die in einer Vorstellung am meisten rühren, zu erst zeigen."

For recent titles dealing with the *Fragmente*, cf. Emil Adler, *Herder und die deutsche Aufklärung* (Wien-Frankfurt-Zürich: Europa-Verlag, 1968), pp. 85–94, and Dieter Lohmeier, *Herder und Klopstock: Herders Auseinandersetzung mit der Persönlichkeit und dem Werk Klopstocks* (Bad Homburg: Verlag Gehlen, 1968), pp. 74–89.

The texts of both *Literaturbriefe* and *Fragmente* are also available in Joseph Kürschner's *Deutsche National-Litteratur*: see Bd. 64, *Lessings Werke*, ed. R. Boxberger, VII (Berlin-Stuttgart: W. Spemann, n.d.), and Bd. 76.1, *Herders Werke*, ed. Hans Lambel, III, 1 (ibid., n.d.). See now the *Literaturbriefe* also in the authoritative new edition by Herbert G. Göpfert, Lessing, *Werke*, V (Munchen: C. Hanser, 1973).

118. André-Pierre le Guay de Prémontval, a French Huguenot refugee, appears to have been a rather self-sufficient though largely inconsequential member of the Berlin Academy. He had read there two papers on May 16, 1754 on the principle of sufficient reason and on the law of continuity within the context of Wolff's philosophy. He congratulated Michaëlis on his winning the 1759 prize on the "Influence of opinions on language and vice versa" and boasted to Michaëlis of having voted for him after having himself authored the topic — which was probably due, instead, to Maupertuis, who had indeed formulated it as early as 1748, at the very beginning of his *Réflections*. The topic was also discussed by Condillac, with reference to Maupertuis as its instigator, in his *Cours d'histoire*, Book III, last chapter (part of the *Cours d'études*). Cf. H. Aarsleff, "The Tradition of Condillac" (1974), p. 134.

119. . . . *oder von den Bestandtheilen derselben und von dem Redesatze* (Zürich: Orell, Geßner).

120. Cf. Jellinek, II, p. 453. Also Fleischmann, pp. 357–9.

121. According to Jellinek, II, pp. 453–4, and Fleischmann, p. 358, agrees.

122. Cf. Jellinek, II, p. 476.

123. "Aber da einige derselben den Satz einführen; andere ihn unterordnen und ver-

binden, so folget natürlich, daß mit der erstern Art das Zeitwort vorne, mit der andern es am Ende gestellt werde" (p. 100). Relative pronouns, however, do have the "power" of determining end-position (p. 95). Cf. Fleischmann, pp. 357–9.

124. Cf. Fleischmann, pp. 58 and 64 for theory and §§ 24 and 29 of historical documentation. For more on the *Nachtrag* see my chapter 3 *passim* and pp. 176–8.

125. Jellinek, II, p. 454.

126. *Deutsche Sprachlehre, zum Gebrauche der kuhrpfälzischen Lande* (Mannheim: Akademische Schriften, 1775); [Jakob Domitor], *Grundris einer dauerhaften Rechtschreibung* (Manheim [sic]: Kurfürstliche Hofbuchdruckerei, 1776); *Kern der deutschen Sprachkunst und Rechtschreibung* (Mannheim: Kr. Fridr. Schwan'en, Kurpfälzischer Hofbuchhändler, 1780).

127. Jellinek, II, p. 455: One could call the *subjectum* and the *praedicatum* "den vordern und hintern Begriff" according to Aichinger, *Versuch*, p. 120.

128. Jellinek, II, p. 451.

129. Jellinek, II, p. 452, § 590.

130. Published both separately and as part of 2d vol. of *Der Teutsche Sprachforscher*, allen Liebhabern ihrer Muttersprache zur Prüfung vorgelegt, 2 Bde. (Stuttgart: J. B. Mezler, 1777, 1778).

131. *Sprachforscher*, II, p. 132, cited by Jellinek, I, p. 281.

132. Jellinek, II, p. 458.

133. It is only for the sake of bibliographic completeness that we wish to enter here the title J. H. Schlegel, *Abhandlung über die Vortheile und Mängel des Dänischen, verglichen mit dem Deutschen und Französischen. Aus dem Dänischen, nebst einigen Anmerkungen und einer Abhandlung des Uebersetzers* (Schleswig: J. F. Hansen, 1763). Gottlieb Benedikt Funk (1734–1814) is the translator and author of the important "Erörterungen" in this translation, which had considerable impact on Adelung.

134. Cf. H. Aarsleff, "The History of Linguistics and Professor Chomsky," *Language*, 46 (1970), 570–85 on Du Marsais' debt to Locke, and H. M. Bracken, "Chomsky's Cartesianism," *Language Sciences*, No. 22 (Oct. 1972), 11–17.

135. Cf. Du Marsais, *Oeuvres choisies* (Paris: Pougin, 1797; reprt. Stuttgart-Bad Cannstatt: Frommann-Holzboog, 1971, Grammatica Universalis 5:1–3), vol. V, pp. 1–96: see pp. 6–7. Du Marsais went on immediately after the words just quoted: "les premiers excitent l'attention et la curiosité, ceux qui suivent la satisfont successivement." "C'est par cette manière que l'on a commencé, dans notre enfance, à nous donner l'exemple et l'usage de l'élocution. D'abord on nous a montré l'objet, ensuite on l'a nommé. . . . Après le nom . . . on ajoutoit les mots qui le modifioient, qui en marquoient les qualités ou les actions " (ibid.).

136. *Deutsche Sprachlehre. Zum Gebrauche der Schüler in den Königlich-Preußischen Landen* (Berlin: Ch. Voss, 1781, 1792, 1795, 1800, 1806, 1816). I use the 1816 ed. (apparently a reprinting of 4th ed., 1800), where the chapter on word order occupies pp. 421–44. *Umständliches Lehrgebäude der deutschen Sprache*, 2 Bde. (Leipzig: J. G. I. Breitkopf, 1782). This was the only edition. The 2 vols. are further divided into 4 "Abschnitte." The last or 4th Abschnitt deals "Von den Syntaxe oder Redesatz," pp. 275–612 of vol. 2. Syntax is divided into: (1) Connecting single words with one another; (2) "Von der Folge der Wörter"; (3) "Von den Sätzen." The section on word order is on pp. 503–65. The 4 "Abschnitte" are preceded by a historical "Vorrede" and followed by a section on Orthography.

137. 1. Von der Folge der Wörter überhaupt, §§ 759–84 (pp. 503 on) in *UL*, II; 2. Von

der Wortfolge nach der Gemüthstellung des Redenden, §§ 785–805; 3. Von der Inversion oder der Abweichung von der gewöhnlichen Wortfolge um des Nachdruckes willen, §§ 806–10 (through p. 565). Pp. 566–612 of *UL* contain ch. 3, "Von den Sätzen."

138. Cf. Jellinek, II, pp. 460–1. And see pp. 459–64 for the remainder of Jellinek's critique of Adelung.

139. *DS* 1781, p. 530; *UL*, pp. 546–9. Fleischmann, pp. 364–5, 368.

140. See Theo Vennemann, "Theoretical Word Order Studies," *Papiere zur Linguistik*, 7 (1974), p. 10, and "Topics, Subjects, and Word Order," *Historical Linguistics*, eds. J. Anderson and Ch. Jones (Amsterdam: North Holland, 1974), vol. II, pp. 347 and 358.

141. On Beauzée's law, see my *CTC*, pp. 266–7.

142. Jellinek, II, p. 459, fn. 2: "Auf 'Gottscheds und aller übrigen Sprachlehren, welche ihm in der grammatischen Kunst ähnlich sind,' mit einem 'z.B.' zu verweisen ist geradezu perfid; G. ist kein Beispiel, sondern eine Ausnahme."

143. Cf. Jellinek, II, p. 462.

144. Jellinek, II, pp. 462–3.

145. See, also, *DS* 1795, pp. 539 and 556, *DS* 1816, p. 441 §§ 806–7.

146. On Natural Serialization see the exposition of Vennemann's terminology under Contemporary Theory in Chapter 3, p. 152.

147. Jellinek, II, 485.

148. This § corresponds, with different wording but with the same example, to § 809 of *UL*. It is irrelevant that these examples are out of place in the *Sprachlehre*, since they do not relate logically to the point of the paragraph in which they appear, which is to define the use of complete clauses as subject, thus causing the inversion of the normal subject, as exemplified in *Daß er heute kommen wird, weiß ich*.

Chapter 3: Modern Theory and Its Nineteenth-Century Background

1. *Vollständige Grammatik der neuhochdeutschen Sprache* (Berlin: G. Reimer, 1833, 5 Bde., reprt. Berlin: W. de Gruyter, 1967), 5. Bd. As to Bernhardt as one of Bauer's sources, see fn. 5 below.

2. *Vollständige Grammatik*, 6. Hauptstück, 3. Abschnitt, vol. V, p. 1, and S. H. A. Herling, "Über die Topik der deutschen Sprache," 1821. See my pp. 97f. on term *Topik*.

3. Johann Friedrich Wilhelm Jerusalem (1709–89), *Über die deutsche Sprache und Litteratur. An ihro königliche Hoheit die verwittwete Frau Herzogin von Braunschweig und Lüneburg* (Berlin: Rottmann, 1781; reprt. Leipzig: Xenien-Verlag, 1910). This 30-page pamphlet was an answer to *De la littérature allemande* by Frederic the Great, written at his request in the form of a letter to his sister.

Karl Wilhelm Kolbe (1747–1835), *Über den Wortreichtum der deutschen und französischen Sprache, und beider Anlage zur Poesie* (Leipzig: C. H. Reclam, 1806, 2 vols.; Berlin: Realschulbuchhandlung, 1818–20², 3 vols.).

4. Cf. my *CTC*, pp. 372 and 375.

5. The tracing of Bauer's sources is made awkward by his practice of mentioning titles only on the early occasions, even if these occurred four tomes before. Bernhardt is indicated only in tomes I and II as the author of a *Sprachlehre* (Frankfurt. 1825). Cf. Bauer, I, p. 541 fn.; II, pp. 190 fn., 572 fn., 620 fn. He is one of his most frequently cited sources. The title must mean Fr. K. Bernhardt's *Deutsche Grammatik für den höhern Unterricht* (Frankfurt/M.: Hermann, 1825, 1828²). As to the other authors cited by

Bauer, see, for titles, Bauer IV, p. 4: Herling, *Grundregel des deutschen Styls* (Frankfurt/M., 1827); Bauer II, p. 671: Geo. Albr. Phil. Lorberg, *Zusätze zu J. C. A. Heyse's Lehrbüchern der dt. Sprache* (Wiesbaden: Ritter, 1828[2]).

6. *Ausführliche deutsche Grammatik als Kommentar der Schulgrammatik* (1837, 2 Bde.), 2. neuarbeitete Ausgabe (Prag: F. Tempsky, 1870, 2 Bde.; reprt. Hildesheim-New York: G. Olms, 1969, 2 vols.). There was also an original 3 Bde. ed. (Frankfurt/M., 1836–9). See vol. II of 1969 reprt., ch. 6, §§ 280–90, "Wortfolge," pp. 423–78. And cf. Gerhard Haselbach, *Grammatik und Sprachstruktur. K. F. Beckers Beitrag zur Allgemeinen Sprachwissenschaft in historischer und systematischer Sicht* (Berlin: W. de Gruyter, 1966). In the Introduction to his classic essay on the order of words, Henri Weil (1844) confessed to have received stimulus to writing on that subject from the example of two German grammarians, Herling (1830) and Becker, who in their grammars had "not confined themselves to establishing the usual construction of German, but have sought the reasons for its manifold inversions." See, now, the reprt. of Ch. W. Super's trans. of Weil, *The Order of Words in the Ancient Languages Compared with that of the Modern Languages*, edited with an introduction by A. Scaglione. Amsterdam Classics in Linguistics, 14 (Amsterdam: John Benjamins, 1978).

7. These theoretical foundations were laid by Becker in his *Organism der Sprache (als Einleitung zur deutschen Grammatik)* (Frankfurt/M.: Kettembeil, 1827, 1841[2]; reprt. Hildesheim-New York: Olms, 1970). The subtitle was dropped in the 2d ed. See, in particular, §§ 60, 122, 123, pp. 229–30, 586–96 on "Einfacher Satz," "Wortstellung," and "Inversion."

8. *System der Sprachwissenschaft*, ed. by H. Steinthal (Berlin: Dümmler, 1856). Cf. Leo Weisgerber, *Grundzüge der inhaltbezogene Grammatik* (Düsseldorf: Schwann, 1962[3]), pp. 344f.

9. The recent study by Klaus Fleischmann, *Verbstellung und Relieftheorie* (München: Fink, 1973), can serve as a useful guide in this area, despite a rather unconvincing theoretical framework. See especially pp. 33–65 for what follows. Fleischmann concentrates on the question of end-position of the verb in subordinate clauses; more important, his reconstruction of the main theses is inaccurate in some details and also incomplete.

10. For an overview of the polemics on this subject cf. Frank L. Borchardt, "Petrarch: The German Connection," in A. Scaglione, ed., *Francis Petrarch, Six Centuries Later: A Symposium* (Chapel Hill: U.N.C. Press, 1975), pp. 418–31.

11. Cf. Tomanetz, p. 54: "Für die ahd. selbständigen HS. lässt sich wol als allgemeine Regel hinstellen, dass das Prädicat von dem betonten Wort angezogen wird, also zweite Stelle einnimmt." P. 102: "Die oben gegebene Entwicklung lässt mich nicht daran glauben, dass unsere jetzige WStllg. des NS. ursprünglich die des HS. war und der HS. von ihr zu seiner jetzigen abgewichen sei." He would find the evolution of the two types exceedingly complicated by the idea that the dependent clause first would have deflected from the original pattern and then returned to it. He refers to Delbrück, *Syntaktische Forschungen* III, 76 for the thesis of the verb at the end in Old Indic main clauses, and also to Behaghel, *Germania* 23, 284 as independently and contemporaneously reaching the same conclusion as Delbrück concerning the present order of the *Nebensatz* being the original order for all clauses (p. 102). Tomanetz reiterated his opposite conclusion in his critical review of Ries 1880 in *Deutsche Literaturzeitung*, 2 (1881), 275f.

12. "Zur Lehre von der deutschen Wortstellung," *Forschungen zur deutschen Philologie: Festgabe für Rudolf Hildebrand* (Leipzig, 1894), pp. 34–51. As one can see, the 1880s and 1890s were productive years for positive research and speculation on our subject. I shall add here a sample of painstakingly detailed presentation of such results

for the use of the school public: Daniel Sanders, *Satzbau und Wortfolge in der deutschen Sprache* (Weimar: Emil Felber, 1895²). One more interesting detail: Fourquet 1974, p. 315, attributes to O. Erdmann's 1886–98 *Grundzüge* and to his even earlier *Untersuchungen über die Syntax der Sprache Otfrids* (Halle/S.: Buchhandlung des Waisenhauses, 1874–76, 2 vols.; reprt. Hildesheim: Olms, 1973) the first realization of the principle, independently arrived at by Fourquet himself in 1938, that the traditional contrast of *gerade/ungerade Folge* or *Inversion* was irrelevant, and that the correct analysis of a sentence had to be based on first, second, or last position of the verb.

13. Cf. Hirt, *Indogermanische Grammatik*, VII (Heidelberg: C. Winter, 1936), p. 142: "The word order of Indo-European was to all appearances free"; Meillet, *Introduction à l'étude comparative des langues indoeuropéennes* (Paris: Hachette, 1937⁸), p. 365: "The order of words had an expressive, not a syntactic value; it belonged to rhetoric, not to grammar." See Paul J. Hopper 1975, p. 15.

14. Behaghel, "Zur deutschen Wortstellung," *Zeitschrift für dt. Unterricht*, 6 (1892), 265–67; "Zur deutschen Wortstellung," *Wiss. Beihefte zur Zeitschrift des Allgemeinen dt. Sprachvereins*, 3. Reihe (1896–1901), Heft 17/18 (1900), pp. 233–51; "Zur Stellung des Verbs im Germanischen und Indogermanischen," *Zeitschrift für vergleichende Sprachforschung*, 56 (1929), 276–81; "Zur Wortstellung des Deutschen," *Curme Volume of Linguistic Studies* (Philadelphia, 1930), pp. 29–33; "Von deutscher Wortstellung," *Zeitschrift für Deutschkunde* (= *Zs. f. dt. Unterricht*), 44 (1930), 81–89; *Deutsche Syntax: Eine geschichtliche Darstellung* (Heidelberg: Carl Winter, 1923–32, 4 vols.), vol. IV: Wortstellung, Periodenbau. Behaghel is also well known for his theory that the arrangement of relatively free parts of the sentence, especially sequences of complements and adverbial phrases, obeys definable criteria of rhythm, typically the Law of the Growing Members (*Gesetz der wachsenden Glieder*). In my *CTC*, pp. 238–9, 266–8, 391, I have traced this important speculative concern back to Beauzée and Gamaches and then on to Jespersen's Principle of Relative Weight (to which one could now add John R. Ross's principle of "Heavy Noun Phrase Shift": "A long and complicated noun phrase obligatorily moves to the end of the sentence" — cf. *Where the Rules Fail: A Student's Guide. An Unauthorized Appendix to Marina K. Burt's From Deep to Surface Structure*, Department of Linguistics, Univ. of Michigan, published by The Linguistic Club, Indiana Univ., 1972, pp. 18–20).

15. Cf. Fleischmann, pp. 40–42.

16. Biener, "Zur Methode der Untersuchungen über deutsche Wortstellung," *Zeitschrift für deutsches Altertum und deutsche Literatur*, 59, NF 47 (1922), 127–44; "Wie ist die neuhochdeutsche Regel über die Stellung des Verbums entstanden?," *ZfdAuL*, 59, NF 47 (1922), 165–79; "Die Stellung des Verbums im Deutschen," *ZfdAuL*, 63, NF 51 (1926), 225–56; "Veränderungen am deutschen Satzbau im humanistischen Zeitalter," *Zeitschrift für deutsche Philologie*, 78 (1959), 72–82.

17. Cf. Emilija Grubačić, *Untersuchungen zur Wortstellung in der deutschen Prosadichtung der letzten Jahrzehnte*. Zagreber germanistische Studien, 2 (Zagreb: Universität, Philosophische Fakultät, Abt. f. Germanistik, 1965), for full discussion and analysis of uses in modern German, and O. Behaghel, *Syntax* (1932), IV, pp. 66ff. and 125–44 for the earlier periods.

18. "Die Stellungsgesetze des Verbum finitum bei Cicero" (Bonn).

19. Linde gave the figures of 35% in main clauses and 61% in dependent clauses for verbal end-position in Cicero's *De republica*, 60+% and 75% respectively as averages for Cato, Cicero, Sallust; and H. G. Koll determined 66.7 versus 88% respectively for Object + Verb (rather than Verb + Object) in main clauses versus dependent clauses in

Cicero, *Catilin.* I, 20–26 and 81.8 versus 90.9% in his *De legibus* II, 1–2. Cf. Scaglione, *CTC*, pp. 364–6. Also, Scaglione, "Dante and the Medieval Theory of Sentence Structure," in J. J. Murphy, ed., *Medieval Eloquence* (Berkeley-Los Angeles: U.C. Press, 1978), pp. 252–69: See pp. 267–8 on lesser incidence of SOV in main clauses than in secondary clauses in Dante.

20. Stolt, *Die Sprachmischung in Luthers Tischreden: Studien zum Problem der Zweisprachigkeit.* Acta Universitatis Stockholmiensis, Stockholmer Germanistische Forschungen, Bd. 4 (Uppsala, 1964). Cf., also, Fritz Tschirch, *Spiegelungen: Untersuchungen vom Grenzrain zwischen Germanistik und Theologie* (Berlin: Erich Schmidt, 1966), "Die Sprache der Bibelübersetzung Luthers damals. Die Sprache der Bibelübersetzung Luthers heute," pp. 53–67, 68–108.

The biblical model seems to have exerted a more decisive impact on the verbal position of Old High German translations: cf. especially Jörg Lippert, *Beiträge zu Technik und Syntax ahd. Übersetzungen, unter besonderer Berücksichtigung der Isidorgruppe und des ahd. Tatian* (München: W. Fink, 1974).

21. Cf. Peter von Polenz, *Geschichte der deutschen Sprache* (Berlin: W. de Gruyter, 1972^8), pp. 92–3.

22. *L'ordre des mots dans la phrase latine* (Paris). Cf. my *CTC, s.v.*

23. *Untersuchungen über die deutsche Verbstellung in ihrer geschichtlichen Entwicklung.* Germanische Bibliothek, II. Abteilung: Untersuchungen und Texte, 21. Bd. (Heidelberg: Carl Winter, 1926).

24. *Die Aufgaben der neuhochdeutschen Wortstellungslehre* (Halle/S.: E. Karras, 1909; Diss. München), esp. pp. 707 ff.; *Die Haupttypen der heutigen neuhochdeutschen Wortstellung im Hauptsatz* (Strassburg: K. J. Trübner, 1914); see, also, his *Einführung in die Syntax* (Heidelberg: C. Winter, 1914).

25. Behaghel, *Deutsche Syntax IV* (1932), pp. 106–8 objected to both Maurer's and Hammarström's (1928) uses of sources because they lumped together two- and three-element verb phrases and they did not take into account that only those cases are significant in which the rhythm does not have a determining impact, or in which the rhythmical patterns are violated.

26. Examples: *wie er die ze friunt gewan* — Gottfried von Strassburg 4189; *wie ein scœniu meit wære in Burgonden ze wunsche wol getân* — Nibelungenlied 44, 2; *daz er mir sîn liut und sîn lant allez bevalch in mîne hant* — Gottfried von Strassburg 4181; *daz sie dich bekennen den einen gewâren got* — Myst. II, 154, 32; *daz er sô lîhte gewandelt wirt an betrüebnisse, an zorne und an ergerunge.* H. Paul, § 187 i, p. 139. I use the 14th ed. of Paul's manual (Halle/S.: Max Niemeyer, 1944).

27. "Über ein Gesetz der indogermanischen Wortstellung," *Indogermanische Forschungen*, 1 (1892), 333–436. The ground for the formulation of this 1892 law had been cleared by an earlier paper, "Der griechische Verbalaccent," *Zeitschrift für vergleichende Sprachforschung*, 23 (1877), 457–70, in which Wackernagel had examined the established enclitic status of some Greek bisyllabic finite verbs, to conclude that in the origin the Greek finite verb had been more generally atonic.

It may seem surprising that Fleischmann overlooked Wackernagel's decisive contribution, as he also failed to trace Delbrück's ideas any further back than 1911. On the impact of Wackernagel's law see, briefly, R. P. Ebert 1978, pp. 34–35.

Wackernagel 1892, pp. 425–8 deals with his conviction that "Altindisch, Latein und Litauisch stellen das Verbum regelmäßig ans Ende des Satzes" (427), and goes over the literature on the rule of end-position for *Nebensatz*, second position for *Hauptsatz* in German. He finds that, so far as he can see, all the scholars concerned about this rule (which he finds paradigmatically expounded in Oskar Erdmann, *Grundzüge der deutschen Syntax nach ihrer geschichtlichen Entwicklung* [Stuttgart: J. G. Cotta, I, 1886], pp. 181 ff., esp. 193 fn. and 195, and, for Old German, also especially Karl Tomanetz, *Die Relativsätze bei den ahd. Übersetzern des 8. u. 9. Jahrhunderts* [Wien: C. Gerold's Sohn, 1879], pp. 54 ff., and in the *Anzeiger für deutsches Alterthum und deutsche Litteratur*, 16 [1890], 381 — but this latter piece by Tomanetz, *Anzeiger*, 16, pp. 379–84, is only a book review of Max Rannow, *Der Satzbau der ahd. Isidor im Verhältnis zur lateinischen Vorlage*, and contains no general theoretical statement; see, instead, by Tomanetz, the important review of John Ries, *Die Stellung vom Subject und Prädicatsverbum im Hêliand*, in *Deutsche Literaturzeitung*, 2, 8 [1881], 275f.) are united in assuming that the rule was not original to Germanic, and that in particular Bergaigne, Ries, and (mark this) even Behaghel affirm that the original situation was end-position of the verb for all clauses: Abel Bergaigne, "Essai sur la construction . . . ," *Mémoires de la Societé de Linguistique de Paris*, 3 (Paris, 1878), 1–51, 124–54, 169–86, Index p. 422: See pp. 139 ff., esp. 140; Behaghel, "Die neuhochdeutschen Zwillingswörter," *Germania. Vierteljahrsschrift für d. Alterthumskunde*, 23 (N.R. 11) (Wien, 1878), 257–92: see p. 284; John Ries, *Die Stellung von Subject und Prädicatsverbum im Hêliand*, (1880), pp. 88 ff. In Wackernagel's words: "Trotzdem sind alle Forscher, die sich eingehender mit diesem germanischen Stellungsgesetz beschäftigt haben, so viel ich sehe, darin einig, die sich hier äußernde Scheidung der beiden Satzarten für unursprünglich zu erklären. Bergaigne etc. behaupten, daß die Endstellung des Verbums, wie sie im Nebensatz vorliegt, ursprünglich allen Sätzen eigen gewesen und in den Hauptsätzen nur allmählich durch eine später aufgekommene entgegengesetzt wirkende Regel verdrängt worden sei" (p. 426).

Further on (p. 427) he stated that "Nun ist es aber ganz unwahrscheinlich, daß die Grundsprache das Verbum im Hauptsatz und im Nebensatz verschieden betont, aber doch in beiden Satzarten gleich gestellt hätte. Und weiterhin müssen wir auf Grund des früher Vorgetragenen erwarten, daß in der Grundsprache das Verbum des Hauptsatzes, weil und insofern es enklitisch war, unmittelbar hinter das erste Wort des Satzes gestellt worden sei. Mit andern Worten: das deutsche Stellungsgesetz hat schon in der Grundsprache gegolten. Dabei muß man sich gegenwärtig halten, daß nicht bloß die Sätze, die wir als Nebensätze ansehen, sondern alle als hypotaktisch empfundenen im Altindischen und somit, wie wir wohl annehmen dürfen, in der Grundsprache betontes Verbum hatten, also unter allen Umständen die Endstellung des Verbums sehr häufig vorkommen mußte."

28. *Grundlagen*, p. 35. See Delbrück, *Germanische Syntax*, II: *Zur Stellung des Verbums*, in *Abhandlungen der könig. sächs. Ges. der Wissenschaften*, phil.-hist. Kl., XXVIII, 7 (Leipzig: Teubner, 1911); *Grundlagen der neuhochdeutschen Satzlehre — Ein Schulbuch für Lehrer* (Berlin-Leipzig: Vereinigg. Wissensch. Verleger, 1920). Both Fleischmann, pp. 65–8, and Fourquet, p. 14, go no further back than these titles for the Delbrück thesis, but one must start at least as early as Delbrück's *Vergleichende Syntax der idg. Sprachen*, 3. Teil (1900), this "Teil" being vol. V. of Karl Brugmann and Berthold Delbrück, *Grundriß der vergleichenden Grammatik der indogermanischen Sprachen* (Strassburg: K. J. Trübner, 5 Bde., 1886–1900). Delbrück's first statements were summarized in K. Brugmann's *Kurze vergleichende Grammatik der indogermanischen Sprachen auf Grund des fünfbändigen Grundriß der v. G. d. i. S. von K. B. u. B. D. verfasst* (Strassburg: K. J. Trübner, 1904), pp. 683–4: "besonders im erklärenden Aussagesatz . . . war in uridg. Zeit, wie es scheint, Endstellung [des Verbum finitum] am beliebtesten, und zwar scheint das Verbum habituell den Objektsakkusativ unmittelbar

vor sich gehabt zu haben. . . . " Furthermore, one must remember that this position of Delbrück's was essentially an extension of his 1888 peremptory conclusion, in *Syntaktische Forschungen*. V: *Altindische Syntax* (Halle/S.: Buchhandlung des Waisenhauses, 1888; reprt. Darmstadt: Wissenschaftliche Buchgesellschaft, 1968), p. 17, that in *Altindisch* "das Verbum tritt an das Ende des Satzes." And this, in turn, goes back to his *Die Altindische Wortfolge aus dem Çatapathabrāhmaṇa* (Halles/S.: Buchhandlung des Waisenhauses, 1878). Nevertheless, his ideas on these matters did not jell in definitive form until 1911, as we shall see.

29. Biener 1922 confirmed these views of Delbrück concerning the shift from last to second place, and contributed to their diffusion. Cf. Fleischmann, p. 67.

30. Hermann Wunderlich — Hans Reis, *Der deutsche Satzbau* (Stuttgart-Berlin: J. C. Cotta Nachf., 1924–25[3], 2 Bde.). But Wunderlich's position along such lines had been developed independently of Delbrück in much earlier years: See Wunderlich, *Der deutsche Satzbau* (Stuttgart: J. C. Cotta Nachf., 1892, 1901[2], 2 vols.): Id., *Unsere Umgangssprache in der Eigenart ihrer Satzfügung dargestellt* (Weimar-Brelin: E. Felber, 1894, 1896); Id., "Der Abgeordnete von Bismarck als Redner," *Zeitschrift d. allg. dt. Sprachvereins*, 10 (1895), 98–110; Id., *Die Kunst der Rede, in ihrer Hauptzügen an den Reden Bismarcks dargestellt* (Leipzig: S. Hirzel, 1898).

31. Curiously enough, in his authoritative 1886 *Syntax* Erdmann adduced for the opposite end two arguments that have become standard supports of the Wackernagel-Delbrück thesis. While offering an interesting attempt at an explanation why the German verb moved to the end (pp. 193–7), Erdmann held second position to be the norm (p. 181, beginning of Vierter Abschnitt: Stellung des Verbums im Satze), and declared himself unconvinced by Delbrück's 1878 and Behaghel's 1878 hypothesis that last position was the original rule: "Dass aber die Stellung des Verbums am Ende des Satzes in allen Fällen als die ursprünglich regelmässige anzusehen sei, wie es Delbrück *Syntakt. Forsch*. III, 76 für das Altindische, und danach auch Behaghel *Germania* 23, S. 284 für das Germanische aufstellten, lässt sich aus den erhaltenen deutschen Sprachdenkmälern nicht erweisen. Ich nehme also an, dass sie für den Nebensatz sekundär allmählich entwickelt sei im Gegensatze zu dem Typus I" [i.e., the normal second position] (fn. p. 193). How, then, did such a secondary development take place? Whatever the reason, it offered "ein Mittel zur Unterscheidung der Satzarten, das um so brauchbarer and wünschenswerter war, als durch die satzverbindenden Worte diese Unterscheidung in den meisten Fällen nicht genügend ausgedrückt wurde, da ja die meisten unterordnenden Conjunctionen auch als Demonstrativa oder Interrogativa in selbständigen Sätzen gebraucht werden konnten und noch heute gebraucht werden können" (p. 195). Recently, linguists again have turned their attention to this peculiarity of German morphology and syntax precisely within this context of explaining the need for further syntactic differentiation through word order.

Further on, and still more significantly, Erdmann formulates the rule whereby the qualifiers of the verb that come to the extreme right of the clause when the verb is in second position will immediately precede the verb in last-but-one position in the secondary clause: "Die . . . in selbständigen Sätze am Schlusse stehenden Bestimmungen des Verbums erhalten also in Nebensätzen die vorletzte Stelle und kommen so mit dem Verbum, dessen nächste Bestimmung sie bilden, auch räumlich zusammen": . . . *er war stets . . . ein Mann, er hielt dort die Fahne . . . hoch, er zog der Gefahr . . . entgegen* become *weil er stets . . . ein Mann war, wo er die Fahne . . . hoch hielt, daß er der Gefahr . . . entgegen zog.*

This fact is now being cited in support of last position of the verb as the general original rule. The presence of the *Rahmenkonstruktion* in Old Germanic is said to confirm Wackernagel's and Delbrück's theses, insofar as only the finite part (unstressed hence enclitic) of the verbal phrase has changed place, moving from last to second spot, whereas the nonfinite elements, separable prefixes, and nominal predicates have remained at the end, where they once accompanied the finite form in a tight whole. Furthermore, when the finite verb stays at the end, it *follows* the other parts of the verb phrase. Cf. R. P. Ebert, *Historische Syntax des Deutschen* (1978), p. 39, with bibliography.

32. Cf. Fleischmann, pp. 313–15. Cf. Ebert 1978, 3.1.3, pp. 25–28.

33. Fleischmann, pp. 315–6. But for OHG see K. Tomanetz, *Die Relativsätze bei den ahd. Übersetzern des 8. u. 9. Jahrh.* (1879), p. 54: "geht der Nebensatz voran, so wird das Verbum des Hauptsatzes attrahiert, gerade so wie im selbständigen HS., nur dass hier ein Nebensatz die Stelle des an der Spitze des HS. stehenden betonten Wortes einnimmt."

Incidentally, Fleischmann, p. 305, also reminds us that in Middle High German the use of the infinitive form in lieu of a participle comes with the modals *dürfen, können, mögen, wollen, müssen, sollen*, and also *heißen, lassen, hören*, and *sehen*. The coupling of such modal "infinitives" with the infinitive they govern produces the *Doppelinfinitiv*, and the ordering of the elements of the resulting group of auxiliary + modal + verb remains, as we have seen, somewhat controversial at least until the middle of the eighteenth century.

34. *L'ordre des éléments de la phrase en germanique ancien: Étude de syntaxe de position*. Publications de la Faculté des Lettres de l'Université de Strasbourg, 86 (Paris: Les Belles Lettres, 1938).

35. Cf. Scaglione, *CTC*, pp. 351–4, 365, with reference to the methods of A. Bergaigne, J. Marouzeau, and H.-G. Koll for the analysis of Latin and French.

I should represent the pivotal function of the German verb with the following formula designed to define the "inverted" sequence: X^1VSX^{-1}, where ^{1} means one element of X (X being "everything else" but S and V), and X^{-1} "everything else" minus ^{1}, i.e., minus that one complemental element that has taken first place.

36. This is an argument against the assumption that last position was adopted to mark dependence by itself. It was simply retained and reinforced as a further clarifying marker of dependence, in addition to a sometimes insufficiently clear conjunction or pronoun.

37. Hans Reis, "Uber althochdeutsche Wortfolge," *Zeitschrift für deutsche Philologie*, 33 (1901), 212–38 and 330–49; Paul Diels, *Die Stellung des Verbums in der älteren althochdeutschen Prosa*. Diss. Berlin (Berlin: Mayer and Müller, 1906).

38. Fourquet, "Genetische Betrachtungen über den deutschen Satzbau," in Werner Besch *et al.*, eds., *Studien zur deutschen Literatur und Sprache des Mittelalters. Festschrift für Hugo Moser zum 65. Geburtstag* (Berlin: E. Schmidt, 1974), pp. 314–23. Cf. R. P. Ebert, *Historische Syntax des Deutschen* (1978), pp. 35–37.

39. Although most of the terminology is explained as we go along, the prospectuses of summary nomenclature in § 4 of this chapter can be used for general reference.

40. Thomas G. Winner, Introduction to Iurii M. Lotman, *Struktura khudozhestrennogo teksta* (Providence: Brown U.P., 1971), p. vii. Joseph Vachek, *A Prague School Reader in Linguistics* (Bloomington: Indiana U.P., 1964), p. i, gives 1928–1948 as the "'classical' period of the Prague linguistic group," but the same author, *The Linguistic School of Prague* (ibid., 1966), p. 11, gives 1929–1939 for the same. One must be aware that the label, "structuralism," extended to these related but different schools, as well as to American Bloomfieldian and post-Bloomfieldian linguists, is a collective term that became current only in the late fifties and early sixties.

41. See my *CTC*, pp. 338–45 on Weil, and my new edition, with introduction, of Weil's essay in Ch. W. Super's translation (Amsterdam: J. Benjamins, 1978). The gap between Weil and Mathesius had been filled, in the context of the present discussion, by the psychologism of the Kantian School leading from J. F. Herbart through H. Steinthal, W. Wundt, and Karl Bühler. Cf. my introduction to Weil's 1978 edition, pp. ix–xii.

42. See Mathesius' several articles on English and comparative word order, 1907–1942, in the Bibliography.

43. Firbas, "Some Thoughts . . . ," *SPFFBU*, Ř.J., 6 (1957), p. 94, fn. 9.

44. Georg von der Gabelentz, "Ideen zu einer vergleichenden Syntax. Wort und Satzstellung," *Zeitschrift für Völkerpsychologie und Sprachwissenschaft*, 6 (1869), 376–84: cf. esp. p. 378.

45. Firbas, "Some Notes on the Problem of English Word Order from the Point of View of Actual Sentence Analysis," *SPFFBU*, Ř.J., 5 (1956), 93–107 (in Czech).

46. "Thoughts on the Communicative Function of the Verb in English, German, and Czech," *Brno Studies in English*, 1 (1959), 39–68, continued in "More Thoughts on the Communicative Function of the English Verb," *SPFFBU*, Ř.J. A7, 8 (1959), 74–96. Somewhat later, Firbas confirmed in a brief note the results reached by Eva Dvořáková to the effect that "within a Czech sentence, a thematic situational adverb [e.g., *yesterday* in English *I came across an important monograph yesterday*] unmistakably tends to occupy a basically thematic position, that is, to occur initially; a transitional adverb . . . [will in turn] occur medially; and a rhematic situational element tends to occupy a basically rhematic position, to occur finally. This is in agreement with the well-known fact that functional sentence perspective (= FSP) acts as the main word-order principle in Czech, and makes the order of words in Czech appear to be a far more important means of FSP than the word-order in English." Cf. Dvořáková, "Poznámky k Postavení . . . [Notes on the Situational Adverbs in English and Czech from the Point of View of FSP]," *SPFFBU*, Ř.J. A9, 10 (1961), 141–50, and Firbas, "Ještě k Postavení . . . [Another Note on the Position of the Situational Adverbs in English and Czech]," ibid., 153–55. I feel that, when compared with Firbas 1956, this pair of notes points up the difficulties one incurs in applying the provocative notions of the Prague functionalists, including the dangers of impressionism and subjectivism in the way thematic and rhematic assessments are distributed.

47. The distinction between subject and topic has been much discussed in recent years, as witnessed by the collective volume edited by Charles N. Li, *Subject and Topic*. Papers presented at the Symposium on Subject and Topic at the Univ. of California, Santa Barbara, March 1975 (New York: Academic Press, 1976).

48. Beneš, "Die Verbstellung im Deutschen, von der Mitteilungsperspektive her betrachtet," *Philologica Pragensia*, 5 (1962), 6–19 and then again in *Muttersprache*, 74 (1964), 9–21; "Die Besetzung der ersten Position im dt. Aussagesatz," in *Fragen der strukturellen Syntax und der kontrastiven Grammatik — Sprache der Gegenwart*, Bd. 17 (Düsseldorf, 1971), pp. 160–82; "Thema-Rhema Gliederung und Textlinguistik," in *Studien zur Texttheorie und zur deutschen Grammatik — Sprache der Gegenwart*, Bd. 30 (Düsseldorf, 1973), pp. 42–62.

49. Review of Blinkenberg, *L'ordre des mots*, 1, in *Archiv für das Studium der neueren Sprachen*, 160 (1931), 135–39.

50. Tesnière, *Éléments de syntaxe structurale* (Paris: Klincksieck, 1959, 1965^2), pp. 22f.

51. See, especially, the first two volumes of this work, under the respective titles *Grundzüge der inhaltbezogene Grammatik* (Düsseldorf: Pädagogischer Verlag Schwann,

1962[3]), pp. 360–402, particularly 360–66, and *Die sprachliche Gestaltung der Welt* (ibid.), pp. 366–70, 374–76, 411–13.

52. The first conception of this work went back to the years 1944–45, and its composition to 1947–48. The author says (1961) that he was pleased to discover how far it harmonized with the work of the contemporaneous American linguists, with whom he had remained unacquainted. The expression *innere Form* comes from a chapter title in Humboldt's *Über die Verschiedenheit des menschlichen Sprachbaus*, 1830–35, meaning the "conceptual," *begriffliche Form* as distinct from the "outer" or phonetic form, *lautliche, äussere Form*, but still in a "structural," not "semantic" sense, as with Weisgerber — with reference here to Weisgerber, *Muttersprache und Geistesbildung*, 1929, p. 86. Cf. Glinz, "Vorbemerkungen zur 2. Auflage," p. 4.

53. Cf. for this credit M. Bierwisch 1963 p. 169 fn. 27, and E. Beneš 1962–64 pp. 9–10. Beneš also mentions H. Ammann, *Die menschliche Rede, 2. Teil: Der Satz* (Lahr/B., 1928) and E. Drach, *Grundgedanken* 1937, for earlier attempts to introduce the distinction into German and, as two Russian Germanists who have recently applied the distinction to German, K. G. Kruschelnizkaja 1956 and 1957 and O. I. Moskalskaja, *Grammatika nemeckogo jazyka* (Moscow, 1956), pp. 121ff.

54. Besprechung von Gunther Ipsens *Zur Theorie des Erkennens, Indogermanische Forschungen*, 46 (1928), 254–55. The phrases in square brackets are Boost's.

55. The terminology on the *Rahmenkonstruktion* is by Guchmann 1969, pp. 79–84. See my Chapter 3, Section 4 for Guchmann's examples. The *Gliedsatz* is declared not to lend itself to such clear distinctions. Cf. my Bibliography for the titles of the authors listed here. I have been unable to locate Volker Beyrich, "Historiche Untersuchungen zur Ausklammerung," *Wissenschaftliche Studien des pädagogischen Instituts Leipzig*, Heft 1 (1967), pp. 88–89, cited by U. Engel 1970.

56. Weinrich, *Tempus — Besprochene und erzählte Welt* (Stuttgart: W. Kohlhammer, 1964), esp. ch. 9: "Relief im Satz," pp. 211–37, for the theoretical statement.

57. Weinrich, p. 220. Cf. Behaghel, *Deutsche Syntax*, IV, p. 6.

58. See Weinrich's ch. 9, pp. 211–37. For a faithful summary and discussion of this theory, cf. Fleischmann, pp. 34 and 73–81.

59. *Tempus*, p. 226. The rule of back-shifting of the verb must, then, be modified through the awareness that after some verbs (*dicendi, credendi* . . .) the verb of the governed clause can resume a second place if the conjunction is omitted. In other words, dropping or deleting the subordinating conjunction causes the clause to revert to a main clause form — in a case, we could add, of restored asyndetic paratactic juxtaposition.

60. Greenberg, "Some Universals of Grammar with Particular Reference to the Order of Meaningful Elements," in Greenberg, ed., *Universals of Language* (Cambridge, Mass.; M.I.T. Press, 1963[1]), pp. 58–90, (1966[2]), pp. 73–113.

I find rather unconvincing the following assessment of Greenberg's laws as applied to French nominal groups, which is found in the most recent comprehensive study of the noun-adjective coupling: "If we apply Greenberg's analysis to French, a rather confusing picture of its system emerges: Whereas French agrees with the majority of languages in putting the demonstrative before the noun while the adjective generally follows the noun (NA), it is slightly in the minority in putting the numeral before the noun under the same conditions. Even more importantly, whereas French 'normally' or 'most frequently' puts the adverb before the adjective (and in this is in the minority, as far as NA languages are concerned), this position for the adverb is, I will maintain, semantically marked." Linda R. Waugh, *A Semantic Analysis of Word Order: Position of the Adjective in French* (Leyden: E. J. Brill, 1977), p. 42.

61. E. C. Traugott, "Diachronic Syntax and Generative Grammar," *Language*, 41 (1965), 402–15; Id., "Toward a Grammar of Syntactic Change," *Lingua*, 23 (1969), 1–27.

62. On this question of nonlinearity in the deep structure, Ramat, p. 26 and fn. 6, quotes Vennemann 1974, "Topics, Subjects, and Word Order," and concludes: "Tatsächlich existieren aber in der Tiefenstruktur nur hierarchische Verhältnisse und Beziehungen semantischer Elemente. . . . Der Einwand wurde von dem Germanisten William G. Moulton gegen das Referat von J. R. Ross am 10. Internationalen Kongress der Linguisten erhoben." (With reference to Ross's paper on "Gapping.") By J. R. Ross, see also the more recent "Some Cyclically Ordered Transformations in German Syntax," in Johannes Bechert *et al.*, eds., *Papiere zur Linguistik*, 7 (1974), pp. 50–79.

63. The seminal text for case-grammar is, of course, Fillmore, "The Case for Case," in Emmon Bach and R. T. Harms, *Universals in Linguistic Theory* (New York: Holt, Rinehart and Winston, 1968), pp. 1–88, but see, specifically, his *Indirect Object Constructions in English and the Ordering of Transformations* (The Hague: Mouton, 1965).

64. Cf. David Crystal, *Linguistics* (Harmondsworth, Eng.: Penguin, 1971), pp. 234, 236–38.

65. Fourquet, *La construction de la phrase allemande* (Paris, 1959, mimeo.); Id., "Strukturelle Syntax und inhaltbezogene Grammatik," in Helmut Gipper, ed., *Sprache, Schlüssel zur Welt. Festschrift für Leo Weisgerber* (Düsseldorf: Pädagogischer Verlag Schwann, 1959), pp. 134–45. I have been unable to locate the first of these titles (obviously a noncommercial publication). As to the second, it is hardly relevant to the issue. Apparently Bierwisch was not familiar with Fourquet's main work; this confirms that his conclusions are purely synchronic and theoretical, not based on historical considerations — as he clearly implies.

66. "An Explanation of Drift," in Charles N. Li, ed., *Word Order and Word Order Change* (Austin: U. of Texas Press, 1975), pp. 269–305: See 271–76.

67. Fries, "On the Development of the Structural Use of Word Order in Modern English," *Language*, 16 (1940), 199–208; Lakoff, "Another Look at Drift," *Linguistic Change and Generative Theory*, eds. Robert P. Stockwell and Ronald K. S. Macaulay (Bloomington: Indiana U. Press, 1972), pp. 172–98.

68. "Natural generative grammar, therefore, assumes its deepest representations of sentences not to be linearly ordered," p. 26 of Vennemann, "Explanation in Syntax," in John P. Kimball, ed., *Syntax and Semantics*, II (New York — London: Seminar Press, 1973), pp. 1–50. Simple page references given henceforth will be to this article. Cf. also Vennemann, "Rule Inversion," *Lingua*, 29 (1972), 209–242 for argument against linear ordering of underlying structures of sentences, and G. Hudson, "Is Deep Structure Linear?" (1972).

69. Vennemann in Kimball, p. 48. Besides the title in fn. 71 below, representations by Bartsch and Vennemann of their theory are contained in several papers, some as yet unpublished, listed on p. 31 of Bartsch and Vennemann, eds., *Linguistics and Neighboring Disciplines* (Amsterdam-Oxford: North Holland, 1975).

70. R. A. Ogle 1974, pp. 159–64, chides Vennemann for his claim of having been the first both to ask and to answer this question. Ogle's counterclaim is that both achievements must be awarded, at least implicitly, and at least for the more general formula "Why do natural languages have the kinds of word order that they do?," to Joseph Emonds' 1969 "extremely important thesis" *Root and Structure-Preserving Transformations* (M.I.T. unpublished diss.), where the answers are obtained "with transformation rules alone," and "simply assuming . . . a linearly ordered base." Indeed, Emonds is said to provide "the strongest evidence yet available that left-to-right order

must be assigned in underlying structure" (Ogle, pp. 160, 163). If this be true, Du Marsais must have been saying something right. Ogle also credits Emonds with successfully tackling the issue of syntactic ambiguity (Vennemann's point of departure) in the form of "constructional homonymity" as raised by Chomsky (*Syntactic Structures*).

71. Likewise, *It was raining annoyingly* (one could barely see the road) versus *Annoyingly it was raining* (only slightly, but we couldn't wear our new summer outfits); *Intelligently* [or *Prudently*] *Sam sold his copy of Marx' Capital*. These further examples are in R. Bartsch and T. Vennemann, *Semantic Structures: A Study in the Relation Between Semantics and Syntax*. Athenäum-Skripten: Linguistik (Frankfurt/M.: Athenäum Verlag, 1972, 1973²), p. 21. Somewhat subtler but equally significant examples of the distinction between sentence adverbials and manner adverbials: *Allegedly, he seduced her*; *He frivolously seduced her*; *He seduced her skillfully*.

72. J. R. Ross, "Gapping and the Order of Constituents" (1970).

73. *Vereórte* is our artificial grapheme to read a *véreor te*, which in the Archipoeta rhymes with *mórte*, and *meliórme* likewise for *mélior me* rhyming with *enórme* in Gauthier de Châtillon. Cf. D'Arco Silvio Avalle, *Preistoria dell' endecasillabo* (Milano-Napoli: Ricciardi, 1963), pp. 17–8.

74. Cf. Vennemann, "Theoretical Word Order Studies: Results and Problems," in J. Bechert *et al.*, eds., *Papiere zur Linguistik*, 7 (Kronberg: Scriptor, 1974), 5–25: See p. 18; and Id., "Topics, Subjects, and Word Order: From SXV to SVX Via TVX," in John Anderson and Ch. Jones, eds., *Historical Linguistics. Proceedings of the 1st Int. Congress of Historical Linguistics, Edinburgh, Sept. 1973* (Amsterdam: North Holland, 1974), vol. II, pp. 339–76: See p. 371. Furthermore, concerning the older diagram, it must be added that SVO can also shift to SOV (see second diagram), as is happening in Modern Chinese: Charles N. Li and Sandra A. Thompson, "An Explanation of Word Order Change SVO → SOV," *Foundations of Language*, XII (1974), 201–14, and Charles N. Li, ed., *Word Order and Word Order Change* (1975), p. 166.

75. Li and Thompson 1974 criticize Vennemann for arbitrarily excluding, besides FWO → SVO, also "SVO → SOV, or SOV → FWO, or FWO → OSV."

76. Bartsch and Vennemann, *Semantic Structures*, p. 136.

77. Lehmann, "Contemporary Linguistics and Indo-European Studies," *PMLA*, 87, 5 (Oct. 1972), 976–93, esp. 982–7. For Marouzeau's assessment of *romanus homo* see my *CTC*, pp. 352–3.

78. Lehmann 1972, pp. 986 and 983 for the Hittite quote and the explanation, respectively.

79. "À la recherche de l'essence du langage," *Diogène*, 51 (1965), 22–38: See p. 29.

80. IX, iv, 23–4 and 25. For other authors and more details see my *CTC*, p. 76 and more generally pp. 74–96.

81. "À la recherche," p. 27.

82. "Implications of Language Universals for Linguistics," in Greenberg, ed., *Universals of Language* (M.I.T. Press, 1963), pp. 208–19: See p. 213.

83. Lehmann, "On the Rise of SOV Patterns in New High German," in K. G. Schweisthal, ed., *Grammatik, Kybernetik, Kommunikation: Festschrift für A. Hoppe* (Bonn: Dümmler, 1971), pp. 19–24, and *PMLA* (1972), 984–7.

84. "These clauses exemplify natural constituent order and natural serialization in the verbal complex:

{ V { Aux { Mod } } }   { [V [Aux [Mod]]] in OV languages
                                 [[[Mod] Aux] V] in VO languages"

"but *John has wanted to bring it* and somewhat less naturally in German: (*daß*) *Hans es hat bringen wollen*" (p. 43 and fn.).

85. Lehmann, art. in Schweisthal, *op. cit.*, p. 19.

86. Vennemann, in *Lingua* (1972), pp. 232–4. One finds here, p. 234, the explanation of the behavior of the speaker (especially the young one) as "misunderstanding" of the basic rule, i.e., OV (dependent clauses) → VO (main clauses) is misunderstood as VO (main) → OV (dependent), as if a shift were to be operated where in reality the main rule is simply preserved.

87. The specific rules are conveniently summarized in the diagrams in *Lingua* 29 (1972), 234 fn.:

(*re* I,D — Indirect, Direct Object)
    OV languages = {I,D} → ID
    VO   "   = {I.D} → DI

English is consistent, German archaic (still with ID)

(*re* Temporal, Instrumental, Directional Adverbs)
    OV = {TA, IA, DA} → TA IA DA
    VO = {TA, IA, DA} → DA IA TA

(*re* Main Verb, Auxiliary, Modal)
    OV = {MV, Aux}   → MV Aux
          {MV, Mod}   → MV Mod
    VO = {MV, Aux}   → Aux MV
          {MV, Mod}   → Mod MV

(similarly, *re* Head Nouns and Modifiers, such as relative clauses)
    OV = {Mf, HN} → MfHN
    VO = {Mf. HN} → HNMf

Here German has progressed toward VO.

Separable particles are not discussed by Vennemann. They behave like Aux and Mod.

The classification of German as basically SOV is now broadly accepted. J. Koster 1975, p. 111 observes: "Since Bach and Bierwisch it has been assumed that German is an SOV language." Reference here is to Emmon Bach 1962 and Manfred Bierwisch 1963.

88. Bartsch and Vennemann, *Semantic Structures*, p. 135.

89. Dauzat, *Histoire de la langue française* (Paris, 1930), p. 432, and *Le génie de la langue française* (Paris, 1943, 1947^2), p. 229.

90. Cf. Vennemann in Kimball, p. 29, and p. 31 for next quote. Vennemann, it should be added, may be too peremptory in postulating a causal relationship between weakness or absence of flection and fixed order; some languages display both a preference for fixed order as "normal" and a rich flectional system, as Russian does (though Russian can by no means be regarded as a fixed order language), while others, like Bulgarian or, perhaps even better, Macedonian, have neither one nor the other characteristic. Nevertheless, the rule (or "tendency") may be regarded as generally valid, while apparent exceptions will have to be analyzed by accounting for particular substitute devices having the function of syntactic markers (such as the repetition or *reprise* of an object noun through an inflected pronoun in Bulgarian, Macedonian, or Albanian — as well as in the Romance languages: Cf. French *cet homme je le connais bien*).

91. Cf. my *CTC*, esp. ch. 1 and Conclusion. On the virtual "confirmation" of the ancient viewpoint, cf. E. Lerch, *Historische französische Syntax*, vol. III (Leipzig, 1934), p. 250: "Soweit in der Wortstellung einer Sprache Freiheit herrscht, gehört die Wortstellung in das Gebiet der Stilistik; soweit sie geregelt worden ist, gehört sie in die Syntax."

92. *CTC*, esp. pp. 235–238, drawing on Arnaldo Pizzorusso, *Teorie letterarie in Francia: Ricerche sei-settecentesche* (Pisa, 1968), ch. 10: "J.-A. Du Cerceau e la teoria delle inversioni poetiche," pp. 401–429.
   Further material on the subject can be found in Vennemann, "Analogy in Generative Grammar: The Origin of Word Order," in Luigi Heilmann, ed., *Proceedings of the XI International Congress of Linguists, Bologna-Florence, 1972* (Bologna: Il Mulino, 1974, 2 vols.), II, pp. 79–83, and "An Explanation of Drift," in Charles N. Li, ed., *Word Order and Word Order Change* (1975), pp. 269–305, with further bibliography.
93. "On the Change from SOV to SVO: Evidence from Niger-Congo," in Charles N. Li, ed., *Word Order and Word Order Change*, pp. 115–47.
94. Lehmann, "Proto-Germanic Syntax," in F. van Coetsen and H. Kufner, eds., *Toward a Grammar of Proto-Germanic* (Tübingen: Max Niemeyer, 1972), pp. 239–68.
95. Cf. Vennemann, "An Explanation of Drift" (1975). And see his other 1973 papers (besides the one in Kimball): "Language Type and Word Order," paper read at the Symposium on Typology, Prague, August 14–17, 1973, reproduced by Linguistic Agency, University of Trier, 1973; and "Topics, Subjects, and Word Order: From SXV to SVX via TVS," in Anderson and Jones.
96. "The Position of Relative Clauses and Conjunctions," *Linguistic Inquiry*, 5 (1974), 117–36. The quote in the text is from Vennemann 1975, p. 290.
97. Vennemann has VDI, which I assume to be a slip.
98. Cf., also, Vennemann, "Theoretical Word Order Studies: Results and Problems," *Papiere zur Linguistik*, 7 (1974), 5–25, from the LSA annual meeting, San Diego, December 1973. We could add that the operator → operand movement governs a manifold hierarchy of relations; for example, *diese zehn rote Kugeln* is harmonic with SOV. The demonstrative *diese*, as the most generic determinant (relating to the whole nominal phrase (NP), not just the noun) is the most distant to the left, just as it would be the most distant to the right in the mirrorlike opposite pattern demanded by a consistent SVO or VSO language, like Yoruba. Cf. Hansjakob Seiler, *Das linguistische Universalienproblem in neuer Sicht*. Rhein.-Westphäl. Akad. der Wiss., Vorträge G. 200 (Opladen, 1975), p. 12.
99. "A Structural Principle of Language and Its Implications," *Language*, 49, 47–66.
100. "Verb Anchoring and Verb Movement," in Li, *Word Order and Word Order Change*, pp. 439–62: See p. 439.
101. Cf. also James D. McCawley, "English as a VSO Language," *Language*, 46, 2, Part I (June 1970), 286–99.
102. Cf. Pavao Tekavčić, *Grammatica storica dell'Italiano*, vol. II: *Morfosintassi* (Bologna: Il Mulino, 1972), p. 691 for the last three examples.
103. In *Tutte le opere*, ed. F. Flora (Milan: Mondadori, 1952^3), vol. I. For examples of (. . .) VS patterns in the Romance languages, see fn. 2 in my Introduction.
104. Pirandello, *Quaderni di Serafino Gubbio operatore* (1915), in *Tutti i Romanzi* (Milan: Mondadori, 1941, reprt. 1944).
105. Cf. Rebecca Posner, *op. cit.*, pp. 174–5.
106. Gerhard Rohlfs, *Historische Grammatik der italienischen Sprache und ihrer Mundarten* (Bern: Francke, 1949–54, 3 vols.), III, pp. 217f., cited by Vennemann, "Topics etc.," in Anderson and Jones, p. 363; and see *Papiere zur Linguistik*, 7, p. 17, for generalizations on the question.
107. Pavao Tekavčić 1972, p. 689, points out another SXV feature of German in the preservation of the semantic contact between simple and preposition-compounded verbs, whereas in the Romance languages the derivatives have lost such contacts and have become autonomous lexical units without the possibility of serving as models for

further formations: see Italian *cedere, incedere, concedere, decedere; indurre, dedurre, condurre; arrivare, derivare* . . . versus *einkommen, herauskommen; wegfahren, abfahren.* . . .

108. Cf. Fourquet 1974, p. 320: *Da hast du recht* and *da du recht hast* are given as examples that "we have in OHG the possibility of using demonstratives as relative pronouns or conjunctions, because the position of the verb is the marker of a subordinate clause. This phenomenon survives in NHG." We have, then, a sort of circle: Morphologically distinct subordinating conjunctions, pronouns, or adverbs are relatively unneeded because verb last position is a sufficient marker; conversely, the last is needed in the absence of the former.

109. Jakobson, "Implications of Language Universals for Linguistics," in Greenberg, ed., *Universals of Language* 1966^2, pp. 263–78.

110. W. Klein, "Eine Theorie der Wortstellungsveränderung. Einige kritische Bemerkungen zu Vennemanns Theorie der Sprachentwicklung," *Linguistische Berichte*, 37 (1975), 46–57.

111. *Journal of Indo-European Studies*, Monograph No. 1 (Butte, Montana: JI-ES, 1975).

112. Cf. P. Ramat 1976, p. 31.

113. Ramat 1976, p. 35 fn. 37.

114. Klaus-Peter Lange, "Problems with OV/VO Word Order," in Maria-Elisabeth Conte *et al.*, eds., *Wortstellung und Bedeutung, Akten des 12. Linguistischen Kolloquiums, Pavia 1977*, Bd. 1 (Tübingen: M. Niemeyer, 1978), pp. 13–22.

115. In M.-E. Conte *et al.*, eds., *Wortstellung und Bedeutung*, 1978, pp. 3–11. Professor Dezsö (b. 1927) is a linguist at the University of Debrecen in Hungary, and the author of several typological studies.

116. Paul J. Hopper, *The Syntax of the Simple Sentence in Proto-Germanic* (The Hague-Paris: Mouton, 1975).

117. Traditional grammar had not realized the importance of patterns of negation, starting with the position of *nicht*, for the deep understanding of the peculiarities of German thinking processes and linguistic structures. Among contemporary linguists no one has exploited this aspect more methodically and fully than J.-M. Zemb, *Les structures logiques de la proposition allemande: Contribution à l'étude des rapports entre le langage et la pensée* (Paris: O.C.D.L., 1968), a logico-philosophical treatise of "semantic structuralism" that hinges systematically on the analysis of negation starting with the very first chapter, "La négation," and uses it to throw light into the depths of German syntactic "irrationality" and "anarchism." It may strike the reader as, at least in part, a sophisticated attempt to transfer to the plane of higher formal analysis the prejudicial approach inherited from the tradition of French classicism.

118. G. O. Curme, *A Grammar of the English Language, I: Syntax* (Boston: D. C. Heath, 1931), p. 351, gives such modifier-modified compounds as *hóme-màde, táble-lèg, éar-rìng, éyelàshes* as "the oldest type of expression in the language. . . . Such words arose at a time when there was no inflection, so that the fixed word-order alone indicated the grammatical relations." On this complex question seen from a comparative viewpoint, see now Greta D. Little, "Does Word Order in Noun Compounding Reflect Sentential Syntax?," *The Second LACUS Forum*, ed. by Peter A. Reich (Columbia, S.C.: Hornbeam, 1976), pp. 249–54.

119. Brecht, "Über die Wiederherstellung der Wahrheit," p. 194 of *Schriften zur Politik und Gesellschaft 1919–1956* (Frankfurt/M.: Suhrkamp, 1968).

NOTES ☐ 211

120. See Curme 1922, pp. 584–98 for his detailed, well-exemplified modern analysis of word-order rules.

121. Curme 1922, pp. 389–91, §§ 234–6.

122. Sudermann, *Teja*, 11, cited by Curme 1922, p. 585.

123. The verb is defined as *Funktionszentrum* of the clause (*das strukturell-syntaktische Zentrum*) in the *Kleine Enzyklopädie — Die deutsche Sprache* (Leipzig: VEB Bibliographisches Institut, 1979, 2 vols.), II, p. 909. This well-informed compilation gives an extremely detailed, up-to-date theory of sentence and clause structure, vol. II, pp. 908–78 (978–93 on deep structural analysis, including the generative methods). The material is interestingly assembled according to the following rubrics: "Die Grundformen der Satzintonation: die Intonationsmuster; die Grundformen der Satzgliederung: die Baumuster (z.B. die topologischen Modelle der Verbstellung, der Feldgliederung, der Wortgruppenordnung, der Teilsatzordnung); die Grundformen der Satzfügung: die Fügungsmuster . . . ; die Grundformen der kommunikativen Funktionen des Satzes: die elementaren Kommunikationsmuster (z.B. die Satztypenmodelle des Aussage-, Frage- und Heischesatzes)" (p. 908). Under *Stilistik*, vol. II, pp. 1075–84, one finds a comprehensive treatment of *asyndetische* and *syndetische Parataxe*, *Hypotaxe*, and *Periode*.

124. Drach 1940^3, p. 12; Weisgerber, *Grundzüge* 1962, p. 361.

125. (*Dudens*) *Grammatik der deutschen Gegenwartssprache*, eds. Paul Grebe *et al.* (Mannheim: Bibliographisches Institut, Dudenverlag, 2. verb. Aufl. 1966, 1973). The current way of viewing the central feature of the sentence, the position of the verb, is to regard second position as neutral or unmarked, the others as marked. The function of last position is to designate the introductory particle as a (subordinating) conjunction or a relative pronoun, hence the clause itself as dependent. The function of first position is to mark the clause as imperative, interrogative, or conditional.

126. *UL*, II, § 809, p. 560.

127. Quoted in Ladislao Mittner, *Grammatica della lingua tedesca* (Milano: Mondadori, 1941^5), p. 159.

128. (Berlin: W. de Gruyter, 1972^8), pp. 95–6.

129. For this nomenclature Polenz cites Tesnière, *Éléments de syntaxe structurale*, 1959 ed., pp. 22f. See my fn. 50 above.

130. Cf. Heinrich Weber, *Das erweiterte Adjektiv- und Partizipialattribut im Deutschen*. Linguistische Reihe, 4 (München: Max Hueber, 1971).

131. As one last bibliographic item, of especial interest for its theoretical context (Russian) and because it provides an articulate up-to-date framework, I should like to mention Wladimir Admoni, *Der deutsche Sprachbau* (München: C. H. Beck'sche Verlagsbuchhandlung, 1970^3, translated from the 1966, Moscow-Leningrad Russian original), pp. 268–302, on general sentence structure and word order. Admoni has authored some major papers on our subject (see bibliography), and can serve as a good example of the way traditional grammar, proceeding with a quantitative, analytic-inductive, empirical method, can still produce authoritative results.

Today's grammarian can operate either by an all-out commitment to modern linguistic methods and principles or by an enlightened allegiance to traditional school methods. Either choice can yield respectable results, even though the latter may miss the intellectual challenges offered by the former. But our subject is fraught with particular perils, because one can still come across some performances that will disappoint in all respects, even from the hand of otherwise well-informed practicioners. As an example I shall briefly dwell on Moritz Regula, *Kurzgefaßte erklärende Satzkunde des Neuhochdeutschen* (Bern-München: Francke, 1968), esp. pp. 187–95 on "Wortstellung." Regula begins by stating a *Gundprinzip* that curiously reminds us of Adelung's *Gundgesetz*: "The known or given (*Gegebenes*) comes first, and we gradually progress from the less to the more important (*Bedeutungsvolles*), to end with the most important by its meaning (*Sinnwichtigstes*), hence with an ascending rhythm according to the Law of Growing Members, with final drop in tone (*Tonabfall*)" (p. 187). It is, at first sight, an attractive and clever recapitulation, in a neat synthetic formula, of the principles of Adelung, Wackernagel, Behaghel, and Delbrück, not without a touch of Aristotelian logic and Prague functionalism in the reminder of the proposition as moving from the known to the unknown. But, in the light of Jellinek's critique of Adelung and of our realization of the contradictory nature of ascending-descending structures in German syntax (as we have observed above in greater detail), the formula is simply untrue to fact, since it correctly applies only to subordinate clauses.

Contradictory as the above rule may appear to be with regard to the realities of the language, it is further contradicted by the theoretical implications of the following rule with which Regula attempts to predicate the "inversions" — and here he seems to revert to the traditional dichotomy of affective versus rational arrangement: "When emotion intervenes, the ordering of words mirrors the emotional state of the speaker; in contrast with the reasoned arrangement of the members, what impresses the speaker most strongly pushes itself to the front, giving top and first place to what predominates in the affections." ("Im *Affekt* spiegelt die Wortstellung die Gefühlslage des Sprechenden wider: im Gegensatz zur reflectierenden Anordnung der Glieder schleudert sich das, was den Redenden am stärksten bedrängt, zuerst hinaus: Spitzenstellung der Affektdominante" — ibid., p. 187.) We then ask: What is the most important place in the sentence, the first or the last, as stated in the previous rule? Or could it be that the effect of the affective movement is to move the point of emphasis from the end to the beginning? Regula does not say this, since it would carry with it an insoluble difficulty, but there seems to be no other way of reconciling the ascending rhythm with the first position of the "inverted" complements under emotional stress.

The problem is that in the light of both modern and traditional stylistic speculation it is difficult to subsume the "inversions" of German under the category of emotion in a general way. If the direct order (*gerade Wortfolge*) of the unemotional speech (*affektfreie Rede*, p. 188) wants the grammatical subject in first place, it is arduous to class *gestern kam ich zu spät* within the emotionally determined. What emotion, and what amount of it, is carried by *gestern*? And Regula remains entirely within the traditional framework when he refers to the first-positioning of other complements than the subject as *Inversion* or *versetzte Wortfolge* (p. 188) — with the consequent sending of the subject immediately after the verb — as a result of emotion, expressive needs, or *reprise* — *Affekt, Expressivität, oder Anknüpfung* (ibid.). To be more precise, there is here a new twist in regard to the old tradition, since he calls all these factors "psychological," whereas the *reprise* or recall tying up with the last thing mentioned (*Anknüpfung*) is clearly reminiscent of Condillac's (and Henri Weil's) perception of the logical train of thought that carries on the discourse through a formal *liaison des idées*. (In the light of modern philosophico-psychological speculation, Wilhelm Martin Esser, "Grammatische und Psychologische Kategorien in der deutschen Satzanalyse," *Der Deutschunterricht*, 13, 3 (1961), 5–16, is of some interest as a recent discussion of what in the tradition has been the question of *Gemüthsstellung* (Adelung) or affective language versus the normal *ordo naturalis* of plain grammar.)

Finally, we find a new echo of the Behaghel thesis in Regula's statement (p. 193) that the end-position of the verb in the subordinate clause (*Gliedsatz*, as distinct from the *Freisatz*) was made dominant by "the powerful influence of Latin." We might prefer to hear that all that Latin did was to reinforce the original thrust of German construction and throw it back, as it were, toward its origins, thus partially contributing to freeze the already begun process of drifting from XV to VX. Correctly enough, however, Regula notes that the influence of dialects and everyday speech is felt in the literary language when, especially after the populist moods first brought in by the *Sturm und Drang*, it started looking with favor on *Retouchen oder Nachträge* in secondary clauses, such as *wie die Kräfte wachsen in der Not* etc. (pp. 194–5).

BIBLIOGRAPHY

BIBLIOGRAPHY

A Selected Bibliography

Abbreviations:
ASnS = *Archiv für das Studium der neueren Sprachen und Literaturen*
BGdS = *Beiträge zur Geschichte der deutschen Sprache und Literatur* (Hall/S.)
ZfD = *Zeitschrift für Deutschkunde*
ZfdA = *Zeitschrift für deutsches Altertum und deutsche Literatur*
ZfdP = *Zeitschrift für deutsche Philologie*
ZfdU = *Zeitschrift für deutschen Unterricht*
ZfvS = *Zeitschrift für vergleichende Sprachforschung*
WBZAS = *Wissenschaftliche Beihefte zur Zeitschrift des Allgemeinen deutschen Sprachvereins*
Das Ringen = Hugo Moser, ed. *Das Ringen um eine neue deutsche Grammatik.* (Wege der Forschung, 25.) Darmstadt: Wissenschaftliche Buchgesellschaft, 1962.

I. Primary Sources

Adelung, Johann Christoph. *Deutsche Sprachlehre.* Zum Gebrauche der Schüler in den Königlich-Preußischen Landen. Berlin: Ch. Voß, 1781. [1782, 1795, 1800, 1806, 1816.]
———. *Umständliches Lehrgebäude der deutschen Sprache.* Leipzig: J. G. I. Breitkopf, 1782.
Aichinger, Carl Friedrich. *Versuch einer teutschen Sprachlehre.* Frankfurt-Leipzig: J. P. Kraus, 1753; Wien: P. Kraus, 1754.
Albertus, Laurentius. (Albrecht von Schlägel?) *Teutsch Grammatick oder Sprachkunst* per Laurentium Albertum Ostrofrancum. 1573. Ed. Carl Müller-Fraureuth. *Die deutsche Grammatik des Laurentius Albertus.* (Ältere deutsche Grammatiken in Neudrucken, 3.) Strassburg: K. J. Trübner, 1895.
Algarotti, Francesco. *Saggi,* ed. Giovanni da Pozzo. Bari: Laterza, 1963.

Basedow, Johann Bernhard. *Neue Lehrart und Uebung in der Regelmäßigkeit der Teutschen Sprache.* Kopenhagen: J. B. Ackermann, 1759.

Bauer, Heinrich. *Vollständige Grammatik der neuhochdeutschen Sprache.* Berlin: G. Reimer, 1822, 5 Bde. Reprt. Berlin: W. de Gruyter, 1967.

Becker, Karl Ferdinand. *Ausführliche deutsche Grammatik als Kommentar der Schulgrammatik.* Frankfurt/M., 1836–9, 3 vols.; Prag: F. Tempsky, 1870[2], 2 vols. Reprt. Hildesheim-New York: G. Olms, 1969, 2 vols.

Beyträge zur critischen Historie der deutschen Sprache, Poesie und Beredsamkeit, hrsgn. von einigen Mitgliedern der Deutschen Gesellschaft in Leipzig. (Ed. J. C. Gottsched.) Leipzig, 1732–44, 8 vols. Reprt. Hildesheim-New York: G. Olms, VIII, 1970.

Bödiker, Johann. *Grundsätze der deutschen Sprache im Reden und Schreiben . . .* Kölln an der Spree: Ulrich Liebpert, 1690. Rev. by Johann Leonhard Frisch, Berlin: Christoph Gottlieb Nicolai, 1723, 1729, and new rev. ed. by J. J. Wippel, ibid., 1746.

Bodmer, Johann Jakob. *Critische Abhandlung von dem Wunderbaren in der Poesie . . . in einer Vertheidigung des Gedichtes Joh. Miltons. . . .* Zürich: C. Orell, 1740. Reprt. Stuttgart: J. B. Metzlersche Verlagsbuchhandlung, 1966.

———. *Critische Betrachtungen über die poetische Gemählde der Dichter, mit einer Vorrede von J. J. Breitinger.* Zürich: C. Orell, 1741.

———. *Die Grundsätze der deutschen Sprache, oder von den Bestandtheilen derselben und von dem Redesatze.* Zürich: Orell, Geßner u. Co., 1768.

Bodmer, Johann Jakob, and J. J. Breitinger. *Die Discourse der Mahlern, 1721-2,* ed. Theodor Vetter, Erster Teil. Frauenfeld: J. Huber, 1891. Reprt. Hildesheim-New York: G. Olms, 1969.

Braun, Heinrich. *Anleitung zur deutschen Sprachkunst.* München: J. Friedrich Ott, 1765; J. N. Fritz, 1775[3].

Breitinger, Johann Jakob. *Critische Dichtkunst* (1740). Reprt. Stuttgart: J. B. Metzler, 1966, 2 Bde.

Buffier, Claude. *Examen des préjugés vulgaires,* in *Cours des sciences.* Paris: Cavelier et Giffard, 1732. Reprt. Geneva: Slatkine Reprints, 1971. Also in *Oeuvres philosophiques du P. Buffier,* ed. Francisque Bouillier. Paris: Charpentier, 1843.

Clajus, Johannes. *Grammatica germanicae linguae ex bibliis Lutheri germanicis et aliis eius libris collecta.* 1578. Ed. Friedrich Weidling, *Die deutsche Grammatik des J. Clajus.* (Ältere deutsche Grammatiken in Neudrucken, 2.) Strassburg: K. J. Trübner, 1894. Reprt. of 1578 ed. Hildesheim-New York: G. Olms, 1973.

Condillac, Étienne Bonnot de. *Oeuvres philosophiques,* ed. Georges Le Roy. Paris: Presses Universitaires de France, 1947–51, 3 vols.

Diderot, Denis. *Oeuvres complètes,* ed. J. Assézat, I. Paris: Garnier, 1875.

Dornblüth, Augustin. *Observationes oder gründliche Anmerckungen über die Art und Weise eine gute Übersetzung besonders in die teutsche Sprach zu machen.* Augsburg: Mattheus Rieger, 1755.

Ernesti, Johann August. *Initia rhetorica.* Leipzig, 1750; C. Fritsch, 1784[2].

———. *Initia doctrinae solidioris.* Leipzig, 1734–5, 1745, 1776, 1783, 1796.

Fabricius, Johann Andreas. *Philosophische Oratorie, das ist: Vernünftige Anleitung zur . . . Beredsamkeit.* Leipzig: bey denen Cörnerischen Erben, 1724, 1739.

Fulda, Friedrich Carl. *Grundregeln der Teutschen Sprache.* In vol. II of *Der Teütsche Sprachforscher, allen Liebhabern ihrer Muttersprache zur Prüfung vorgelegt.* Stuttgart: J. B. Metzler, 1777–8, 2 vols. [Also published separately.]

Girbert, Johann. *Deütsche Grammatica oder Sprachkunst, aus denen bey dieser Zeit gedruckten Grammaticis*. . . . Mülhausen/Thüringen: Johann Hüter, 1653.

Gottsched, Johann Christoph. *Versuch einer critischen Dichtkunst* (1730, 1737²), in G., *Ausgewählte Werke*, eds. J. and B. Birke, VI.1–2. Berlin-New York: W. de Gruyter, 1973. 1751 ed. reprt. Darmstadt: Wissenschaftliche Buchgesellschaft, 1962.

———. *Grundlegung einer deutschen Sprachkunst*. Leipzig: Bernh. Christoph Breitkopf, 1748, 1749², 1752³, 1757⁴ with new title *Vollständigere und neuerläuterte deutsche Sprachkunst*, 1762⁵, 1776⁶. Ed. Herbert Penzl (1762 ed.) in Gottsched, *Ausgewählte Werke*, ed. P. M. Mitchell, VIII.1–2. Berlin-New York, W. de Gruyter, 1978.

———. *Ausführliche Redekunst* (1736, . . . 1759⁵, rev. ed. of *Grundriß zu einer vernunfftmäßigen Redekunst*, 1729), ed. Rosemary Scholl, in Gottsched, *Ausgewählte Werke*, ed. P. M. Mitchell, VII.1. Berlin-New York: W. de Gruyter, 1975.

Gueintz, Christian. *Deutscher Sprachlehre Entwurf*. Göthen: im Fürstenthume Anhalt, 1641.

Hamann, Johann Georg. *Kreuzzüge des Philologen* (1762) in vol. II (1950) of *Sämtliche Werke*, ed. Joseph Nadler. Wien: Thomas-Morus-Presse, im Verlag Herder, 1949–57, 6 vols.

———. *Schriften*, ed. Friedrich Roth. Berlin: G. Reimer, 1821–43, 8 vols.

———. *Schriften zur Sprache*, ed. Joseph Simon. Frankfurt/M.: Suhrkamp, 1967.

Heinsius, Theodor. *Teut, oder theoretisch-praktisches Lehrbuch der gesammten deutschen Sprachwissenschaft*. Berlin: Duncker u. Humblot, 1821, 1821–5³, 5 vols. in 3, 1825–32⁴, 5 vols.

Helwig, Christoph (Helvicus). *Libri didactici grammaticae universalis, latinae, graecae, hebraicae, chaldaicae*; and German version *Sprachkunste*: I. *Allgemeine*, II. *Lateinische*, III. *Hebraische; teutsch geschrieben durch Weyland den* . . . *Herren Christophorum Helvicum*. Giessen: Caspar Chemlin, 1619.

Hemmer, Jakob. *Deutsche Sprachlehre, zum Gebrauche der Kuhrpfälzischen Lande*. Mannheim: Akademische Schriften, 1775.

Hempel, Christian Friedrich. *Erleichterte Hoch-Teutsche Sprachlehre*. Frankfurt-Leipzig: J. G. Garben, 1754.

Herder, Johann Gottfried. *Fragmente über die neuere deutsche Literatur* (1766–7) in vol. I (1877) of *Sämtliche Werke*, eds. Bernhard Suphan *et al*. Berlin: Weidmannsche Buchhandlung, 1877–1913, 33 vols.

Herling, Simon Heinrich Adolph. "Über die Topik der deutschen Sprache." *Abhandlungen des frankfürtischen Gelehrtenvereins für deutsche Sprache*, III (Frankfurt a/M.: Franz Varrentrapp, 1821), 296–362.

———. *Erster Kursus eines wissenschaftlichen Unterrichts in der deutschen Sprache*. Frankfurt/M.: J. C. Hermann, 1828.

———. *Syntax der deutschen Sprache*. Frankfurt/M.: J. C. Hermann, 1830–2, 3 vols.

Hübner, Johann. *Kurtze Fragen aus der Oratoria*. Leipzig: Gleditsch, 1701, 1706².

Jerusalem, Johann Fr. W. *Über die deutsche Sprache und Litteratur. An ihro königliche Hoheit die verwittwete Frau Herzogin von Braunschweig und Lüneburg*. Berlin: Rottmann, 1781. Reprt. Leipzig: Xenien Verlag, 1910.

Klopstock, Friedrich Gottlieb. *Sämmtliche sprachwissenschaftliche und ästhetische Schriften*, eds. A. L. Back and A. R. C. Spindler. Leipzig: Friedrich Fleischer, 1830, 6 Bde. [= 13–18 of *Sämmtliche Werke*, eds. Back-Spindler. Leipzig: Bde. 1–12 by Göschen, 13–18 by Fleischer, 1823–30.] "Von der Wortfolge" in Bd. 2 (14); "Von der Darstellung" and "Von der Sprache der Poesie" in Bd. 4 (16).

Kolbe, Karl Wilhelm. *Über den Wortreichtum der deutschen und französischen Sprache, und beider Anlage zur Poesie.* Leipzig: C. H. Reclam, 1806, 2 vols.; Berlin: Realschulbuchhandlung, 1818–20[2], 3 vols.

Lamy, Bernard. *La rhétorique ou l'art de parler.* Paris: A. Pralard, 1675, . . . ; Amsterdam: Paul Marret, 1699. Reprt. Sussex Reprints, Brighton: Univ. of Sussex Library, 1969.

Leibniz, Gottfried Wilhelm. *Unvorgreiffliche Gedanken betreffend die Ausübung und Verbesserung der teutschen Sprache,* in *Philosophische Werke,* eds. A. Buchenau and Ernst Cassirer, II. Leipzig: F. Meiner, 1924[2].

Lessing, Gotthold Ephraim. *Briefe, die neueste Litteratur betreffend,* in *Sämtliche Schriften,* eds. Karl Lachmann and Franz Muncker, VIII. Stuttgart: Göschen, 1892[3]. Reprt. Berlin: W. de Gruyter, 1968.

Longolius, Johann Daniel. *Einleitung zu gründtlicher Erkäntniß einer jeden, insebesonderheit aber der teutschen Sprache.* Budissin: David Richter, 1715.

Le maître de la langue allemande ou nouvelle grammaire allemande méthodique et raisonnée composée sur le modèle des meilleurs auteurs de nos jours et principalement sur celui de Mr. le Prof. Gottsched. Strasbourg: Amand König, 1754, 1758[2], 1760[3], 1763[4], 1766[5], 1769[6], 1774[7], 1778[8], 1782[9].

Maupertuis, Pierre-Louis Moreau de. *Réflexions sur l'origine des langues et la signification des mots.* Paris, 1748, then in his *Oeuvres,* I, Dresden, 1752.

Meiner, Johann Werner. *Versuch einer an der menschlichen Sprache abgebildeten Vernunftlehre oder philosophische und allgemeine Sprachlehre.* Faksimile-Neudruck der Ausgabe Leipzig 1781, ed. H. E. Brekle. Stuttgart-Bad Cannstatt: Frommann-Holzboog, 1971.

Melanchthon, Philip. *Elementa latinae grammatices.* Lipsiae: Nicolaus Faber, 1530, 1538; Parisiis: Robertus Stephanus, 1533, 1539, 1550; Basileae: Johannes Oporinus, 1552, 1557; Lipsiae: Valentinus Papa, 1557.

Michaelis, Johann David. *De l'influence des opinions sur le langage et du langage sur les opinions.* Bremen, 1762. Reprt. Stuttgart-Bad Cannstatt: Frommann-Holzboog, 1970.

Morhof, Daniel Georg. *Unterricht von der teutschen Sprache und Poesie.* Kiel: J. Reumann, 1682; Lübeck-Frankfurt: J. Wiedermeyer, 1700, 1702, 1718. Reprt. of 1700 ed., ed. Henning Boetius. Bad Homburg: Gehlen, 1969.

Müller, Johannes, ed. *Quellenschriften und Geschichte des deutschsprachigen Unterrichtes bis zur Mitte des 16. Jahrhunderts.* Gotha: E. F. Thienemann, 1882.

Neukirch, Benjamin. *Anweisung zu teutschen Briefen.* Leipzig: Thomas Fritsch, 1709, 1721, 1727; Leipzig: J. P. Roth, 1735, . . . 1745; Nürnberg: J. Stein, 1741, 1751[2], 1755[3].

Ölinger, Albert. *Underricht der HochTeutschen Spraach: Grammatica seu Institutio verae germanicae linguae* . . . 1573, 1574. Ed. Willy Scheel, *Die deutsche Grammatik des A. Ö.* (Ältere deutsche Grammatiken in Neudrucken, 4.) Halle/S.: M. Niemeyer, 1897.

Der Patriot. Hamburg, Jan. 5, 1724 — Dec. 28, 1726, 1737–8[2], 3 vols. Reprt. ed. W. Martens. Berlin: W. de Gruyter, 1969–70, 4 vols.

Piper, Paul. *Die Schriften Notkers und seiner Schule.* Freiburg/B.-Leipzig: J. C. B. Mohr, 1895, 3 vols.

Ramshorn, Ludwig. *Lateinische Grammatik.* Leipzig: F. C. W. Vogel, 1824, 1830[2].

Ritter, Stephan. *Grammatica germanica nova, usui omnium aliarum nationum hanc linguam affectantium inserviens, praecipue vero ad linguam gallicam accommodata.* . . . Marburg: Rudolph Hutwelcker, 1616.

Roth, Georg Michael. *Systematisch deutsche Sprachlehre*. Giessen, 1799.
──── . *Grundriß der reinen allgemeinen Sprachlehre*. Frankfurt, 1815.
Sacy: See Silvestre.
Sapir, Edward. *Language: An Introduction to the Study of Speech*. New York: Harcourt, Brace & Co., 1921.
Saussure, Ferdinand de. *Cours de linguistique générale*. Paris: Payot, 1949^3.
Schottelius, Justus Georgius. *Teutsche Sprachkunst*. Braunschweig: Balthasar Gruber, 1641.
──── . *Ausführliche Arbeit von der Teutschen Haubt-Sprache*. Braunschweig: Christoff Friederich Zilliger, 1663. Reprt. ed. Wolfgang Hecht. Tübingen: M. Niemeyer, 1967, 2 vols.
Silvestre, Antoine-Isaac, baron de Sacy. *Grundsätze der allgemeinen Sprachlehre in einem allgemein faßlichen Vortrage*. Trans. **Johann Severin Vater**. Halle/S.-Leipzig: Ruff, 1804.
Steinbach, Christ. Ernst. *Kurtze und gründliche Anweisung zur deutschen Sprache, vel succincta et perfecta grammatica linguae germanicae nova methodo tradita*. Rostochii et Parchimi: Georg Ludwig Fritsch, 1724.
Stieler, Kaspar. *Kurze Lehrschrift von der Hochteutschen Sprachkunst*, Anhang von: *Der Teutschen Sprache Stammbaum und Fortwachs oder Teutscher Sprachschatz . . . gesamlet von dem Spaten*. Nürnberg: Johann Hoffmann, 1691.
Vater, Johann Severin. *Lehrbuch der allgemeinen Grammatik besonders für höhere Schul-Classen*. Halle/S.: Renger, 1805.
Wahn, Hermann. *Kurtzgefassete Teutsche Grammatica oder ordentliche Grund-Legung der Teutschen Sprach-Lehre*. Hamburg: in Verlegung des Autoris, gedruckt bey Ph. L. Stromer, 1723.
Weil, Henri. *The Order of Words in the Ancient Languages Compared with that of the Modern Languages* (1844), trans. Ch. W. Super, ed. A. Scaglione. (Amsterdam Classics in Linguistics, 14.) Amsterdam: John Benjamins, 1978.
Wolff, Christian. *Vernünfftige Gedancken von den Kräfften des menschlichen Verstandes*, in *Gesammelte Werke*, eds. J. École *et al.*, I, 1. Hildesheim: G. Olms, 1965, 1973.

II. Secondary Sources

Aarsleff, Hans. "The Tradition of Condillac: The Problem of the Origin of Language in the 18th century and the Debate in the Berlin Academy before Herder." In Dell Hymes, ed. *Studies in the History of Linguistics: Traditions and Paradigms*. Bloomington-London: Indiana U. Press, 1974, pp. 93–156.
Admoni, Wladimir Grigorjewitsch. *Der deutsche Sprachbau*. München: C. H. Beck'sche Verlagsbuchhandlung. 1970^3. (Trans. from 1966 Moscow—Leningrad Russian original.)
──── . *Die Entwicklungstendenzen des deutschen Satzbaus von heute*. (Linguistische Reihe, 12.) München: Max Hueber, 1973.
──── . "Über die Wortstellung im Deutschen." In *Das Ringen*, pp. 376–80.
──── . "Die Struktur des Satzes." In *Das Ringen*, pp. 381–98.
──── . "Die umstrittenen Gebilde der deutschen Sprache von heute: III. Das erweiterte Partizipialattribut." *Muttersprache*, 74 (1964), 321–32.
──── . "Der Umfang und die Gestaltungsmittel des Satzes in der deutschen Literatursprache bis zum Ende des 18. Jahrhunderts." *BGdS*, 89 (1967), 144–99.

Adolf, Helen. "Intonation and Word Order in German Narrative Style." *Journal of English and Germanic Philology*, 43 (1944), 71–9.

Alston, R. C. *A Bibliography of the English Language from the Invention of Printing to the Year 1800*. Leeds, Eng.: E. J. Arnold, 10 vols. 1965–72 and Supplement 1973.

Antoine, Gérald. *La coordination en français*. Paris: D'Artrey, 1959–63, 2 vols. Diss. Paris 1954.

Avalle, D'Arco Silvio. *Preistoria dell'endecasillabo*. Milano-Napoli: Ricciardi, 1963.

Bach, Adolf. *Geschichte der deutschen Sprache*. Leipzig: Quelle u. Meyer, 1938; Heidelberg: Quelle u. Meyer, 1949[4] . . . , 1965[8], 1970[9].

Bach, Emmon. "The Order of Elements in a Transformational Grammar of German." *Language*, 38 (1962), 263–9. [trans. by G. W. Weber as "Die Stellung der Satzglieder in einer Transformationsgrammatik des Deutschen." In Hugo Steger, ed. *Vorschläge für eine strukturale Grammatik*. Darmstadt: Wissenschaftliche Buchgesellschaft, 1970, pp. 109–20.]

———. "Questions." *Linguistic Inquiry*, 2 (1971), 153–66.

Bacquet, Paul. *La structure de la phrase verbale à l'époque alfrédienne*. (Publications de la Faculté des Lettres de l'Univ. de Strasbourg, 145.) Paris: Les Belles Lettres, 1962.

Baechtold, Jacob. *Geschichte der deutschen Literatur in der Schweiz*. Frauenfeld: T. Huber, 1892, reprt. 1919.

Bartsch, Renate and Theo Vennemann. *Semantic Structures. A Study in the Relation Between Semantics and Syntax*. (Athenäum-Skripten: Linguistik.) Frankfurt/M.: Athenäum Verlag, 1972, 1973[2].

———, eds. *Linguistics and Neighboring Disciplines*. Amsterdam-Oxford: North Holland, 1975.

Behaghel, Otto. "Die neuhochdeutschen Zwillingswörter." *Germania. Vierteljahrsschrift für d. Alterthumskunde*, 23, N.R. 11 (Wien, 1878), 257–92.

———. "Zur deutschen Wortstellung." *ZfdU*, 6 (1892), 265–7.

———."Zur deutschen Wortstellung." *WBZAS*, 3. Reihe, 1896–1901, Heft 17/18 (1900), 233–51.

———."Zur Stellung des Verbs im Germanischen und Indogermanischen." *ZfvS*, 56 (1929), 276–81.

———. "Von deutscher Wortstellung." *ZfD*, 44 (1930), 81–89.

———. "Zur Wortstellung des Deutschen." In James T. Hatfield *et al.*, eds. *Curme Volume of Linguistic Studies*. Baltimore: Waverly Press, 1930, pp. 29–33.

———. *Deutsche Syntax: Eine geschichtliche Darstellung*. Heidelberg: C. Winter, 1923–32, 4 vols.

Beneš, Eduard. "Die Verbstellung im Deutschen, von der Mitteilungsperspektive her betrachtet." *Philologica Pragensia*, 5 (1962), 6–19; reprt. in *Muttersprache*, 74 (1964), 9–21.

———. "Die funktionelle Satzperspektive im Deutschen." *Deutsch als Fremdsprache*, 4 (1967), 23–28.

———. "On Two Aspects of Functional Sentence Perspective." *Travaux Linguistiques de Prague*, 3 (1968), 267–74.

———. "Die Ausklammerung im Deutschen als grammatische Norm und als stilistischer Effekt." *Muttersprache*, 78 (1968), 289–98.

Biener, Clemens. "Zur Methode der Untersuchungen über deutsche Wortstellung." *ZfdA*, 59, NF 47 (1922), 127–44.

———. "Wie ist die neuhochdeutsche Regel über die Stellung des Verbums entstanden?" *ZfdA*, 59, NF 47 (1922), 165–79.

———. "Die Stellung des Verbums im Deutschen." *ZfdA*, 63, NF 51 (1926), 225–56.

———. "Veränderungen am deutschen Satzbau im humanistischen Zeitalter." *ZfdP*, 78 (1959), 72–82.

Bierwisch, Manfred. *Grammatik des deutschen Verbs*. (Deutsche Akademie der Wissenschaften zu Berlin: *Studia Grammatica*, 2.) Ost-Berlin: Akademie-Verlag, 1963, 1966^3, 1973^8.

———. "Regeln für die Intonation deutscher Sätze." *Studia Grammatica*, 7: *Untersuchungen über Akzent und Intonation im Deutschen*, hrsg. Manfred Bierwisch. Ost-Berlin: Akademie-Verlag, 1966, pp. 99–201.

Blackall, Eric A. *The Emergence of German as a Literary Language, 1700–1775*. Cambridge: U. Press, 1959. 2d ed. with a new bibliographical essay, Ithaca & London: Cornell U. Press, 1978. German ed. *Die Entwicklung des Deutschen zur Literatursprache, 1700–1775*. Stuttgart: Metzlersche Verlagsbuchhandlung, 1966, with updated bibliography by Dieter Kimpel.

Blümel, Rudolf. *Die Aufgaben der neuhochdeutschen Wortstellungslehre*. Halle/S.: E. Karras, 1909. Diss. München.

———. *Die Haupttypen der heutigen neuhochdeutschen Wortstellung im Hauptsatz*. Strassburg: K. J. Trübner, 1914.

———. *Einführung in die Syntax*. Heidelberg: C. Winter, 1914.

Bolinger, Dwight. *Forms of English: Accent, Morpheme, Order*. Cambridge: Harvard U. Press, 1965: "Linear Modifications," pp. 279–307. [from *PMLA*, 67 (1952), 1117–44.]

Bonfante, Giuliano. "Proposizione principale e proposizione dipendente in indoeuropeo." *Archivio Glottologico Italiano*, 24 (1930), 1–60.

Boost, Karl. *Neue Untersuchungen zum Wesen und zur Struktur des deutschen Satzes. Der Satz als Spannungsfeld*. Berlin: Akademie-Verlag, 1955, 1964^5.

Brekle, Herbert E. "The Seventeenth Century." In Thomas A. Sebeok, ed. *Current Trends in Linguistics*, 13/1: *Historiography of Linguistics*. The Hague-Paris: Mouton, 1975, pp. 277–382.

Condoyannis, George E. "Word Order in Colloquial German." *Monatshefte*, 36 (1944), 371–77.

Coseriu, Eugenio. "L'arbitraire du signe: Zur Spätgeschichte eines aristotelischen Begriffes." *ASnS*, 204, 2 (1967–8), 81–112.

Curme, George O. *A Grammar of the German Language*. New York: Macmillan, 1922.

Delbrück, Berthold. *Syntaktische Forschungen, III: Die altindische Wortfolge aus dem Çatapathabrāmaṇa*. Halle/S.: Buchhandlung des Waisenhauses, 1878.

———. *Syntaktische Forschungen, V: Altindische Syntax*. Halle/S.: Buchhandlung des Waisenhauses, 1888; reprt. Darmstadt: Wissenschaftliche Buchgesellschaft, 1968.

———. *Vergleichende Syntax der indogermanischen Sprachen*, I–III; 3.–5. Bde. of *Karl Brugmanns Grundriß der vergleichenden Grammatik der indogermanischen Sprachen*. Strassburg: K. J. Trübner, 1893–1900.

———. *Germanische Syntax*, II: *Zur Stellung des Verbums*. In *Abhandlungen der kön. sächs. Ges. der Wissenschaften*, phil.-hist. Kl., XXVIII, 7. Leipzig: Teubner, 1911.

———. *Grundlagen der neuhochdeutschen Satzlehre. Ein Schulbuch für Lehrer*. Berlin-Leipzig: Vereinigung wissenschaftlicher Verleger, 1920.

De Mauro, Tullio. *Une introduction à la sémantique*, trans. L.-J. Calvet. Paris: Payot, 1969. [Original ed. *Introduzione alla semantica*. Bari, 1966^2.]

Diels, Paul. *Die Stellung des Verbums in der älteren althochdeutschen Prosa.* Berlin: Mayer & Müller, 1906. [Diss. Berlin.]

Dinser, Gudula, ed. *Zur Theorie des Sprachveränderung.* Kronberg: Scriptor, 1974.

Drach, Erich. *Grundgedanken der deutschen Satzlehre.* Frankfurt/M.: M. Diesterweg, 1937, 1939², 1940³; reprt. Darmstadt: Wissenschaftliche Buchgesellschaft, 1963.

———. "Hauptsatz und Gliedsatz." In *Das Ringen*, pp. 269–79. [Extracts from pp. 15–21, 28–31 of *Grundgedanken.*]

Dressler, Wolfgang. "Eine textsyntaktische Regel der idg. Wortstellung." *ZfvS. 83* (1969), 1–25.

(Duden). *Der Grosse Duden, 4: Grammatik der deutschen Gegenwartssprache.* Eds. Paul Grebe *et al.* Mannheim: Bibliographisches Institut, Dudenverlag, 1966², 1973.

Dünninger, Josef. "Geschichte der deutschen Philologie." In Wolfgang Stammler, ed. *Deutsche Philologie im Aufriß,* 1. Berlin: E. Schmidt, rev. ed. 1957², pp. 83–222.

Dvořáková, Eva. "On the English and Czech Situational Adverbs in Functional Sentence Perspective." *Brno Studies in English,* 4 (1964), 129–40.

Ebert, Robert P. "On the Notion 'Subordinate Clause' in Standard German." In C. Corum *et al.,* eds. *You Take the High Node* etc. [See J. R. Ross 1973.]

———. *Historische Syntax des Deutschen.* Stuttgart: Metzler, 1978.

Engel, Ulrich. "Studie zur Geschichte des Satzrahmens und seiner Durchbrechung." In Hugo Moser, ed. *Studien zur Syntax des heutigen Deutsch. Paul Grebe zum 60. Geburtstag.* Düsseldorf: Pädagogischer Verlag Schwann, 1970, pp. 45–61.

———. "Regeln zur 'Satzgliedfolge' — Zur Stellung der Elemente im einfachen Verbalsatz." *Linguistische Studien,* I. Sprache der Gegenwart, 19. Düsseldorf: Pädagogischer Verlag Schwann, 1972, pp. 17–75.

———. *Syntax der deutschen Gegenwartssprache.* Berlin: E. Schmidt, 1977.

Erben, Johannes. "Prinzipielles zur Syntaxforschung, mit dem besonderen Blick auf Grundfragen der deutschen Syntax." In *Das Ringen*, pp. 505–26.

Erdmann, Oskar. *Grundzüge der deutschen Syntax nach ihrer geschichtlichen Entwicklung.* Stuttgart: J. G. Cotta, 1886–98, 2 vols., 2d vol. ed. by Otto Mensing.

Fillmore, Charles J. "The Case for Case." In Emmon Bach and T. R. Harms, eds. *Universals in Linguistic Theory.* New York: Holt, 1968, pp. 1–88.

Finck, Franz Nikolaus. *Der deutsche Sprachbau als Ausdruck deutscher Weltanschauung.* Marburg: Elwert, 1899.

———. *Die Haupttypen des Sprachbaus.* Leipzig — Berlin: Teubner, 1909.

Firbas, Jan. "Some Notes on the Problem of English Word Order from the Point of View of Actual Sentence Analysis" (in Czech), *Sborník Prací Filosofické Fakulty Brněnské University,* Řada Jazykovědná, 5 (1956), 93–107; "Some Thoughts on the Function of Word Order in Old English and Modern English" (in English), ibid., 6 (1957), 72–98.

———. "Thoughts on the Communicative Function of the Verb in English, German, and Czech." *Brno Studies in English,* 1 (1959), 39–68; "From Comparative Word Order Studies." *Brno Studies in English,* 4 (1964), 111–26.

Flämig, Walter. "Grundformen der Gliedfolge im deutschen Satz und ihre sprachlichen Funktionen." *BGdS,* 86 (1964), 309–49.

Fleischmann, Klaus. *Verbstellung und Relieftheorie.* (Münchener Germanistische Beiträge, 6.) München: W. Fink, 1973.

Forsgren, Kjell-Åke. "Zur Theorie und Terminologie der Satzlehre. Ein Beitrag zur Geschichte der deutschen Grammatik von J. C. Adelung bis K. F. Becker, 1780–1830." Diss. Goteborg, 1973.

Fourquet, Jean. *L'ordre des éléments de la phrase en germanique ancien: Étude de syntaxe de position.* (Publications de la Faculté des Lettres de l'Univ. des Strasbourg, 86.) Paris: Les Belles Lettres, 1938.

———. "Zur neuhochdeutschen Wortstellung." In *Das Ringen*, pp. 360–75. [Trans. of *L'ordre des elements*, pp. 21–32.]

———. "Die Strukturanalyse des deutschen Satzes. Sprachwissenschaftliche Analyse und Sprachunterricht." In Hugo Steger, ed. *Vorschläge für eine strukturale Grammatik des Deutschen.* Darmstadt: Wissenschaftliche Buchgesellschaft, 1970, pp. 151–65. [Trans. of "L'analyse structurale de la phrase allemande. Analyse linguistique et enseignement des langues." *Langage et comportement*, 1 (1965), pp. 49–60.]

———. "Genetische Betrachtungen über den deutschen Satzbau." In Werner Besch *et al.*, eds. *Studien zur deutschen Literatur und Sprache des Mittelalters. Festschrift für Hugo Moser zum 65. Geburtstag.* Berlin: E. Schmidt, 1974, pp. 314–23.

Frei, Henri. *La grammaire des fautes.* Paris: Geuthner, 1929.

Fries, Charles C. "On the Development of the Structural Use of Word-Order in Modern English." *Language*, 16 (1940), 199–208.

Garin, Eugenio. *Geschichte und Dokumente der abendländischen Pädagogik.* Hamburg: Rowohlt: 1964–7, 3 vols.: Mittelalter; Humanismus; Von der Reformation bis John Locke.

Glinz, Hans. *Die innere Form des Deutschen. Eine neue deutsche Grammatik.* Bern-München: Francke, 1952, 1961².

———. *Deutsche Syntax.* Stuttgart: J. B. Metzler, 1965.

Gosewitz, Uta. *Wort- und Satzgliedstellung. Eine Bibliographie (in Auswahl).* (Germanistische Linguistik, 73.3.) Hildesheim: G. Olms, 1974.

Greenberg, Joseph H. "Some Universals of Language with Particular Reference to the Order of Meaningful Elements." In J. H. Greenberg, ed. *Universals of Language.* Cambridge, Mass.: M.I.T. Press, 1966², pp. 73–113.

Grosse, Siegfried. "Die deutsche Satzperiode." *Der Deutschunterricht*, 12 (1960), 66–82.

Grubačić, Emilija. *Untersuchungen zur Wortstellung in der deutschen Prosadichtung der letzten Jahrzehnte.* (Zagreber germanistische Studien, 2.) Zagreb: Universität, Philos. Fak., Abt. Für Germanistik, 1965.

Guchmann, Mirra M. "Grammatische Kategorie und typologische Forschungen." *Zeichen und System der Sprache* (2. Internationales Symposion "Z.u.S.d.S.," Magdeburg 1964.) Bd. 3. Berlin: Akademie-Verlag, 1966, pp. 262–73.

———. *Der Weg zur deutschen Nationalsprache.* 2 Bde. Berlin: Akademie-Verlag, 1964–69.

Haarmann, Harald. *Grundzüge der Sprachtypologie.* Stuttgart: Kohlhammer, 1976.

Haiman, John. *Targets and Syntactic Change.* The Hague-Paris: Mouton, 1974.

Hammarström, Emil. *Zur Stellung des Verbums in der deutschen Sprache.* Lund: Gleerupska Universitetsbokhandeln (Håkan Ohlssohn), 1923.

Hartung, Wolfdietrich. *Die zusammengesetzten Sätze des Deutschen.* (Deutsche Akademie der Wissenschaften zu Berlin: *Studia Grammatica*, 4.) Ost-Berlin: Akademie-Verlag, 1964.

Harweg, Roland. "Zum Verhältnis von Satz, Hauptsatz und Nebensatz." *Zeitschrift für Dialektologie und Linguistik*, 38 (1971), 16–46.

Haselbach, Gerhard. *Grammatik und Sprachstruktur. K. F. Beckers Beitrag zur Allgemeinen Sprachwissenschaft in historischer und systematischer Sicht.* Berlin: W. de Gruyter, 1966.

Hijmans, B. L., Jr. *Inlaboratus et facilis: Aspects of Structure in Some Letters of Seneca*. Leiden: Brill, 1976.

Hirt, Hermann. *Indogermanische Grammatik*, V–VII Teile. Heidelberg: C. Winter, 1929–36.

Hjelmslev, Louis "Rôle structural de l'ordre des mots." *Journal de Psychologie*, 43 (1950), 54–8.

Hoberg, Ursula. "Probleme der Wortstellung." In Otmar Werner and Gerd Fritz, eds. *Deutsch als Fremdsprache und neuere Linguistik*. München: Max Hueber, 1975, pp. 67–80.

Hopper, Paul J. *The Syntax of the Simple Sentence in Proto-Germanic*. The Hague-Paris: Mouton, 1975.

Hudson, Grover. "Is Deep Structure Linear?" In George Bedell, ed. *Explorations in Syntactic Theory — UCLA Papers in Syntax*, 2. Los Angeles: U. of California Press, 1972, pp. 51–77.

Hyman, Larry M. "On the Change from SOV to SVO: Evidence from Niger-Congo." In Charles N. Li, ed. *Word Order and Word Order Change*. Austin: U. of Texas Press, 1975, pp. 115–47.

Isačenko, Alexander V. and Hans-Joachim Schädlich. "Untersuchungen über die deutsche Satzintonation." *Studia Grammatica, 7: Untersuchungen über Akzent und Intonation im Deutschen*, hrsg. Manfred Bierwisch. Ost-Berlin: Akademie-Verlag, 1966, pp. 7–67.

Jakobson, Roman. "À la recherche de l'essence du langage." *Diogène*, 51 (1965), 22–38.

———. "Implications of Language Universals for Linguistics." In Greenberg, ed. *Universals of Language*. Cambridge, Mass.: M.I.T. Press, 1963, pp. 208–19; 1966[2], pp. 263–78.

Jellinek, Max Hermann. *Geschichte der neuhochdeutschen Grammatik von den Anfängen bis auf Adelung*. Heidelberg: C. Winter, 1913–4, 2 vols.

Jespersen, Otto. *Progress in Language, with Special Reference to English*. London: S. Sonnenschein; New York: Macmillan, 1894.

Kefer, Michel. "Die Erforschung der Entwicklung des nhd. Satzbaus anhand der quantitativen und der sprachtypologischen Methode." *Revue des langues vivantes*, 40 (1974), 528–39.

Kiefer, Ferenc. "On the Problem of Word Order." *Computational Linguistics*, 7 (1968), 45–65. Also in M. Bierwisch and K. E. Heidolph, eds. *Progress in Linguistics: A Collection of Papers*. The Hague-Paris: Mouton, 1970, pp. 127–42.

Kirkwood, H. W. "Aspects of Word Order and Its Communicative Function in English and German." *Journal of Linguistics*, 5 (1969), 85–107.

Kleine Enzyklopädie — Die deutsche Sprache. Leipzig: VEB Bibliographisches Institut, 1970, 2 vols.

Koster, Jan. "Dutch as an SOV Language." *Linguistic Analysis*, 1 (1975), 111–36.

Kuhn, Hans. "Zur Wortstellung und -betonung im Altgermanischen." *BGdS*, 57, (1933), 1–109.

Kuno, Susumu. "The Position of Relative Clauses and Conjunctions." *Linguistic Inquiry*, 5 (1974), 117–36.

Lakoff, Robin. "Another Look at Drift." In R. P. Stockwell and R. K. S. Macaulay, eds. *Linguistic Change and Generative Theory*. Bloomington: Indiana U. Press, 1972, pp. 172–98.

Langen, August. "Deutsche Sprachgeschichte vom Barock bis zur Gegenwart." In Wolfgang Stammler, ed. *Deutsche Philologie im Aufriß*, I. Berlin: Erich Schmidt, rev. ed. 1957[2], pp. 931–1356.

Lee, Duk Ho. "Die Problematik der Zweitstellung des Verbum finitum im Deutschen." *Colloquia Germanica* (Bern: Francke, 1975), 118–42.
Lehmann, Winfred P. "On the Rise of SOV Patterns in New High German." In K. G. Schweisthal, ed. *Grammatik, Kybernetik, Kommunikation: Festschrift für A. Hoppe.* Bonn: Dümmler, 1971, pp. 19–24.
———. "Contemporary Linguistics and Indo-European Studies." *PMLA*, 87, 5 (1972), 976–93.
———. "Proto-Germanic Syntax." In F. van Coetsen and H. Kufner, eds. *Toward A Grammar of Proto-Germanic.* Tübingen: M. Niemeyer, 1972, pp. 239–68.
———. "A Structural Principle of Language and Its Implications." *Language*, 49 (1973), 47–66.
———, ed. *Syntactic Typology. Studies in the Phenomenology of Language.* Austin-London: U. of Texas P., 1978. [Sections by Lehmann, S. Kuno, Ch. N. Li on word order in various languages.]
Lerch, Eugen. *Historische französische Syntax*, III. Leipzig: O. R. Reisland, 1934 (1925–34, 3 vols.).
Lévy, Paul. *La langue allemande en France; pénétration et diffusion des origines à nos jours*, I. Lyon: IAC, 1950.
Li, Charles N., ed. *Word Order and Word Order Change.* Austin: U. of Texas Press, 1975.
——— and Sandra A. Thompson. "An Explanation of Word Order Change SVO → SOV." *Foundations of Language*, 12 (1974), 201–14.
Lippert, Jörg. *Beiträge zu Technik und Syntax ahd. Übersetzungen.* München: Fink, 1974.
Mathesius, Vilém. "Studie k dějinám anglického slovosledu [Studies in the History of English Word Order]." *Věstník České Akademie*, 16 (1907), 261–74; 17 (1908), 195–214, 299–311; 18 (1909), 1–12; 19 (1910), 125–30, 496–519.
———. "Ze srovnávacích studií slovosledných [On Some Problems Concerning the Comparative Studies of Word-Order]." *Časopis pro moderní filologii*, 28 (1942), 181–90, 302–7.
Mattausch, Joseph. *Untersuchungen zur Wortstellung in der Prosa des jungen Goethe.* Berlin: Akademie Verlag, 1965.
Maurer, Friedrich. *Untersuchungen über die deutsche Verbstellung in ihrer geschichtlichen Entwicklung.* (Germanistische Bibliothek, 2: Untersuchungen und Texte, 21.) Heidelberg: C. Winter, 1926.
McCawley, James. "English as a VSO Language." *Language*, 46 (1970), 286–99.
McKnight, George. "The Primitive Teutonic Order of Words." *Journal of English and Germanic Philology*, 1 (1893), 136–219.
Mittner, Ladislao. *Grammatica della lingua tedesca.* Milano: Mondadori, 1933, 1941[5].
Mounin, Georges. *Saussure.* Paris: Séghers, 1968.
Nehring, Alfons. "Studien zur Theorie des Nebensatzes, I." *ZfvS*, 57 (1930), 118–58.
Ogle, Richard A. "Natural Order and Dislocated Syntax: An Essay in the History of Linguistic Ideas." Diss. U.C.L.A., 1974.
Panfilov, Vladimir. "Linguistic Universals and Sentence Typology." In *Theoretical Aspects of Linguistics.* Moscow: USSR Academy of Sciences, 1977, pp. 78–89.
Paul, Hermann. *Mittelhochdeutsche Grammatik.* Halle/S.: Max Niemeyer, 1944[14].
Polenz, Peter von. *Geschichte der deutschen Sprache.* Berlin: W. de Gruyter, 1972[8].
Posner, Rebecca. *The Romance Languages: A Linguistic Introduction.* Garden City, N.Y.: Doubleday & Co., 1966.
Primmer, Adolf. *Cicero numerosus. Studien zum antiken Prosarhythmus.* (Oester-

reichische Akademie der Wissenschaften, Philos.-hist. Kl., Sitzungsberichte, 257.) Wien, 1968.

Pullum, Geoffrey K. "Word Order Universals and Grammatical Relations." In Peter Cole and Jerrold M. Sadock, eds. *Syntax and Semantics, 8: Grammatical Relations.* New York-San Francisco-London: Academic Press, 1977, pp. 249–77.

Ramat, Paolo. "Ist das Germanische eine SOV-Sprache?" In Leonard Forster and H.-G. Roloff, eds. *Akten des V. Internationalen Germanisten-Kongresses, Cambridge, Eng. 1975,* Bd. 2, Heft 2. Bern: H. Lang, 1976, pp. 25–35.

Rath, Rainer. "Trennbare Verben und Ausklammerung. Zur Syntax der deutschen Sprache der Gegenwart." *Wirkendes Wort*, 15 (1965), 217–32.

Regula, Moritz. *Kurzgefaßte erklärende Satzkunde des Neuhochdeutschen.* Bern-München: Francke, 1968.

Reis, Hans. "Über althochdeutsche Wortfolge." *ZfdP*, 33 (1901), 212–38, 330–49.

Reis, Marga. "Syntaktische Hauptsatz-Privilegien und das Problem der deutschen Wortstellung." *Zeitschrift für germanistische Linguistik*, 2 (1974), 299–327.

Richter, Elise. *Zur Entwicklung der romanischen Wortstellung aus der lateinischen.* Halle/S.: M. Niemeyer, 1903.

Rohlfs, Gerhard. *Historische Grammatik der italienischen Sprache und ihrer Mundarten.* Bern: Francke, 1949–54, 3 vols.

Ross, John R. "Gapping and the Order of Constituents." In M. Bierwisch and K. E. Heidolph, eds. *Progress in Linguistics.* The Hague: Mouton, 1970, pp. 249–59.

———. "The Penthouse Principle and the Order of Constituents." In Claudia Corum, T. C. Smith-Clark, and A. Weiser, eds. *You Take the High Node and I'll Take the Low Node.* Papers from the Comparative Syntax Festival: The Differences Between Main and Subordinate Clauses, 12 April 1973 — Chicago Linguistic Society: Ninth Regional Meeting (Chicago: Chicago Linguistic Society, 1973), pp. 397–422.

———. "Some Cyclically Ordered Transformations in German Syntax." In Johannes Bechert *et al.*, eds. *Papiere zur Linguistik*, 7 (Kronberg: Scriptor Verlag, 1974), pp. 50–79.

Sanders, Gerald A. "Constraints on Constituent Ordering." *Papers in Linguistics*, 2 (1970), 460–502.

Sandmann, Manfred. *Subject and Predicate. A Contribution to the Theory of Syntax.* Edinburgh: Edinburgh U. Press, 1954.

———. "Zur Frühgeschichte des Terminus der syntaktischen Beiordnung." *ASnS*, 206 (1969–70), 161–88.

Sandys, John Edwin. *A History of Classical Scholarship.* Cambridge: U. Press, 1903–8, 3 vols., II: *From the Revival of Learning to the End of the 18th Century (in Italy, France, England, The Netherlands)*; III: *The 18th Century in Germany, and the 19th Century in Europe and the United States.*

Scaglione, Aldo. *Ars grammatica.* (Janua Linguarum, Series minor, 77.) The Hague-Paris: Mouton, 1970.

———. *The Classical Theory of Composition, from Its Origin to the Present: A Historical Survey.* (N.C. Studies in Comparative Literature, 53.) Chapel Hill: U.N.C. Press, 1972.

———. "Dante and the Medieval Theory of Sentence Structure." In J. J. Murphy, ed. *Medieval Eloquence.* Berkeley-Los Angeles: U.C. Press, 1978, pp. 252–69.

———, ed. *Francis Petrarch, Six Centuries Later: A Symposium.* (N.C.S.R.L.L., 159.) Chapel Hill: U.N.C. Press, 1975.

Schanze, Helmut, ed. *Rhetorik. Beiträge zu ihrer Geschichte in Deutschland vom*

16.–20. Jahrhundert. Frankfurt/M.: Athenäum Fischer Taschenbücher, 1974 [biblio. pp. 221–355].

Schneider, Carl. *Die Stellungstypen des finiten Verbs im urgermanischen Haupt- und Nebensatz.* Heidelberg: C. Winter, 1938.

Schwartz, Arthur. "The VP-Constituent in SVO Languages." In John P. Kimball, ed. *Syntax and Semantics*, I. New York-London: Seminar Press, 1972, pp. 213–35.

Šimko, Ján. "K teórii slovosledného štúdia [Concerning the Theory of Word-Order Study]." *Časopis pro moderní filologii*, 39 (Prague, 1957), 281–86.

Skalička, Vladimír. "La fonction de l'ordre des éléments linguistiques." *Travaux du cercle linguistique de Prague*, 6 (Prague, 1936), 129–33.

Staal, J. F. *Word Order in Sanskrit and Universal Grammar. Foundations of Language*, Suppl. 2 (1967).

Steele, Susan. "On Some Factors That Affect and Effect Word Order." In Charles N. Li, ed. *Word Order and Word Order Change.* Austin: U. of Texas Press, 1975, pp. 197–268.

Steinhausen, Georg. *Geschichte des deutschen Briefs: Zur Kulturgeschichte des deutschen Volkes.* Berlin: R. Gartner, 1889–91, 2 vols.

Stockwell, Robert P. "Motivations for Exbraciation in Old English." In Charles N. Li, ed. *Mechanisms of Syntactic Change.* Austin-London: U. of Texas Press, 1977, pp. 292–314.

Stojanova-Jovčeva, Stanka. "Untersuchungen zur Stilistik der Nebensätze in der deutschen Gegenwartssprache." *BGdS*, 100 (1979), 40–178.

Stolt, Birgit. *Die Sprachmischung in Luthers Tischreden: Studien zum Problem der Zweisprachigkeit.* (Acta Universitatis Stockholmiensis, Stockholmer Germanistische Forschungen, 4.) Uppsala, 1964.

Tekavčić, Pavao. *Grammatica storica dell'italiano*, II: *Morfosintassi.* Bologna: Il Mulino, 1972.

Tesnière, Lucien. *Éléments de syntaxe structurale.* Paris: Klincksieck, 1959, 1965².

Thurot, Charles. "Notices et extraits . . . pour servir à l'histoire des doctrines grammaticales au Moyen Age." In *Notices et extraits des manuscrits de la Bibliothèque Impériale et autres Bibliothèques*, XXII, 2 (Paris, 1868).

Tomanetz, Karl. *Die Relativsätze bei den ahd. Übersetzern des 8. und 9. Jahrhunderts.* Wien: C. Gerold's Sohn, 1879.

Traugott, Elizabeth C. *A History of English Syntax: A Transformational Approach to the History of English Sentence Structure.* New York: Holt, Rinehart & Winston, 1972.

Tschirch, Fritz. *Spiegelungen. Untersuchungen vom Grenzrain zwischen Germanistik und Theologie.* Berlin: Erich Schmidt, 1966.

Ulvestad, Bjarne. "Vorschlag zur strukturellen Beschreibung der deutschen Wortstellung." In Hugo Steger, ed. *Vorschläge für eine strukturale Grammatik des Deutschen.* Darmstadt: Wissenschaftliche Buchgesellschaft, 1970, pp. 166–201. [Trans. of "A Structural Approach to the Description of German Word-Order." *Årbok for Universitetet i Bergen.* Humanistisk Serie 1, 1960, pp. 1–28.]

Unger, Rudolf. *Hamanns Sprachtheorie im Zusammenhange seines Denkens.* München: O. Beck, 1905.

Uspenskij, Boris P. *Principles of Structural Typology.* The Hague: Mouton, 1968.

Velde, Marc van de. "Zur Wortstellung im Niederländischen und im deutschen Satz." *Linguistische Studien*, I. (Sprache der Gegenwart, 19.) Düsseldorf: Pädagogischer Verlag Schwann, 1972, pp. 76–125.

Vennemann, Theo. "Rule Inversion." *Lingua*, 29 (1972), 209–42.

——. "Explanation in Syntax." In John P. Kimball, ed. *Syntax and Semantics*, II. New York-London: Seminar Press, 1973, pp. 1–50.

——. "Analogy in Generative Grammar." In Luigi Heilmann, ed. *Proceedings of the XI International Congress of Linguists, Bologna-Florence 1972*. Bologna: Il Mulino, 1974, 2 vols., II, 79–83.

——. "Topics, Subjects, and Word Order: From SXV to SVX Via TVX." In John Anderson and Ch. Jones, eds. *Historical Linguistics. Proceedings of the 1st International Congress of Historical Linguistics, Edinburgh, Sept. 1973*. Amsterdam: North Holland, 1974, 2 vols., II, 339–76. [trans. as "Zur Theorie der Wortstellungsveränderung: Von SXV zu SVX über TVX" in DINSER 1974, pp. 265–314.]

——. "Theoretical Word Order Studies: Results and Problems." In J. Bechert *et al.*, eds. *Papiere zur Linguistik*, 7 (Kronberg: Scriptor, 1974), pp. 5–25.

——. "An Explanation of Drift." In Charles N. Li, ed. *Word Order and Word Order Change*. Austin: U. of Texas Press, 1975, pp. 269–305.

Wackernagel, Jacob. "Der griechische Verbalaccent," *Zeitschrift für vergleichende Sprachforschung auf dem Gebiete der indogermanischen Sprachen*, 23, NF 3 (1877), 457–70.

——. "Uber ein Gesetz der indogermanischen Wortstellung." *Indogermanische Forschungen*, 1 (1892), 333–436.

Waterman, John T. *A History of the German Language*. Seattle-London: U. of Washington Press, 1966, 1976^2.

Watkins, Calvert. "Preliminaries to the Reconstruction of Indo-European Sentence Structure." In Horace G. Lunt, ed. *Proceedings of the 9th International Congress of Linguists, Cambridge, Mass. 1962*. The Hague: Mouton, 1964, pp. 1035–42.

——. "Towards Proto-Indo-European Syntax: Problems and Pseudo-Problems." In S. B. Steever *et al.*, eds. *Papers from the Parasession on Diachronic Syntax*. Chicago: Chicago Linguistic Society, 1976, pp. 305–26.

Waugh, Linda R. *A Semantic Analysis of Word Order: Position of the Adjective in French*. Leiden: E. J. Brill, 1977. [See bibliography for full listing of Roman Jakobson's 50-odd papers bearing on word order.]

Weber, Heinrich. *Das erweiterte Adjektiv- und Partizipialattribut im Deutschen*. (Linguistische Reihe, 4.) München: Max Hueber, 1971.

Weinrich, Harald. *Tempus. Besprochene und erzählte Welt*. Stuttgart: W. Kohlhammer, 1964.

Weisgerber, (Johann) Leo. *Die ganzheitliche Behandlung eines Satzbauplanes*. Düsseldorf: Pädagogischer Verlag Schwann, 1962. [34 pp.]

Wunderlich, Hermann. *Der deutsche Satzbau*. Stuttgart: J. G. Cotta Nachf., 1892, 1901^2, 2 vols. [1924^3, 2 vols., bearb. von **Hans Reis**.]

——. *Unsere Umgangssprache in der Eigenart ihrer Satzfügung dargestellt*. Weimar-Berlin: E. Felber, 1894, 1896.

——. *Die Kunst der Rede, in ihren Hauptzügen an den Reden Bismarcks dargestellt*. Leipzig: S. Hirzel, 1898.

—— and Hans Reis. *Der deutsche Satzbau*. Stuttgart-Berlin: J. G. Cotta Nachf., $1924–5^3$, 2 vols.

Zemb, J.-M. *Les structures logiques de la proposition allemande: Contribution à l'étude des rapport entre le langage et la pensée*. Paris: O.C.D.L., 1968.

INDEXES

SUBJECT INDEX

Abwandelungen (complements), 44
Accent, 107
"Adverbial" coordinating conjunctions, 173
Affect, affective, 72, 78, 102, 155
Ambiguity, 73, 76, 79, 95, 153f., 162–164
Amtsstil, Beamtenstil, 16, 96. *See also Kanzleistil*
Analytical order, 42, 53
Anti-Ciceronian, 17
Arbitraire du signe: 56, 58, 191; arbitrariness of word order, 57
Ascending construction, 81, 102f., 126, 131
Asyndetic, 8f., 211 fn. 123
Ausklammerung (exbraciation), 111, 113, 177
Auxiliary: 4, 33, 39 (separation), 34 (final), 35 (*haben*), 38 (Schottel), 43 (before Stieler), 44 (Stieler), 45 (Longolius), 46 (Wahn), 47 (Steinbach), 61 (Gottsched), 66 (final), 68 (Hempel), 81 (Fulda's contradiction on government), 83 (id.), 86 (Adelung), 88 (id.), 102 (Jerusalem), 115 (Maurer), 116 (*haben* in MHG), 157 (final with SOV), 165 (in Old Italian), 166 (id.), 203 fn. 33 (in MHG groups)

Beauzée's Law, 87, 197 fn. 141
Behaghel's Law, 117, 175, 199 fn. 14
Behaghel's Second Law, 164
Bestimmend/Bestimmt, 80, 83, 85, 100–103. *See also Unbestimmt*
Bestimmungen, 95
Brevity, 17, 21, 95
Bureaucratic style. *See Amtsstil, Kanzleistil*

Case grammar, 145
Ciceronianism, 24, 26f., 139
Clarity, 21, 25f., 74, 89
Colon, 11, 13, 34
Comma, 11f.
Comment, 130, 141, 155f. *See also* Topic
Complements, 4, 44, 52, 60, 63, 79f., 84, 86f., 94, 100, 106f., 119, 126, 130, 134, 136, 138, 155, 163f., 172f., 175f., 199 fn. 14
Composition, 5, 11, 28, 97, 161
Compound verbs, 4, 33
Concessive construction, 92

233

234 □ INDEX

Conditional constructs, *Konditionalsatz,* 10, 49, 64
Conjunctions: 14, 20f., 23 (Gottsched), 25 (*connectio verbalis*), 26f. (Dornblüth), 35 (Laurentius Albertus), 37 (with subjunctive in Schottel), 43 (order), 44f. (with subjunctive in Stieler), 61 (no *Rücksendung* when *daß* omitted, Gottsched), 74 (Herder on omitting), 141 (Weinrich: omission); adverbial (coordinating), 173f.; coordinating, 45 (Longolius), 49 (*Beyträge* I), 91 (Adelung), 123 (Fourquet); subordinating, 8, 10, 36 (Claius), 45, 46 (Wahn's classification), 47 (with *Rücksendung* in Steinbach), 50 (*Beyträge* I), 62 (Gottsched), 65f. (id.), 69 (H. Braun), 78 (Bodmer), 84 (Adelung's list), 89f. (Adelung), 93 (Adelung on *Rücksendung*), 105 (Bauer), 116 (H. Paul), 120 (Delbrück), 135 (Glinz), 140 (weak in German), 160 (c. and hypotaxis), 173 (G. O. Curme), 175 (Fleischmann), 180 (and *Satzklammer*), 194 fn. 111 (and cut style), 202 fn. 31 (O. Erdmann), 210 fn. 108 (Fourquet on OHG), 211 fn. 125 (Duden)
Constituents, 146, 154, 159, 168
Construction (*constructio*), 33, 39, 47, 98
Coordination, *Koordination,* 11, 15, 100, 105
Cut style (*coupé*), 20f., 23, 25f., 70, 105, 139, 194 fn. 111

Dative + accusative, 126
Declension, 94f.
Deep structure, 54, 143–146, 149, 151–153, 158, 172, 190 fn. 60, 206 fn. 62
Dependent clause. *See* Subordination
Descending order, 81, 131
Determinant/determined, 30, 71, 137
Direct order, *gerade Folge,* 42, 55, 61, 73, 74, 178, 199 fn. 12
Distanzstellung, 176
Double infinitive, 124, 147, 176, 203 fn. 33
Drift, 150f., 154, 162f., 167–169

Ellipsis, 33, 100
Embedding, 102, 146
Emotion, 52, 69, 70

Emphasis (*Betonung*), 46, 52, 69, 72, 74, 78, 84, 91, 94, 103, 107, 111, 114, 139f., 149, 155, 183 fn. 2
Encapsulation, Incapsulation, 10f., 16, 19, 39, 66, 84, 93, 134f.
Enclisis, 118, 169, 171, 200 fn. 27, 203 fn. 31
Es-construct: 148; Disappearing *es,* 142f.
Extended attribute, 180

Flection, inflection, 41, 71, 73, 75f., 106, 117f., 121, 132, 150, 156, 162, 164–167, 169, 190 fn. 60, 208 fn. 90, 210 fn. 118
Focalization, focus, 129f., 145, 156, 175
Free word order, 42, 114, 117, 126, 129, 132, 152, 154, 156, 159, 161, 167, 194 fn. 111
Functional sentence perspective, 128–130, 170f.
Future tense, 41

Gapping, 144
Gesetz der wachsenden Glieder. See Behaghel's Law
Gestalt, 109, 127, 138

Hauptsatz, 12, 14, 45, 98
Heldensprache, 28, 287 fn. 56
Hochsprache, 16
Hypotaxis: 7f., 10f., 32, 34, 51, 59, 62, 65, 67, 99, 140, 160, 211 fn. 123; syndetic, asyndetic, 8–10, 211 fn. 123
Hypothetical construction, 34, 92

Indirect construction, 92; *ungerade Gliedfolge,* 178
Indirect discourse, *indirekte Rede,* 45, 69, 84
Infinitive, 64, 80, 88
Inflection. *See* Flection
Interrogation, question, 49, 93
Intonation, 119, 129, 167, 174
Inversion: 4, 46, 51 (Du Cerceau), 55 (id.), 52 and 56 (Gottsched), 84 (Adelung), 89 (Adelung, in verb phrase), 91 (Adelung, interrogative), 98f. (Herling), 106 (Becker), 125 (with pronouns), 129 (Prague School), 194 (Algarotti), 198f. fns. 6 and 12; for emphasis or emotion, 69f.,

72-78, 102f. (Kolbe and Bauer), 104 (Bauer), 127, 134, 195 fn. 117; optional, 48; XVS, 32, 29, 42 (in Latin), 45, 48 (XVS and SOV in Steinbach), 49, 92 (Adelung), 95f. (id.) 130, 160f., 165f. (in Italian), 173f., 178, 183 fn. 2, 197 fn. 148, 198 fn. 6, 199 fn. 12, 203 fn. 35

Juxtaposition, 8, 10, 26

Kanzleistil, 16, 20–23, 25–27, 38f., 62, 66, 89, 93, 122, 135, 160, 180, 187 fn. 56, 194 fn. 111
Kernsatz, 135, 177
Kurialstil, 10, 16

Latin influx, 109, 111–113, 122
Lexicalization rules, 152
Linearity, 42, 54, 57f., 141, 144f., 151–153, 190 fn. 60, 191 fns. 66 and 67, 206 fns. 62, 68, and 70

Mécaniciens, 53f., 73f., 76, 194 fn. 111
Métaphysiciens, 53, 56, 61, 73, 76, 104, 194 fn. 111
Mittelfeld, 134, 177
Modal, 4, 38, 61, 64, 86, 102, 124, 157, 166

Nachfeld, 134, 177
Nachsatz, 14, 179
Nachtrag, 78, 100, 111, 113, 120, 129, 139, 147, 163, 174, 176–178, 213
Natural generative grammar, 54, 151, 158
Natural order, *ordo naturalis*, 46, 55, 156
Nebensatz, secondary clause, 4, 12, 45 (Longolius), 14 (Meiner), 51 and 61f. (absent in Gottsched), 67 (Dornblüth), 77 (Bodmer), 78 (Bodmer and Basedow), 84 and 94 (Adelung), 98 and 100 (Herling), 104f. (Bauer), 110 (John Ries), 111 (Biener), 115 (Maurer), 121 (MHG), 135 (Burdach), 175 (Drach), 188 fn. 12 (Laurentius Albertus), 198 fn. 11 (Tomanetz, Behaghel, Delbrück), 200 fn. 27 (Wackernagel), 202 fn. 31 (Erdmann). *See also* Subordination
Nicht-Zweitstellung. See Verb
Numerus, 72

Operator/operand, 86, 169, 172
Optative, 37
Order of prose, prose style, 69, 71
Organicism, 127
OVS, 79

Parataxis: 7f., 11, 59, 99, 105; syndetic, asyndetic, 8–10, 211 fn. 123
Participle: 4, 21, 24, 27, 43, 50, 64–66, 80f., 83, 86, 88f., 124, 157, 165, 166; participial clause, 16
Particles, *trennbare Komposita, Partikeln*: inseparable, 33, 61, 65; separable, 36, 43f., 51, 61, 65f., 86, 88, 104, 121; separated, 46
Period, Periodicity, 11, 13, 20, 23, 26, 28, 67, 74, 84, 100, 103, 139, 160, 167, 179, 192 fn. 76
Phonetic change or grind, 132, 151, 153, 162, 167
Plainness, 17, 19, 25
Poetics, 20
Post-positions, 86
Prague School, 108, 126, 155
Pronoun, 93
Psychological subject, 128
Punctuation theory, 13

Qualifier/qualified, 80, 86f., 106, 154

Rahmen. See Satzklammer.
Relative clauses, 8, 63, 67, 147, 155, 157f., 164
Relative pronouns and adverbs, 14, 46f., 50, 79, 116, 173, 196 fn. 123
Reprise, 94
Rheme, 130, 145, 154, 204 fn. 46
Rhetoric, 20, 22, 28, 106
Russian formalism, 127

Sapic-Whorf theory, 133
Satzklammer, Rahmen. frame: 31, 33, 35f., 38f., 67, 84, 89, 103, 111, 134, 136, 147, 163, 166, 177–180, 183 fn. 2; full frame, 136, 138, 176
Schachtelsatz, 139
Second part of the predicate, 179
Semiotic, 127, 130, 170
Senecanism, 21, 23–25, 74, 139, 186 fn. 44

Sentence structure, 7
Serialization rules, 152, 154, 158, 164, 168, 172, 180
Simultaneity, 42, 57–59, 143, 154, 189 fn. 35, 191 fn. 67
SOV (subject + object + verb), 29, 47, 66–68, 71, 81f., 84, 91, 103, 112, 114, 122, 139, 142, 144, 147, 152, 154–159, 162
Spannsatz, 135, 177
Stirnsatz, 135, 177
Stoic, neo-Stoic style, 17, 21, 26, 186 fn. 44
Structuralism, 108, 126f., 133, 135, 138
Subjunctive, 10, 36f., 41, 45, 61, 63, 69, 140
Subordination: 4, 8, 10 (subjunctive without conjunctions in MHG), 11f. (origin of term), 15 (Herling), 19 (Bodmer), 36 (Claius), 37 (subjunctive), 59 (Condillac), 62 (Gottsched lacking notion of), 78 (Bodmer), 79 (Hemmer), 89–91 (Adelung), 100 (Herling), 105 (id.), 158 (Lehmann), 167 (need for markers), 175 (Fleischmann); subordinate or dependent clauses or constructs, 21 (Neukirch), 29 (SOV), 35 (Ölinger lacking distinction), 63 (Gottsched), 115 (Maurer on auxiliary in), 164 (fronted), 173 (Curme), 210 fn. 108 (in OHG); *Verbindung*, 90
Suspense, 72
SVO (subject + verb + object), 29–31, 47, 60, 67f., 82, 91, 104, 111f., 117, 123, 141–143, 145, 151, 155–158, 161, 164, 167, 174
SVX, 130, 165
SXV, 119, 130, 165
Synchysis, 51
Syntax, 12

Taciteanism, 21, 23, 25, 74
Theme, 130, 144, 204 fn. 46
Theme-rheme, 128, 134, 136, 146, 171, 204 fn. 46

Topic/comment: 126, 128, 130, 134, 141f., 144f., 149, 153–156, 166, 204 fn. 47; topicalization, 149, 153, 162, 169, 174
Topik, 28, 97, 106, 147
Topologie, 147
"Triple infinitive," 36, 88
Transformational-generative grammar, 8, 54, 109, 138, 141, 143, 145f., 151f.
Trivium, 6
TXV, 103
Typology, 86, 122, 126, 141, 143f., 150, 168, 170f.

Unbestimmt/bestimmt, 83, 85, 168

Verb, position of: auxiliary, *see s.v.*; first position (*Spitzstellung*), front-shifting, 10, 34, 45, 114, 129, 149, 158, 171, 175; final position (*Endstellung, Rücksendung*), 13, 31, 35–37, 44–46, 48, 50, 54, 62f., 66f., 69, 78, 80, 84, 91, 93, 109–113, 115f., 118f., 122, 124, 126, 130, 139f., 165, 167f., 171, 173–175, 179, 194 fn. 111, 196 fn. 193, 198 fn. 9, 200f. fn. 27, 202 fn. 31; late position (*Spätstellung, Nichtzweitstellung*), 111, 116, 174, 178; second position (*Zweitstellung*), 48, 78, 110–112, 114–116, 118, 120, 122, 124f., 134, 139, 148, 171, 173–175, 200 fn. 27, 202 fn. 31; verb as central knot of sentence, 47f., 123, 161, 199 fn. 12. *See also Spannsatz, Stirnsatz, Nebensatz,* Subordination
Verbindende Wortfolge, 90, 92, 95, 105
Vorfeld-Mitte-Nachfeld, 134, 137, 146, 177
Vorsatz, 14
VOS, 144
VSO, 68, 142, 144, 149, 155, 164
VSX, 130

Wackernagel's Law, 171
Whole (*Ganzheit*), 137

XVS, 73, 79

INDEX OF PERSONAL NAMES

Italicized numbers indicate pages where main entries occur or begin.

Aarsleff, Hans, 58f., 189, 191, 194 fn. 115, 195 fn. 118, 196 fn. 134
Addison, Joseph, 71, 74
Adelung, Johann Christoph, *19*, 81, *82*-96, 99, 100, 103f., 168, 170, 179
Admoni, Wladimir G., 138, 176, 211 fn. 131
Aichinger, Carl Friedrich, 12, *13*, 45, 48, 64, *68*, 78f., 84, 88
Albertus, Laurentius, *32*-36, 38, 43, 88
Alcamo, Cielo d', 165
Alexander de Villadei, 30, 187 fn. 4
Algarotti, Francesco, 73, 193f. fn. 106
Alsted, Heinrich, *32*, 37
Ammann, H., 128
Aristotle, 51f., 71
Avalle, D'Arco Silvio, 207 fn. 73
Ayer, Cyprien, *11*

Bach, Adolf, *111*
Bach, Emmon, *142*f., 147
Bandello, Matteo, 165
Bartsch, Renate, 29, 151, 159
Basedow, Johann Bernhard, *13*, *78*
Batteux, Charles, 42, 74

Bauer, Heinrich, *28*, 97, *100*, 103-106, 147, 197 fn. 5
Beauzée, Nicolas, 12, 42, 59f., 199 fn. 14
Bech, Gunnar, *147*
Becker, Karl Ferdinand, 100, 104, *106*-108
Behaghel, Otto, 4, 108f., *110*-113, 121f., 139, 168, 199 fn. 14, 200 fn. 25, 201 fn. 27, 202 fn. 31
Beneš, Eduard, 108, *130*, 136, 204 fn. 48, 205 fn. 53
Bergaigne, Abel, 122, 201 fn. 27
Bernhardt, Fr. K., 100, 104, 197 fn. 5
Beyrich, Volker, 205 fn. 55
Beyträge zu einer critischen Historie der deutschen Sprache, 48, *53*-57, 190 fns. 58 and 61
Biener, Clemens, 34, 78, *109*, 111-114, 116, 120, 199 fn. 16, 202 fn. 29
Bierwisch, Manfred, 130, *143*, *146*f., 206 fn. 65
Blackall, Eric A., *16*, 19, and *passim* in fns.
Blinkenberg, Andreas, 103
Blümel, Rudolf, *115*
Boccaccio, Giovanni, 165

238 □ INDEX

Bödiker, Johann, *19*, *43*f., 49
Bodmer, Johann Jakob, *13*, 19f., 28, 51, 53, *70*f., 74, *77*f., 193
Boileau, Nicolas, 16, 54f., , 57, 59
Bolinger, Dwight L., , 129
Boost, Karl, 108, 130, *136*–138, 146
Bopp, Franz, 117
Bouhours, Father Dominique, 19, 55
Braun, Heinrich, *68*
Braune, Wilhelm, *110*
Brecht, Bertolt, *172*
Breitinger, Johann Jakob, 20, *24*, *69*, 74, 193 fn. 95
Brekle, H. E., 188 fns. 9 and 23
Brockes, Barthold Heinrich, 19
Buffier, Claude, 52–54, 56–58
Burdach, Konrad, *109*, 135
Bürger, Gottfried August, 101
Burt, Marina K., 199
Bussy-Rabutin, Roger, 23, 27

Chateaubriand, François René de, 101
Chomsky, Noam, 146, 152, 170, 191 fn. 69
Cicero, Marcus Tullius, 9, 24, 112
Claius, Johannes, 31, *36*
Coclaeus, Johannes, 31
Condillac, Étienne Bonnot de, 12, 15, 41f., 46, 58–60, 74f., 101, 133, 166, 195 fn. 118
Cook, Daniel J., 186 fn. 36
Cordemoy, Géraud de, 41
Corneille, Pierre, 57
Coseriu, Eugenio, 191 fn. 67
Crébillon *fils*, Claude-Prosper Jolyot de, 25
Crystal, David, 206 fn. 64
Curme, George O., 99, *173*, 210 fn. 118

Dante Alighieri, 17, 165
Dascal, Marcelo, 186 fn. 33
Dauzat, Albert, 103, 161
Delbrück, Berthold, 7, 98f., *108*–110, *118*–120, 122, 139, 167, 198 fn. 11, 201 fn. 28, 202 fn. 31
Dezsö, László, *170*
Diderot, Denis, 5, 42, 58f., 74
Dionysius of Halicarnassus, 29f., 187 fns. 1 and 3
Donatus, Aelius, 81
Dornblüth, Father Augustin, 24, *25*f., 28, 66f.

Drach, Erich, 108, *133*f., 137f., 146, 174
Du Cerceau, Jean-Antoine, 51–53, 55, 69, 72, 162
Duden, 177, 178, 211 fn. 125
Du Marsais, César Chesnau, 12, 42, 59, 73, 82, 85, 168, 196 fn. 135
Duret, Claude, *39*

Ebert, Robert P., *177*, 203 fn. 31
Emonds, Joseph, 206f.
Engel, Ulrich, 138, 177
Erdmann, Oskar, *110*, 119, 202 fn. 31
Ernesti, Johann August, *13*
Esser, Wilhelm Martin, 212 fn. 131

Fabricius, Johann Andreas, *50*
Fillmore, Charles J., 145f., 206 fn. 63
Finck, Caspar, 37
Finck-Helwig (Caspar Finck and Christoph Helwig [Helvicus]), 43
Firbas, Jan, 108, *128*, 204 fns. 43, 45, 46
Fléchier, Esprit, 23
Fleischmann, Klaus, 36f., 48, 63, 84, 110, 112f., 120f., *175*, 185, 192, 195f., 198, 203
Forsgren, Kjell-Åke. *11*, 15, 105, 184 fn. 11
Fourquet, Jean, *123*–125, 147, 201 fn. 28, 203 fn. 38, 210 fn. 108
Frei, Henri, 131
Fries, Charles C., 151
Fulda, Friedrich Carl, *80*–83, 88, 170
Funk, Gottlieb Benedikt, 88, 196 fn. 133

Gabelentz, Georg von der, 128
Gamaches, Étienne-Simon de, 199 fn. 14
Girard, Gabriel, 13
Girbert, Johann, 44
Glinz, Hans, 108, *135*f., 138, 145, 205 fn. 52
Goethe, Johann Wolfgang von, 179
Goldast, Melchior Haiminsfeld, 62
Gottsched, Frau (Luise Adelgunde Viktorie Kulmus), *53*f., 190 fn. 58
Gottsched, Johann Christoph, *19*–24, 26–28, 35, 43, *50*–53, 56, 58, *60*–64, 67–69, 74, 77, 88f.
Grebe, Paul, 211 fn. 125
Greenberg, Joseph H., 30, *141*, 145, 154f., 164, 168, 170, 205 fn. 60

Grubačić, Emilija, 199 fn. 17
Gryphius, Andreas, 49f.
Guchmann, Mirra M., 138, 176f., 205 fn. 55
Gueintz, Christian, *37*
Günther, Johann Christian, 50, 52

Haiman, John, 130, 141, *148*f.
Haller, Albrecht von, *24*
Hamann, Johann Georg, *72*–75, 193 fn. 104, 194 fn. 107
Hammarström, Emil, *122*
Harris, Zellig S., 142
Haselbach, Gerhard, 198 fn. 6
Hegel, Georg Wilhelm Friedrich, 18
Heidegger, Martin, 4
Heinsius, Theodor, *11*, *15*
Helwig (Helvicus), Christoph, *32*, 37
Hemmer, Jakob, *14*, 43, *79*, 95
Hempel, Christian Friedrich, *68*, 79
Herder, Johann Gottfried, *72*–77, 103, 133, 194 fns. 108 and 115, 195 fn. 117
Herling, S. H. A., *11*, 14, 97–99, 103–105, 147
Heynatz, Johann Friedrich, 43
Heyse, Johann Christian August, 98f.
Heyse, Karl Wilhelm Ludwig, *107*
Hieber, Gelasius, 187
Hijmans, B. L., Jr., 184
Hirt, Hermann, *110*
Hoffmanswaldau, or Hofmann von Hofmannswaldau, Christian, 52
Hopper, Paul J., *171*, 210 fn. 116
Hübner, Johann, *21*
Humboldt, Wilhelm von, 133
Hyman, Larry M., 162

Jakobson, Roman, 145, 155f., 168, 210 fn. 109
Jellinek, Max Hermann, *15*, 30, 45, 50, 63, 79, 81–83, 88, 91, 95, 99, and *passim* in fns.
Jerusalem, J. F. W., 102, 197 fn. 3
Jespersen, Otto, *117*f., *150*, 162, 199 fn. 14
John of Salisbury, 9

Kandler, Agnellus, 187 fn. 56
Kanitz (usual sp. Canitz), Friedrich Rudolf von, 62
Kant, Immanuel, 98

Kierkegaard, Søren, 3
Klein, Wolfgang, *169*, 210 fn. 110
Klopstock, Friedrich Gottlieb, *24*, 53, *71*f., 104, 193 fn. 95
Kolbe, Karl Wilhelm, 102f., 197 fn. 3
Koll, Hans Georg, 192 fn. 84, 199 fn. 19
Komenský, Jan Amos, 38
Körber, C. A. (M. Belius), 49
Kuno, Susumu, 163

La Grange-Chancel, Joseph, 55
Lakoff, Robin, 151, 162
La Motte, A. Houdar de, 55, 57
Lamy, Bernard, 41
Lange, Klaus-Peter, *170*, 210fn. 114
Lassenius, Johann, 23
Lees, R. B., 142
Lehmann, Winfred P., *150*, 162, 164, 207 fns. 77f. and 83, 208 fn. 85, 209 fn. 94
Leibniz, Gottfried Wilhelm von, 4, *17*f., 185 fns. 29–31
Le Laboureur, Louis, 41
Lemaire, Pierre-Auguste, *11*
Lerch, Eugen, 208 fn. 91
Lessing, Gotthold Ephraim, *24*, 187, 195 fn. 117
Lévy, Paul, 186 fn. 45
Linde, Paulus, 199 fn. 19
Lippert, Jörg, 200 fn. 20
Little, Greta D., 210 fn. 118
Livy, 74
Locke, John, 60, 75
Longolius, Johann Daniel, *12*, *45*f.
Lorberg, G. A. P., 104, 198 fn. 5
Lotman, Iurii M., 203 fn. 40
Luther, Martin, 63, 67, 112, 115

McCawley, James, *144*, 149, 209 fn. 101
Malvezzi, Virgilio, 23
Mann, Thomas, 178
Maro Grammaticus, Vergilius, 51
Marouzeau, Jacques, 155
Mathesius, Vilém, 108, 127f., 144
Maupertuis, Pierre-Louis Moreau de, 58, 195 fn. 118
Maurer, Friedrich, *34*–36, 113, *114*–116
Megenberg, Konrad von, 115
Meillet, Antoine, *110*, 125, 199 fn. 13
Meiner, Johann Werner, *14*
Melanchthon, Philipp, 22, 32, 35, 37, 112

INDEX

Michaëlis, Johann David, 64, 101, 133, 195 fn. 118
Milton, John, 51–53, 70, 193 fn. 95
Mittner, Ladislao, 184 fn. 3, 211 fn. 127
Morhof, Daniel Georg, 41, 49, 69
Moulton, William G., 206 fn. 62
Mounin, Georges, 54
Mügeln, Heinrich von, 116
Müller, Gottfr. Polyk., 23
Müller, Johannes, 31
Mukařovsky, Jan, 127

Neukirch, Benjamin, *21*f., 69
Neumarkt, Johannes von, 109, 116
Nizolius, Marius, *17*
Notker, Labeo, 31

Ogle, Richard A., 58f., 190 fn. 60, 206 fn. 70
Ölinger, Albert, *35*f.
Opitz, Martin, 16, 51, 63, 67

Paul, Hermann, 116
Pirandello, Luigi, 166
Pliny the Younger, 9, 74
Pluche, Noël Antoine, 53, 72
Polenz, Peter von, *10*, 179f., 184, 200, 211
Politz, K. H. L., *15*
Porten, B. J., 112
Porzig, Walter, *137*
Posner, Rebecca, 183 fn. 2
Prémontval, André Pierre le Guay de, 77, 195 fn. 118
Primmer, Adolph, 9
Priscian, 30, 81

Quintilian, Marcus Fabius, 9, 156

Racine, Jean, 57
Ramat, Paolo, *144*f., *169*, 206 fn. 62
Ramshorn, Ludwig, *15*
Ramus (Pierre de la Ramée), 32
Rapin, René, 74
Ratke, Wolfgang (Ratichius), *32*, 37
Regula, Moritz, 212
Reis, Hans, *120*, 140, 202 fn. 30, 203 fn. 37
Repkow, Eike von, 115f.
Richter, Elise, 115, 118, 150, 162
Ries, John, *110*, 115, 118f., 201 fn. 27
Ritter, Stephen, *36*

Rivarol, Antoine de, 5, 53, 77
Rohlfs, Gerhard, 209 fn. 106
Ross, John R., *143*–145, 199, 206 fn. 62, 207 fn. 72
Roth, G. M., *15*
Rousseau, Jean-Baptiste, 55, 57
Rousseau, Jean-Jacques, 74, 101

Sacy, Antoine Isaac Silvestre, baron de, *14*
Saint-Évremond, Charles de Saint-Denis, sieur de, 23, 27
Saint-Simon, Louis de Rouvroy, duc de, 25
Sandmann, Manfred, *11*, 15, 105, 184 fn. 2
Sapir, Edward, *150*, 162
Sapir-Whorf (Theory), 60, 101
Saussure, Ferdinand de, 53f., 56–58, 121, 131f.
Scaglione, Aldo (D.), 188 fn. 11, 198 fn. 10, 200 fn. 19, 203 fn. 35, 204 fn. 41
Schlegel, Friedrich von, 7, 117
Schlegel, J. H., 196
Schönaich, Christoph Otto von, 25
Schottel (Schottelius), Justus Georgius, *17*, 32, *37*f., 44, 48, 188 fn. 25
Sciascia, Leonardo, 165
Seneca, Lucius Annaeus, the Younger, 9, 74
Senecans, 27
Siger of Brabant, 12
Staal, J. F., 190
Steinbach, Christian Ernst, 43, 45, *47*–51, 63, 78
Steinhausen, Georg, 186 fn. 52
Stieler, Kaspar, 43, *44*, 49, 88
Stolt, Birgit, 112, 200 fn. 20
Stromer, Ulrich, 115

Tacitus, 23, 74, 112
Tekavčić, Pavao, 9, 209 fns. 102 and 107
Tesnière, Lucien, 123, *131*
Thiersch, Friedrich von, 7, 11
Thomasius, Christian, *11*, *18*
Thurot, Charles, 31, 184 fn. 13
Tomanetz, Karl, *110*, 119, 198 fn. 11, 201 fn. 27, 203 fn. 33
Traugott, Elizabeth Closs, *143*
Tschirch, Fritz, 200 fn. 20

Ulfila, 114, 126
Ursin, Georg Heinrich, 12

Vater, Johann Severin, 14
Vennemann, Theo, 29, 95, *150*f., 153, 155–157, 159f., 162–164, 167, 169f., 197 fn. 140, 206–209
Vico, Giambattista, 75
Voltaire (F.-M. Arouet), 141
Vossius, Isaac, 41

Wackernagel, Jacob, *110*, 118f., 144, 167, 169, 200f. fn. 27
Wahn, Hermann, 43, *46*, 49
Waterman, John T., 185 fn. 26
Watkins, Calvert, *169*

Waugh, Linda R., 205 fn. 60
Weber, Heinrich, 211 fn. 130
Weil, Henri, 30, 81, 86, 114, 127, 129, 131, 166, 198 fn. 6
Weinrich, Harald, 4, *138*–140, 205 fns. 56–59
Weise, Christian, *16*, 22, 52, 69f.
Weisgerber, Leo, *133*f., 174
Wendland, Ulrich, 186 fn. 44
Winner, Thomas G., 203 fn. 40
Wolff, Christian, *18*
Wunderlich, Hermann, *109*, *120*, 140, 202 fn. 30

Zemb, J.-M., 3, 210 fn. 117